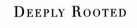

DEEPLY ROOTED

For steve &
THE seeds of change gang —
keep up your good work.

CdS

Aug
2009

DEEPLY ROOTED

UNCONVENTIONAL FARMERS
IN THE AGE OF AGRIBUSINESS

Lisa M. Hamilton

COUNTERPOINT
BERKELEY

Library of Congress Cataloging-in-Publication Data

Hamilton, Lisa M.
  Deeply rooted : unconventional farmers in the age of agribusiness / Lisa M. Hamilton.
    p. cm.
  1. Farmers—Texas—Sulphur Springs—Case studies. 2. Farmers—New Mexico—Abiquiu—
Case studies. 3. Farmers—North Dakota—La Moure—Case studies. I. Title.

  HD8039.F32U646 2009
  338.10973—dc22

                                2008050526

ISBN 978-1-59376-180-6

Cover design by Ann Weinstock
Interior design by Megan Cooney
Printed in the United States of America

COUNTERPOINT
2117 Fourth Street
Suite D
Berkeley, CA 94710

www.counterpointpress.com

Distributed by Publishers Group West

10 9 8 7 6 5 4 3 2 1

Introduction

Balfour, North Dakota

Highway 84 cuts a diagonal line across central North Dakota, a landscape of wheat. It's a lonely road, two lanes stringing together a handful of farm towns small enough to come and go in the space of a sentence. Velva. Voltaire. Bergen. Now Balfour. As I drive I'm looking for something to eat but in vain, and not just because it's Sunday morning. At Balfour there seems to be hope in the form of a roadside café, in front of which a big sign calls TRUCK STOP. Closer up, though, I see in the parking lot what has unintentionally become a sad joke: three trucks "stopped" here years ago and now rusting their way back into the earth. I'll bet the café has been closed for twenty years.

A few houses here are still lived in, but mostly Balfour appears to be closed. Next to the café, a cottage has been swallowed up by the bushes that once formed its hedge. Across the highway on the railroad tracks sit eight empty cars, graffiti spreading across them like cobwebs. Beside the tracks is a collection of abandoned tractors. In the stillness, fluffy seed heads of Canada thistle drift up and then down, tracing the soft curves of the air.

What caught my eye, the reason I pulled over and got out of the car, is an old, wood-shingled church. Built probably in the 1920s, it's a strangely huge building: two stories inside with a third-story bell tower, itself crowned with a steeple that reaches another fifteen feet into the air. At the very top is a delicate wooden cross, backlit by the sun. I soften my eyes to blur the massive building back to some former grandeur. But as my focus returns, I see its white paint peeling off like old skin, and weedy wormwood grown over its path. I see on the building's front the words FOR SALE spray-painted in red beside a phone number with an area code from North Carolina.

As I stand looking at the silent church, a convoy of trucks surges down the highway. According to the names on their cabs they normally transport ag equipment, but today they're hauling out the carnival from the state fair, which closed last night. Blowing down the road comes a candy-colored coupon booth on its side in the back of a flatbed, then a blue-and-lavender kiddie ride broken down to its clanking pieces, then a grown-up ride in red, with flames down its flanks and its outline marked by orange lightbulbs. The colors stream through town at fifty miles an hour.

Wind kicked up by the trucks sends the thistle seed-puffs reeling, their slow dance suddenly plunging and pointed. Watching them, it hits me that the truckers with their blurred faces are the only humans I have seen since I pulled over to look at this place. Of course I know that people live in Balfour; the census says there's a population of twenty, at least as of the year 2000. This town is not dead. What it is is empty. I get in my car and soon I leave, too.

Balfour should be a surprise to no one. In fact, this emptiness is what we've come to expect from farm towns. To those of us passing through, this landscape is not supposed to be about people. It is about wheat as far as the eye can see; or in Iowa, corn for miles on end; or in Texas, such endless cotton that in fall the roadsides turn white as if dusted with snow. We know that things used to be different—that in 1950 there were 162 people living in Balfour; that six days a week there were farmers in those fields and that on Sunday mornings the church was so full that the building didn't seem oversized at all.

But we also know those days are gone. The way things work now, with industrialization and consolidation and combines navigated by GPS, agriculture doesn't really need people anymore—at least not like it used to. As we have mathematized food production, we have reduced its pieces to numbers and its processes to calculations; humans have become mere inputs, useful only when applied efficiently in relation to the outputs they create. Of all those people once filling the church at Balfour, conventional agriculture needs only the handful in the front row. The rest are fat to be trimmed.

———

As a person who writes about agriculture, I spend a fair amount of time in places that have grown quiet over the past fifty years. Gibbon, Minnesota. Bluffton, Georgia. Unincorporated Fremont County, Wyoming. My visits there are not fast-paced. Indeed, I pass most of my time sitting: in the passenger seat of a truck, on the wheel well of a tractor, on whatever flat space is free in the cab of a combine. But as my hosts and I make slow revolutions around a field or drive from one pasture to another, what happens is not dull. What happens is we talk. Or, typically, they talk. On most days the conversation lasts for hours.

"They" are farmers and ranchers, though generally not those from the front row of the church, that select few who remain in conventional agriculture. These are the ones who were trimmed off long ago, or at least by the industry's prescription, should have been. As we sit and talk, the topics are sometimes technical, often political or economic, and always, ultimately, philosophical. And personal. If we start with a discussion of soil microbiology or a comparison of turkey breeds, inevitably we end up in family, history, ecology, faith, beauty, morality, and the fate of the world to come. For them, all those things are linked.

As they see it, agriculture is not an industry on the periphery of modern civilization. It is a fundamental act that determines whether we as a society will live or die. What binds these people is not a particular farming method, but rather the conviction that as humans, the contributions they make are essential. Conventional agriculture doesn't need people for much more than to run the machines and carry the debt, but these people refuse that lifeless role. To the work, they bring their intellects and their consciences, their histories and their concerns for the future. In quiet ways, in quiet places, they have set about correcting the damage that has come from believing agriculture could actually be reduced to numbers alone. The first step: reclaim their place in the center of the equation.

That Sunday morning in Balfour, after I left the abandoned church but before I got back on the highway, I drove into what was

4

left of the town. Beyond a scattering of houses, I came to a building that was newer but not new, non-descript except that its doors were wide open. Outside were a few cars—cars that had arrived there that morning, not two decades ago. It was the town's last working church. Technically it was Lutheran, but the congregation was so small that any person was welcome. What mattered was that they were there at all, listening, talking, praying, and even singing.

If the closed-down face of Balfour represents the disappearing human role in agriculture, then this book is about the people in church that Sunday morning. They are the faithful, the ones who believe, despite everything society shows them, that what they are doing is worth it—that it is vital. When their nation tells them this is the way it is, and this is the way it has to be, they do not just fade away. Instead, they talk, and they pray, and they sing at the top of their lungs. *To hell with what you've decided is convention,* they say. *We are unconventional farmers.*

Sulphur Springs, Texas

The great cities rest upon our broad and fertile prairies. Burn down your cities and leave our farms, and your cities will spring up again as if by magic; but destroy our farms, and grass will grow in the streets of every city in the country.

—Nebraska Congressman William Jennings Bryan,
speaking at the Democratic National Convention of 1896

1

THE FIRST TIME I ever met the dairy farmer Harry Lewis, he talked for two hours straight—over the telephone.

The second time I met Harry Lewis, I stopped him in a hall-way at an all-day conference. The proceedings had just broken for lunch, and as he talked the food line formed before us and then grew, snaking into another room. Two hundred people shuffled by. When finally Harry was done talking, he and I each walked right up to the buffet, helped ourselves to what was left, and took seats warmed by people who had already come and gone from the meal.

The third time I met Harry Lewis (and this I could not be-lieve): five hours straight. For five hours we sat on the porch of his house in Sulphur Springs, Texas, side by side in wicker chairs, fac-ing the yard and the pasture beyond. It was ninety-one degrees and the man didn't sweat, didn't drink, didn't unlace his heavy, black boots, didn't even stand up. He just talked. Had I not stopped him I swear he would have gone long past sundown.

The first time I met Harry's wife, Billye, it was the first thing she said. "Everyone in Hopkins County knows about Harry Leon.

Everybody knows you don't talk to him unless you have some *time*."

Apparently he takes after his late father. It's said that by the end of his life, Harry Senior didn't even stop for periods—he'd just string his words from the porch to the barn to the pasture, his whole day one endless sentence. As Billye was telling me this, a local repairman arrived to deliver a part for their truck. She passed the statement on for confirmation—*You know Harry likes to talk, right?* The man nodded vigorously but still only nodded, as if merely talking about Harry's talking would draw him irrevocably out of his day and into infinite conversation.

That said, this must also be said: Harry is not a droning windbag, the kind with whom conversation feels like slow-moving punishment. If you're on a schedule or need to be somewhere else, the loquaciousness can be maddening. But if you have time to sit back in a wicker chair and just listen, his trip is worth taking.

Partly that's because when Harry talks, it is not just speaking, it is speech. The ideas come spontaneously, but he works strategically: He anchors the big concepts with catch phrases and asks questions that he then answers himself. He spaces his words out for just the right emphasis. He slows his voice to ar-tic-u-late words like pas-ture and man-ip-u-late. When that's not enough, he adds extra syllables, making pro-fi-t or p-rou-d.

The result can be so compelling that I want to rise to my feet and yell *Amen!* Other times he just starts rolling on a topic, seemingly with no idea where he's taking it, and his words get mixed up and his logic gets shaky and the ideas pour out of his mouth, out of control. It's like watching a person run down a hill: his steps propel themselves and he must just trust that they'll keep coming, one after the other, until the ground levels out and the pace slows down and finally all those words make sense again. You ask Harry a question about the organic milk cooperative he is part of, and he'll begin to talk about it, then segue into how Organic has been hijacked by corporations, how those corporations are enabled by corrupt politicians, then into nepotism, populism, the erosion of the Democratic Party since the 1960s, fundamentalist Christians' manipulation of the working man, God's supremacy, Mount Saint Helens, Muhammad Ali, terrorism, Hillary Clinton, Jerry Falwell, Thomas Jefferson, and the mayor of Sulphur Springs, and as you listen your head spins and you've no clue what his point is. You might try to steer him back to the original question, but you can't get a word in.

Then, suddenly, you arrive with him at the 359th degree. You realize that this rambling promenade has brought you right back to where you started, except now you're looking at it from a whole new angle. From speaking of the mayor of Sulphur Springs, he goes to the democracy of his organic milk cooperative, and how being an active member in that democracy allows him finally, after years in the cutthroat dairy industry, to farm the simple way he does in peace. Whether or not he knew *how* he was going to get there, he knew where he was going all along.

And then he's off again.

As Harry's mouth sculpts the important words, his face does acrobatics to match. To raise his eyebrows as high as possible, he will stretch out his eyelids to their limit, nearly closing his eyes. Then he'll tip his head back and look out from the slit at the bottom. (This look he reserves mainly for when talking about corrupt politicians.) Or he will drop the shoulder that's nearest you, lean in confidentially, then squeeze shut the eye on your side and turn his head just enough to look at you with his other eye. When thinking of a point, he will stick a forefinger in his eye and scrunch his entire face up around it, as if taking in delivery of new information through his fingertip.

Best of the acrobatics is when he laughs. It begins with his smile, a wide banner of pink gums and long, shiny, perfect denture teeth. He then closes his eyes tight and makes a laughing sound to match the moment—anything from a snicker to a hoo-haw to a breathless, on-the-verge-of-tears, sort of wheezing sound. Sometimes he laughs so hard that he throws his body forward and folds in half, chest laid on top of thighs, arms tucked up in between, and he rocks back and forth, folding and opening, until he runs out of steam. If you laugh with him, he laughs even harder.

All this laughing and deep thought and suspicion of politicians has carved lines in Harry's face. Technically they are wrinkles, but they come across more as the resting position of some very active skin. Really, by all rights he should be wrinkled like a raisin, being sixty-one years old and at the far end of some very hard living, yet he does not look like an old man. He is tall and thin, and strong. In the morning he might limp a little bit with stiffness, but during the rest of the day his walk could be called a swagger. When he grips with his hands, veins pop up through the smooth skin of his arms. His hair is shorn short and nearly always under a hat, so unnoticeable that its gray color will surprise you when he lifts his cap to wipe his brow.

Also, Harry is black. Or African-American, whichever you prefer. He uses both. On one hand it is an integral part of his story, an element that has shaped his experience of life and farming from the start. He resisted the draft for Vietnam because he felt that the United States had not yet fully made him a citizen. ("Your war? You fight it," he remembered saying. "Show me freedom first.") Around the same time he had what he refers to as a "black power period," and was briefly a Black Panther. He remembers meeting the KKK in his town.

On the other hand, race is not his primary identity. He is first a proud Texan, a proud dairyman, a proud native of Hopkins County, and the current head of the Lewis family. Put simply, he wants to be known as a person, not as a black person. He says he's not very popular with some other African-Americans in his community, because they don't like his philosophy. "I say stop pointin fingers and get to work changin things. Back in the Sixties we used to carry signs sayin WE SHALL OVERCOME. Well, I'm not interested in what we *shall* do. I'm interested in where I am."

The value Harry holds highest, the one that overrides everything else, is that of fairness and equality—in the most literal, fundamental application of the words. Every person gets a life, and every person should have the same fair chance to make that life as good and right as he or she can. Harry is tired of elitist politicians who pronounce themselves important, tired of celebrities and the people who worship them, and sick to death of preachers who claim that we need them to save us. As he sees it, the only true hierarchy is between God and man. "After that," he says, "we all even-steven."

That conviction is what first signaled to me that what Harry had to say was worth listening to. I had a freelance job interviewing and writing short profiles of several dozen members of his organic dairy cooperative. Each one was passionate about being a small farmer in the age of agribusiness, and all were devoted to maintaining a sense of craft in their work despite the industry's pressure to make their farms more like factories. When I called Harry for an interview he spoke about the same ideas as the others, but he linked them to a story bigger than his own, and to a moral code that extended far beyond farming. I asked him who he was, and he replied with the history of dairy farming in Hopkins County, Texas, the history of his own family going back four generations, praise for his wife, for his granddaughter, a treatise on home economics, corporate greed, free enterprise, populism, and a short story about biscuits that demonstrated the power food has to connect people. At the end of our conversation he told me something he had learned from his father, a dairyman before him. The words still ring in my ears. "I learned from him that you worked not to be rich," he said, "but to be free." That's who Harry is.

———•———

The Lewis farm in Sulphur Springs, Texas, is not in the Texas you might imagine. This is not the land of longhorns and lonesome, dusty trails; of oilmen who drive Cadillacs and press the gas with alligator-skin boots. Harry will proudly tell you that this is Texas, but it is *East* Texas—more South than Southwest. While Dallas/Fort Worth is the closest metropolis, eighty miles away, Texarkana is only eighty-five going the opposite direction on the freeway. Shreveport, Louisiana, is just a little farther on back roads. This is the Texas of slow-smoked barbecue, all-you-can-eat catfish, and get-up-and-clap-your-hands gospel music.

All of which means that, when I arrive at the farm one Monday morning in June, I am greeted not by a great desert quiet but by a riot of birds. Scissor-tailed flycatchers loop down out of the trees, their long, showy feathers trailing behind. A striped killdeer pecks through the mud. Barn swallows dart and ping and turn on a dime in the air, so many of them I cannot follow one for longer than a few seconds before it's lost in the crowd. In the branches of the big walnut tree that hangs over the barn, there are dozens more that I can only hear: eastern phoebes, cardinals, a mockingbird mimicking a red-shouldered hawk.

I stand watching them a while, then realize something is wrong: There are *only* birds here. The barnyard is empty of cows, the barn is empty of people. At eight o'clock on Monday morning, even the slowest-moving farm would be in its first stirrings. A dairy farm, though? I would expect activity since the sun rose two hours ago— since *before* the sun rose. Eight is normally time for a dairy farmer's coffee break.

Then again, Harry Lewis is known for doing things his own way. What's more, he is known for being absolutely sure of that way. He doesn't need others to follow him, but he'll be damned if he'll follow them. Mention his name to people in the Texas dairy business and you're likely to get a strong response—some positive, some not so positive. Over time I've learned that in order to see his eccentricity as the gift that it is, a person has to be patient. So I watch the birds some more. I go back to the milk barn and look in the door, listening for a radio or something. Instead, silence. Birds.

I start to wonder what's wrong—I mean, you can't just *not* milk. Then I hear a screen door slap shut at the house, and across the lawn walks Harry's son, Wynton. He says good morning. He has just woken up. Nothing is wrong.

Wynton is over six feet tall and has one of those invincible-looking bodies people possess only at age twenty-three, when they are as strong as they will ever be. This morning he has thrown on a T-shirt with the sleeves cut off and zipped his coveralls only up to his waist, leaving the arms and collar hanging down behind. His dark hair is clipped close to his skull, and over it he wears a black doo-rag. When I first met Wynton I was sure he was a badass, but it turns out he's just shy. As he opens up, he's even quite sweet. When I ask him where the cows are, he says with a chuckle that he was wondering the same thing. He gets on the hulking orange tractor and fires up the motor, then motions for me to come up and sit on the giant wheel well.

Wynton's house, within a stone's throw of the barn, was his late grandfather's house, or at least the one rebuilt on site after a fire some years ago. Harry used to live there, moved years ago to a house built by his late brother on the next property over. The farm driveway is basically the gravelly dead end of the county road. It enters from the west, goes in front of the barn, then the house, then turns to dirt and heads out to the pasture that surrounds the buildings. Tractor rumbling, Wynton and I head down the dirt and into the grass, our eight-inch wheels leaving deep tracks in the soft ground.

The pasture is wide, flat, and round, covered in grass and various other pasture plants. The borders are thick with tall, leafy trees that keep you from seeing very far in any direction. In places strips of trees have even slipped inside the pasture, and this morning that is where Wynton figures the cows are. We approach from the left, slowed by the wet ground but also in no hurry. When the engine's noise reaches the trees, cows appear from out of thin air: moving out of the dark shade, standing up in the tall grass. Even before we get there the first ones walk past us, toward the barn. In retrospect, I believe Wynton was being demure by saying he wondered where they were. I'd bet the cows are in those strips every morning. The process, as it turns out, is less a matter of finding them than of giving them a wake-up call.

Wynton drives the perimeter of the pasture, looping up and down the edges of various strips of trees. As he goes the cows appear and walk. Or they don't, and instead keep lounging or chewing in the shade until the forked arms of the tractor come near enough to roust them into joining the procession back to the barn. At times Wynton gets off the tractor and approaches a cow on foot, hollering if necessary. Is there a secret to it? "No. Once you get them moving, they'll go."

He goes, and they go, and alongside them hundreds of other creatures go in all directions. Out here there are ten times as many birds as there were back at the barn, all swooping and chirping in the morning air. Yellow butterflies flutter around the pink pompom flowers of mimosa trees. Despite the heat the rains have kept the grass lush and green, especially in the shady areas. From my seat the scene is a pastoral fantasy, though I realize that for those directly involved this morning chore is as routine and unremarkable as brushing one's teeth. The cows seem neither happy nor unhappy with it, and the same goes for Wynton. To him, it's just Monday morning at work.

After rousting a few stragglers out of the shade and doing a silent head count, he starts back toward the barn. The cows in front have slowed down, even stopped to graze, and in the rear they are spread out enough that a few can start to slink away. Wynton corrals and hustles them, as much as it is possible to hustle something while on a tractor in mushy grass. He bounces the forklift behind one heifer, swerves behind another that's drifting too far out of line. It's a slow procession, but a procession nonetheless.

Watching from atop the wheel well, I have a good view of the herd. They are various mixtures of various breeds, which means they are golden brown, or black, or white with black spots, or brown with white spots. The biggest ones are no taller than Wynton's shoulders, but mostly their heads come to between his waist and chest. As Harry explains to me later, smaller cows can take the Texas heat. He tells me proudly they are breeding their own cows, and in fact already have two that are native to this very farm. The hulking Holsteins that populate most American dairy farms will stop and lie down as the temperatures rise, but these cows just keep eating. "You can hear them at night," Harry says, mimicking their munching motion with his own mouth.

Looking down at them it occurs to me this is unlike any dairy herd I've seen. At most other dairies in the United States cows are organized into groups by age and kept separate for the sake of efficiency. Here the herd of about eighty animals is milk cows as well as calves, who try to suckle en route to the barn. There are young heifers and heifers ready to be bred, even growing male calves with their sacks starting to fill out and hang behind them. The only thing missing from the family portrait is a bull. This I can understand—dairy farming is all about managing reproduction, and a fourteen-hundred-pound alpha male would not respect the necessary schedule. But I can't understand the calves. The whole point of a dairy farm is to get milk from the mothers; having the calves in with them would be a loss. Over the rumbling engine I ask Wynton, and he gives a simple answer back over his shoulder: "Mamas do a better job raising them than we do."

Later, Harry explains further that the calves' suckling helps their mothers ward off mastitis, an inflammation of the udder that is the bane of dairy farmers everywhere. But mostly his answer is the same as Wynton's. "The mothers take care of the calves better than we can. I mean, we could bottle-feed them, but that's more labor on our part." On a lot of small dairies the children look after the calves, but Wynton's three kids are still all under five years old. To feed the calves they would probably have to hire someone, which would cost money. In the larger equation of the Lewis farm, letting the milk cows take care of the calves makes the most sense.

From the beginning, the Lewis farm has run on this mathematics of frugality—that's what has kept this business afloat for more than fifty years. As much as possible it runs on what's available for free: grass, rain, family members. They have bought the equipment needed to run a modern dairy, things like milking machines, milk tanks, trucks for hauling hay, and a tractor with various implements. They also buy feed, though only as much as necessary. Otherwise they don't upgrade unless they must, and they have no interest in growing the farm. They don't take out loans. Harry's wife, Billye, who is in charge of the farm's finances, put it simply: "We've stayed in business because we've stuck with what we had."

———•———

The white, concrete-brick milk barn was built in 1952, when Harry was six years old. Today there are still bricks in piles around the farm, and I wonder if they are in the same places they were left a half-century ago. Certainly the barn has not been changed. It is tiny, the milking room smaller than my living room, the adjoining room just big enough for the eight-foot-long milk tank, a sink, and space for a person to walk through. The ceiling is low, maybe a foot and a half over the Lewis men's heads; the roof is corrugated tin. The section that hangs over the barnyard entrance is missing tin sheets here and there, and those that remain are in various stages of rust. In the tank room, three panes of a six-pane window have been replaced by a piece of plywood, which itself is now starting to come apart.

I ask Wynton what he thinks of the barn. He gives a soft laugh and a smile of resignation. "It's legendary. Been around longer than I have."

Wynton clearly has plans for, or at least imaginations of, bigger things here. It goes without saying he'd like a better barn, and who knows what else. To that end, roaming the yard and meadows is a herd of Boer goats, which he raises for extra money. At the edge of the pasture's far side he has installed what looks like a kennel for a three-hundred-pound dog. It's a trap for wild pigs. Wynton heard about a guy over in Greenville who pays cash for the pigs so he can turn them out on his leased land and charge people to hunt them.

A month ago there were pigs all over the woods here—that's why Wynton got the trap—but since he put it out he hasn't seen a one.

Today, though, Wynton is sticking with what they have. He is in the dirt yard behind the barn, where the herd now mills about. Most of the yard is under a wooden roof, so at least the ground is dry and solid, but with manure accumulating and flies in abundance it's not as idyllic as the pasture. Homemade fences of wire and steel bars and even some slats of corrugated tin divide the yard into sections: a pen to the left of the barn entrance, where the cows go to be milked; an adjoining pen to the right, where they go after being milked; and this big open space where the rest of the herd hangs around until they get bored and return to the pasture.

Wynton walks among the milling cows, arms at his sides, studying the beasts and making sure they go to the proper places. To steer a cow in one direction he might raise an arm like a traffic cop, but generally the animals know where they belong and go on their own. When all forty-two milk cows are in the pre-milking pen, Wynton clangs the gate shut behind them, tightly. It's a good thing Harry doesn't want to increase his herd size; it's hard to imagine fitting even two more cows in there.

I stroll around to the front of the barn and enter through the hallway into the milking room, where Wynton has started bringing in cows. By the time I get there, Harry has arrived and slipped into the morning's routine. The machine that would automatically deliver grain to the troughs is broken, so Harry is scooping grain from a bucket in the hallway and walking it to each stall, scoop by scoop.

Every workday he wears the same thing: cap, coveralls, and big, black boots that lace up around his calf. Today's cap bears the worn logo of Dairy Farmers of America, the processor they used to sell to. Today's coveralls are faded but clean, with no undershirt and unzipped to midway down his chest. At nine o'clock it's eighty degrees outside, and noticeably warmer in the breezeless barn. Harry loves the heat, would take the days ten degrees hotter if he could. He says it's part of being Texan.

Like most everything else on this farm, the room where they milk the cows is bare bones—working, but with no extras. Each side is divided into four simple stalls, with two steel rails separating each cow from the next. For every two stalls there is a milking machine, a long black hose that splits into four suction nozzles, one for each teat. To get it onto the cow's udder, Wynton bends over and matches teat with nozzle; from there it just slips on. Its pulsating suction is meant to replicate a calf's, but it's mechanical, and hungrier, sucking at the rate of windshield wipers on high. The other end of the hose attaches to a glass tube that runs the perimeter of the room along the ceiling. In it you can see the milk pumping and sloshing back to the tank in the other room. A salesman once tried to sell Harry's father a low-line system, whose tubes would run along the ground and therefore be out of range of an errant bull or other high-flying object. *But would it do anything differently? Harry Senior asked. Won't it carry milk just like this one does?* The salesman said yes. It was just another thing to sell. They stuck with what they had.

At the cow's rear there is a chain that can be draped across the stall and clipped into place, locking her from behind. Sometimes they use it, sometimes they don't. They don't seem to need any of this—the chains end up serving mostly to keep other cows from squeezing into the same stall. Some cows actually have to be nudged back out of the barn when milking is done. The non-Texan in me might sweatily suggest that the animals have been mellowed by heat, but really these cows are naturally sedate. Harry and Wynton don't even cut their horns anymore. It takes too much time and, as Harry says, if the herd is friendly you really don't need to. At one point, Wynton's toddler daughter Anika wanders into the milking room in a diaper and rubber boots. She slips but the padding of her diaper breaks the fall, so she just gets up on her feet and toddles out. The cows keep eating. Harry and Wynton keep milking.

The real risk here is not wild cows but collision. The room seems to be the bare minimum amount of space needed for eight cows, two men, and a lane into which the animals can back out of their stalls and walk to the door. If two cows aim to leave at the same time, one must wait. The concrete is slick with manure and mud from the hooves, and across the floor runs a yellow hose, its extra length twisting into treacherous coils as Wynton and Harry move it here and there to spray down the muck into slurry. Looking on from the doorway to the hall, I feel my worrywart mother rise up in me. It is everything I can do to keep from moving the hose out of the way each time a cow backs out of her stall. When one slips I have to stifle my gasp-and-flinch reflex and override my visions of shattered bones and other disasters. But not a thing goes wrong. Harry and Wynton and their cows have an unspoken choreography that makes it work. The two men crisscross constantly—walking to the grain bucket, pulling the hose, moving the animals—but they never get in each other's way. There is a moment of chaos when a cow decides to squeeze into a stall with another, but then the two animals just stand there uncomfortably until Harry slides the interloper out.

There is another moment, when a cow entering the barn sees me, turns as fast as she can, and runs out. As she goes she slides wildly as if on ice, but buckles her knees and manages to get out. Wynton jumps up and chases after her, slips for a second but makes it out the door clean. He marches the cow back in, and this time when she sees me she jolts forward, running too fast to slip, and flies past me in the doorway, through the hallway, and into the driveway. They let her go. Half an hour later, when the last few cows are being milked, Harry walks out to the driveway and brings her around through the gate and back in to be milked. He doesn't say a word.

Outside of these moments, the two men simply move through their twice-daily routine: put cows in and out of stalls, attach and detach the milking machine, scoop feed. Wynton doesn't talk much during milking, but Harry, working his side of the barn, always has something more to say. Sitting on the metal bars between two stalls to remove the nozzles from a cow, he'll have a thought, look up at me, and talk the thought out for five minutes or ten. He talks about cattle breeding, Paris Hilton, Dick Cheney, raw milk, the Nation of Islam. Each time it's long enough for Wynton to lap his father, turning over the four cows on his side of the barn while his dad's four cows sit idle, chewing their cud. But Wynton doesn't seem to mind. I figure he's used to it.

2

Harry's story begins long before he was born, in a community called East Caney that is about ten miles from the farm. The community dates to just after the Civil War. At that time East Texas was a relatively blank slate, sparsely populated and therefore offering land and opportunity to those seeking refuge from the damage the war had done to the rest of the South. While some white families had moved to places like Hopkins County during the war to protect their slave ownership from Union forces, these areas had never been part of the cotton culture. After the war, it allowed freedmen a fresh start that would have been much more difficult in places whose precedent was plantations.

Throughout East Texas hundreds of communities of former slaves took root, eleven in Hopkins County alone. The freedom colonies, as they came to be known, varied in character and size, but they had a common, defining foundation: their residents owned and farmed their own land. This was at a time when many sharecropping farms throughout the South remained barely indistinguishable from before Emancipation. Black sharecroppers were indebted to the plantation for their livelihood and to the company store for their sustenance. Schools and independent churches were prohibited, for fear they would "spoil" the people as laborers.

But in the freedom colonies, daily life was informed and defined by people's independence. They farmed their own land, and grew or made nearly everything they needed to live. In an interview recorded in *The New Handbook of Texas*, George Frances from the Antioch community in Lee County explained it this way: "I ain't never been to heaven but I'd rather have this here outside of anything I know. I can do anything I want to. All of it's mine. Nothing can be more enjoyable. Chickens crowing, get the eggs, eat the eggs, kill the chickens, and eat the chickens, and go on according to the year."

East Caney was the most prosperous of the eleven freedom colonies in Hopkins County, at one time having four schools and two churches of its own. Homes there were not the shacks of the Jim Crow South but houses with dining rooms and wide hallways—a few of them still stand today. Mary Ross, a resident of Sulphur Springs, recalled to me her grandfather who bought a farm there and built a house that he always kept freshly painted. "He even added some property to the farm when another man was in need of some money," she said. "The man borrowed from my grandfather, and when he didn't pay him back my grandfather foreclosed on him. We always talk about that at family reunions, how they were right out of slavery—I mean, my grandfather remembered being sold with his mother—he couldn't even read or write, and still he foreclosed on that man."

Harry's paternal grandparents, Sam and Bettie Lewis, were longtime residents of East Caney. Shortly after the couple was married in 1887, they bought one hundred acres of farmland. Not long after, when Harry Senior was a child, Sam died. Bettie, left with a houseful of sons and a farm to run, proceeded to buy another hundred acres. How she did so is a mystery to Harry—he says she could barely write her name to sign the deed.

"When I went to the courthouse and read the land transfers and burials, I said, *Wow! Where did they get the money to do this?* How is it that African-Americans were supposed to be making fifty cents, a quarter a day, and yet they're purchasing this kind of acreage? How did they have so much before Martin Luther King got here? I mean, why did they have this then and we don't have it now? As a community, everything we're doin now is *strugglin*."

———•———

By the 1930s and '40s the freedom colonies began to die off. Race played a role in their demise. Some local whites, feeling threatened by the success and independence of the black communities, swindled their land through shady business deals. In other cases they outright harassed black landowners into selling their farms. For the most part, though, places like East Caney disintegrated for the same reasons that rural towns across the country did: there was less money to be made in farming, and more in urban work, so country people migrated to towns and then to cities. During World War II, people left for the military or war-industry work. Some people stayed living in the country but took advantage of the new roads and got jobs or went to school in town, abandoning the business of farming.

For those who chose to remain in agriculture, with each new generation it became harder to stay. A two-hundred-acre farm might have supported Sam and Bettie Lewis, but as their children had children, the number of people dependent on that land multiplied. Either farms were subdivided among subsequent generations, making new parcels that were too small to support a family, or all but one heir had to leave.

By 1940, Harry Senior had married Elvira Harrison and they were living in their own house on the family farm in East Caney. His three brothers were still there, too, and the question of who would ultimately stay had not yet been answered. Then one day two white men in straw hats and khakis drove up to the farm looking for Harry Senior, offering him the chance to buy a farm. Elvira was suspicious it was a trick, perhaps a dangerous one, but they turned out to be legitimate government agents. The federal government had purchased a tract of land from a man named Smith. As part of the wartime effort to increase agricultural production, they were offering nine black families the chance to buy sections of it and build their own farms.

Immediately the Harry Lewises and eight other families bought the nine adjoining farms and formed their own community. Officially it was considered part of Mount Sterling, the preexisting white village with a church and cemetery; today the address is recorded as Sulphur Springs. Always, though, at least for the nine families, the settlement has existed unto itself, a place they called Smith Bottom or, for reasons no one today knows, Chicken Bristle. It was bottomland, which meant rich soil but with the trade-off of being in a flood plain. They didn't mind. What mattered was that it was theirs.

The creek to flood was Rock Creek, a tributary of White Oak Creek. The first time I spoke with Harry he told me proudly that White Oak was the lifeblood of Hopkins County, and that it ran all the way across East Texas and into Lake Texarkana, then on through Louisiana, into the Mississippi and on to the Gulf of Mexico. An apt metaphor, I thought, for how owning the farms at Smith Bottom connected the nine families to something larger than themselves. They all had roots in strong black communities like East Caney, but with Smith Bottom these nine families had their own place to build something new—a freedom community for the twentieth century.

The families of Smith Bottom had or made basically everything they needed—and lived a good life on top of it. They grew gardens with all the vegetables they could eat and raised chickens and rabbits, hogs and milk cows. On weekends the families might get together to butcher a hog, which meant cracklin' cooked fresh and thrown on the table with salt for the kids to eat. At night families would gather at one house or another and listen to the radio— a baseball game with Jackie Robinson, or new episodes of *The Shadow*. The kids tied tin cans together into make-believe freight trains and spun tire casings around the yard for hours on end.

As Harry remembers it, the government regarded Smith Bottom as an experiment in preparing farm families for the new world that was dawning in the 1940s and '50s. The county extension agents taught bookkeeping so the farms could keep up with their loans. The home economics agents came to the farms to teach the wives how to preserve food. They encouraged them to read *McCall's* and *Better Homes and Gardens*, aiming to inculcate them into what

Harry calls the "Ozzie and Harriet lifestyle." Elvira loved it. Harry remembers when on holidays she would set the table with multiple forks at each place setting and make him sit up with a proper napkin in a straight-backed chair. She would bring out the nice glassware and, invariably, Harry Senior would get to talking and gesticulating with his hands and knock a wineglass over, breaking the delicate stem. While he would always promise to replace it, as far as anyone's memory serves he never did.

As much as Elvira liked the Ozzie and Harriet idea, it was not the trappings of modern farm life that mattered. What made the family proud was not money but independence. Most of the parents of children at Harry's school had jobs as maids or laborers, but his father owned a farm and worked for himself. They were not wealthy, but they were free.

While growing up, the mindset of Smith Bottom was all Harry knew and in a sense he took it for granted. Only by leaving home did he realize the value of the farm and the security that it offered. At eighteen he went to Houston to attend Texas State University, inspired by Thurgood Marshall to study law and become a defense attorney. What happened once he got there he describes as a rather aimless time. He switched from law to studying accounting, then marketing, and after riots at the university in 1966, he simply dropped out. Defiant of the draft, he went to a trade school, then went to the streets, did drugs, hung out, all for too long. He always felt out of whack in the city, especially at night. After eighteen years of looking into the nighttime sky above the farm and seeing nothing but moon and stars, he found himself among neon signs and streetlights. It took him sixteen years to realize it, but eventually he came to appreciate what he had left behind. At thirty-four, he moved home.

"When I was young, I didn't want to farm because I didn't want to be confined. You know, when the baseball game's goin, you in the milk barn. Or if you wanna do somethin during the day then you have to do the milkin earlier, and then you have to get up earlier. What I failed to realize at that age: anything you do is confinin, but everything you do don't offer you a sense of freedom. And farming, as we were farming, allowed that. I gradually had a sort of metamorphosis. When I went on drugs that was the bad part, the worst part, but I ended up a country butterfly."

It wasn't until Harry returned to the farm that he learned the full story of Sam and Bettie Lewis in East Caney and went to the courthouse to see their land transfers of a hundred acres at a time. To this day he cannot figure out *how* they managed it, but he says that simply by learning that they *did* do it fundamentally changed the way he saw himself. Coming out of years of believing in black power—"when the fist was the salute"—he no longer felt he could claim to have been cheated out of opportunity. Instead, he realized that opportunity was under his very feet, on his family's farm. I once asked him if he moved home to save the farm and he told me no. He moved back because he needed to be saved, and only the farm could do it.

———

It is an autumn afternoon and Harry and I are driving the back roads of Hopkins County in his enormous Dodge pickup truck. It has double wheels in the rear, which make for a backside that juts out, as slender Harry would put it, like a "Wal-Mart butt." Perhaps because of the truck's girth he drives it loosely, kind of like the way he talks. When the road is clear he rides the center stripe. When a car approaches, he veers off so far that his right wheels sputter in the gravel and grass.

The truck bed is loaded with necessities: tanks of hydraulic fluid for the tractor and boxes of baling twine and a dusty cooler holding bottles of water and grape Powerade. He lives off the latter during the workday, figuring if he wants to eat he'll just save his appetite for dinner. Inside the cab there's a can of Vanilla Coke in the drink holder and a tree-shaped air freshener, scented like watermelon. He keeps a magnifying glass in the glove compartment in case he loses his glasses, something that has happened more than once. We ride with the windows open.

The countryside here is pretty and easy to digest—no stunning vistas but rather a constant flow of creeks and meadows and trees in all shades of green. We pass a herd of brown Jersey cows in a pasture, a house with a broken window, a man working on his garage. We pass by what looks like a vacant house and Harry tells me it is one of the Smith Bottom farms; the owner gave it up and moved to Fort Worth. After some silent dismay, he tells me that when the government set up the farms at Smith Bottom, they figured if two families paid off their farms they could call the program a success. "You know how many did?" he says, beaming. "Five. And they're all still here today."

We're going to visit one of them, which used to be a dairy farm but now runs beef cows. Beef is generally less stressful business, partly because it takes less time and commitment but more so because that allows a person to work another job. The farm is owned by Bobby Gay and her husband of forty-eight years, John. John is originally a city boy, and they say that when he first came here he had cowboy boots and a cowboy hat, but he didn't even know what a cow looked like. It was Bobby who grew up here in the bottom. By the acrobatics of a family tree in a small community, she is the niece of Harry's wife Billye, and yet she is several years Harry's senior—she used to babysit him when they were young. Like most people from Smith Bottom she calls him Leon, his middle name.

Harry is loaning them a hay rake attachment for their tractor, and before he and John finagle it off the machine, John shows me out of the heat and into the house. The kitchen is bright white and simple. On one wall is a wooden plaque with a blessing painted on it. Directly across from it, tacked to the wall, is a bumper sticker that says, I WAS COUNTRY BEFORE COUNTRY WAS COOL. In a space too small for it, between the table and the corner, is a standing freezer. At the counter is Bobby, a short, wide, friendly woman who speaks in a gentle voice and smiles after each point she makes. Her hair is in curlers and she wears a nightshirt that goes down to her knees. On it is a photograph of a kitten and the words NO AUTOGRAPHS, PLEASE. This isn't her usual look. She apologizes to me that she wasn't expecting my company and is getting ready for work, which is at the hospital in Rockwall, an hour away. I comment that it's a long way to go for work.

"Well, no, I just put on some good music. You heard of Willie Nelson?"

I nod.

"Yeah, well, Willie and I go to work together. It ain't bad."

She takes me into the living room and shows me a wall of family photographs: Her and John. Them with their children. Their children with their children. Her father in Western fancy dress, with a black cowboy hat, black shirt, and an enormous belt buckle. On top of the television is a framed photograph of a bull. Harry walks in and sits on the edge of the raised fireplace.

"I just admire him so much," Bobby says about Harry, talking to me but gazing at him. As she speaks, Harry looks at the floor, apparently bashful. "He is a legend, I say. He is an *absolute* treasure."

I'm not sure why, exactly, she is proud of him, and neither one of them fills in the blanks. Instead, Harry starts to lift his head and takes this as his cue to talk. It's about seemingly nothing at first, highlights from a conversation we had about frogs, something about the trash we saw earlier that day. As he talks I hear a murmur.

That's right.

Mmm hmm.

Oh, yeah!

It's Bobby. Her eyes are fixed on Harry.

"Some people might come up to a man's house and say that's all trash," he is saying. "But to them, it's a treasure. You can't walk up and judge someone else's home."

That's right!

"What you might see as trash is to them a treasure."

Eye of the beholder!

Each time Bobby speaks, her voice rises a bit, like a churchgoer during a sermon that's starting to steam. Until now I knew that Harry was different and special—deeply engaging, if hard to follow—but I never quite got him. Rhythm-challenged Yankee that I am, I always thought that those pauses between the points he makes were simply him thinking of what to say next, or a break to emphasize an important message. When he calls I respond with a flat, writerly *hmm*. Bobby, here just short of singing and clapping, completes him and sends him forward. As she does I realize that Harry is more than just an intriguing, quirky farmer with an unusual history and a lot of big ideas. He is a leader, even if only for a small group of people. Among the five remaining Smith Bottom farms, Harry's is the only one that's still a real, working dairy. He's the only one who has kept that part of the dream alive.

Now that he's warmed up, Harry returns, as usual, to the subject of power. As we move into the kitchen Harry explains that in the early days of Smith Bottom, they had their own church and in that church it was the families that made the decisions.

"Nowadays, people follow whatever the preacher says. Even Billye can't understand why I don't listen to the preacher—that's how she was taught. *Well*, I say, *you were taught wrong.*"

Mmmm hm.

"Our church back in the community took these votes. Even when we were just kids, father would pull us in to vote, everyone in the family voted."

Oh, yeah!

"The head deacon would get up and say, *The preacher's askin for a raise. But we've all had a bad year. So we say, you can preach your last two sermons and here's a check. Or, you can stay on as it is. All in favor*"—Harry straightens his shoulders and stiffens his body, hand tight at his side—"everyone stood up like military soldiers and voted yes. *And all those not in favor?* Nothin."

That's right!

"And so we told the preacher, you can take this and go on and we'll wish you well, or you can stay with us."

Yes, yes!

"But today, we've forgotten that preachers come and go. It's the churches that stay. It's the *people* that stay."

Mm, mm, mm.

Bobby nods as she puts two hamburgers on a cookie sheet, to reheat them for dinner before she heads to work. She peels a slice of American cheese and puts it on top of one, then repeats for the other.

"He is a legend in our time," she says, putting the hamburgers in the oven. "The torch has been passing, you see. Harry Leon is carrying on the torch for his farm, his family, his community. It's like if you have a relay race: it don't matter how fast that first runner is if the last runner can't finish the race."

Harry takes the compliment without so much as a nod. When Bobby finishes, he begins again with new energy.

"There was a time when I had cow problems, and my brother was sick," he says. "I had just lost a cow and I was feelin sorry for myself. An old man came by, a farmer, and I told him I just couldn't make it work anymore. Old man said, *How many more cows you have?* I told him forty-two. He told me, *You need to get your ass up and go to work. You got forty-two more chances.*"

Mmm! That's right!

"Old man walked off. I looked at that, and I said, *Damn right. I have forty-two more chances.*"

Forty-two!

"Then four more cows had healthy calves, forty-two went right up to forty-six."

Forty-six!

"He reminded me: That's it, that situation is done. Take what ya got left and put that extra effort into it. If you gonna do this, you got to *move*, 'cause nobody's gonna feel sorry for you, and nobody's gonna give you nothin."

Amen!

3

For decades after the Civil War, cotton was the major crop in Hopkins County. A profitable commodity, it was at least partly responsible for the economic growth in communities like East Caney. But it is also exhausting for both the land and the farmers who work it. As one man recalled in a local history book, by the 1930s, the crop had left Hopkins County a place of "worn-out farms and worn-out people." Gradually irrigation reclaimed land in West Texas and cotton farming moved there.

Looking for a replacement crop, farmers found that Hopkins County had near-ideal dairy conditions. Annual rainfall of forty-four inches made for lush pastures to rival Wisconsin and Vermont. An eight-month-long growing season meant cows could be out on pasture and feed themselves nearly year-round. As farmers switched to dairy farming in the 1930s and '40s, the county came back to life. While cotton had robbed the soil of nutrients, the grazing cows' manure recharged it. The nearly year-round payments of dairy farming provided an income far more reliable than the cotton commodity market.

For the next half-century, milk cows would be the county's primary industry and a source of deep pride for the people there. "The dairy business in Hopkins County has afforded the citizens of the county and the businesses of Sulphur Springs a level of prosperity unequaled in all of the state of Texas," a county promotional guide trumpeted in 1980. "How many towns with a population of twelve thousand people has four home-owned banks, a savings and loan, and other markers prevalent in this city? We have more nice brick homes, new automobiles, and vacations than any group of rural citizens in the state!"

The highest number of dairy farms officially recorded in the county was 507 in 1977, but local estimates range into the seven hundreds. Some people in town will tell you Hopkins was once the top-producing county in the South, perhaps even in the United States. Numbers don't back up the claims, but the county was indisputably number one in the state—the Dairy Capital of Texas.

In the 1950s, dairy became the lifeblood of the Lewis family. For the first decade in Smith Bottom they had sold milk to the local Carnation plant as a sideline to the farm business. Most farms in the county did. Because that milk would be evaporated and canned, it required only minimal, Grade-B standards; the half-can from the family cow passed the test. After the war came a rising demand for fresh milk, Grade-A, but that was a whole different business. Grade-A production required things like cement floors, hot water, and a separate room devoted to cooling equipment— for most farms it would mean building a whole new barn. Then again, the investment promised to return a more stable income and with it a certain prestige. Going Grade-A meant becoming a full-time, first-class dairyman, the proudest position in the local farm community.

To this day Harry speaks about his family's upgrade as a point of pride, remembering that in making the switch his father was counseled and encouraged by other black farmers who promised it would "set him free." The first day they filled cans with Grade-A milk and sold it to the creamery was June 6, 1952. The date rolls off of Harry's tongue.

"Oh, I remember when they built this barn." Harry sits on the rails between stalls in the milk barn, putting iodine on a cow's teats. "I would sit over in the sand pile, taking bricks from the stack and building my own barn. Eventually they'd come and take the bricks away and use them for the big barn. So I'd get more, and do it all over again."

He sits there with a soft, happy look on his face. Then he has a thought, which makes him let go of the udder, stand up, and walk to the tank room. He returns and hands me a little white Styrofoam cup, the kind you use for orange juice in a motel's continental breakfast. The cup is filled with cold milk.

It is an odd moment. The cup itself is a picture of purity, but in a very dirty world. All morning long I've been surrounded by mud and manure. This barn was once painted white, but its walls are now brownish to shoulder-height—spattered from below and smeared by bodies. From this doorway my view is of eight cows' asses, one evacuating as I hold the cold milk in my hand. There are flies on the feed and on the cows, on my arm, on the walls.

But Harry is sure of this moment. He is sure of this farm and what he's doing here. He says his farm is always open to anyone who wants to see how they run things or just sit on the porch and talk. He knows the farm is old-fashioned and a bit run-down, knows there is an old Dodge pickup parked in the meadow and goats playing king of the mountain on a heap of scrap metal rusting in the pasture. He knows people will see a soupy sea of mud where Wynton has scraped the slurry from the barn, especially after the rains this past month. He knows that in addition to seeing the happy cows on green pasture they expect, they will also see things they might not like. Yet when I asked to visit, he said yes without a moment's hesitation.

"Imagine," he says, "if people saw where their milk normally comes from. Imagine if people visited a big, concrete dairy. You know what I call that kind of dairy? I call it a penitentiary. When you're not free to move, then you're incarcerated. Those cows are in a penitentiary." His face twists in disgust.

Harry knows his dairy is different. The difference is, in a word, pasture. Most people who don't think about farming a whole lot would probably assume the milk they drink comes from cows on pasture like in the classic red-barn image of a farm. Those who spend a lot of effort knowing where their food comes from likely know that most milk comes from cows that don't live on pasture. Either way, given the choice, most people would choose the milk from the cow that is on green grass. It's a major part of what people think they are buying when they pay a premium for organic milk.

It is true that the USDA mandates that milk certified as organic come from cows that have access to pasture, but to date that's as specific as they have chosen to be. This has been the source of a long-standing legal and legislative melee between farms and consumers who believe in green grass and farms that fulfill the requirement only as much as organic regulations require. There are even some dairies that have found loopholes large enough to slide in their multi-thousand-cow herds, for which the only thing they have resembling pasture is a lawn in front of the company's office. Farmers and consumers who believe in cows on green grass have campaigned for the USDA to more concretely define the pasture requirement, for instance as a percentage of the cow's diet or the number of days per year it is available, in order to rule out those dairies that do not truly meet the criteria.

For Harry, though, pasture is not quantifiable. It isn't a standard to be met; it is a principle. Either you have it or you don't. "We all realize the golden rule for organics is pasture," he says. "But people take that lightly. They write it on their cartons, but do they do it as religiously as they would wear a Christian cross or hold a Bible or some other holy book? They say, *Yeah, we believe.* But really do they? If they do, do they practice? The word *pasture* must be *practiced.* And if it's not practiced, it's not pasture. And it's not Godly created."

I am intrigued, but not exactly sure what he means. He continues.

"Pas-ture. You can use the word in the same way that you use the word godliness. We all love to use the word G-O-D. You can use pasture the same way—it doesn't change."

"Um, how do you mean?"

"Because God is the creator. And pasture is the foodstuff for his creation. You can't have one without the other. If he created

this heaven and earth, he created pasture. To feed his existence."
Harry's on a roll. "Why was Noah goin around pickin up animals?"
He lets out a great, big laugh. "Heh? Because he knew there would
be a pasture. If there is a God, there is a pasture. Noah did what
God told him to do. He says, *Okay, I'll get the animals*—he didn't
worry about feeding them."

"Because he knew that as long as there was a God there would
be pasture?"

"Pasture! Our Earth is a pasture."

He explains further, how the Earth is made of rock, and that
rock becomes topsoil, and that topsoil is the basis to produce plants
and animals. That is pasture. To Harry, pasture is not simply grass,
it is the natural order of things, the uninterrupted, unadulterated
food chain.

"The seal, it's an underwater animal, but it pastures. And the
whale, if it eats krill, it receives it from the coral reef, which what?
Comes from the topsoil! Just because it's in cold water don't stop it
being topsoil. Because it's producing nourishment to create the krill
to create the enormous animal called the whale, it's pasture."

Pasture is godliness. As Harry talks he twines the two words
together. He disdains the corporations for trying to alter or obscure
the meaning of *pasture* for their own profits, changing the cow to
live on grain and concrete for the sake of their annual reports. In
the same breath he deplores so many churches' commodification of
spiritual belief.

"People try to sell. They sell crosses, they sell Bibles, they sell
images. But *It* ain't a picture, *It* ain't a cross you're wearing around
your neck. You read scripture, that's fine, that's to reinforce. But

you have to get out here and say, I *feel* it. *That's* what It's about. Church is a building, a place to assemble and worship together. But *every day* is God."

He lets the words hang in the air between us.

"I look at him as an invisible. If I see God as I see Jesus Christ, like everybody got him in their house"—he draws his breath, draws his eyebrows straight up in supreme contempt—"well, I know where that's goin. That's one certain people sayin"—he switches to a mocking falsetto—"*This is the way God looks.*"

He switches back to his own voice. "No! This ain't the way God looks *to me*. Visibly, I don't want to see God. I want to see him *invisibly*, moving the mountains. And when *he feels* that the mountains need to move. I can want it now, but it don't work that way. And that's the organic way. I want to rush, but unh-uhh. Be patient, and he'll getcha there. He'll get you there and give you back more than you ever thought you could have.

"Cows, we have modified to use grain instead of pasture because it's a boost feedstuff, and it's faster, and it produces more milk, which is about profit. And stock shares. So we think that is the better way. But from the beginnin we're totally backwards in our thought process. God didn't give us *nothin* to make better—we have destroyed everything that God gave us. In organic we're just tryin to get it back to the way it was. We got to get back to what God has, and then sell *that*. And when you do that you understand that you don't create prosperity. You *receive* it, through your efforts of shepherding."

In my hand is the little white Styrofoam cup, filled with milk. It's close to ninety degrees in the milk barn. I'm sweaty and dirty.

Harry has returned to the stall where a red cow with white spots waits. He is pretending not to watch me and the cup. To be honest I don't even like milk. My sister drinks it by the gallon, but I have refused it ever since I could speak the words to do so. At least this serving is cold.

Lifting the cup to my mouth I see that the liquid is not pure white but slightly yellow, with butterfat. It's chilly on my lips. Creamy, cold, crisp. It tastes like melted ice-cream-flavored milk. I drink it all in two swallows.

"Wow!" I blurt out. I don't ask for one, but I want another cup.

Harry just nods, doesn't even look up as he puts the milker on the red-and-white cow before him. Doesn't need to. I can feel the swagger. When at last he stands up, he looks at me and points to the cow. "That milk is not two hours old," he says. "Went from this cow, straight to you."

After he says that I look at the barn again. It's still old and cramped, with more than its share of flies. The white walls are still messy. And yet, I realize, what milking barn is attractive? What cows do not shit? What dairy farmer has clean coveralls at the end of the day? No dairy is all just pretty cows on green pasture. It's a messy business. The true measure of right and wrong here is not one of manure or mud, but rather of the details. The calmness of the cows and the people. The pace of the work and the attention it allows. Even the shit: most dairy cows have a sticky coating of manure on their backsides and tails. It's the result of replacing pasture with an unnatural diet of grain and the ill health of confinement, both of which can lead to perpetual diarrhea. Harry's cows, on the other hand, defecate solidly. Their feet may be muddy, but their rears are clean.

Cleanliness. Godliness. Pasture. "That word," Harry says, "is going to put farming back like it's supposed to be. So I keep puttin it out there. Tell them people, if you can't go to a farm that's like Mr. Lewis's, that's wide open, something's wrong. It's open house with us every day. But go and see what those penitentiaries do, and you will see that it   ain't   farmin."

4

It's a slow day at the airport rental car center. For the two young guys at the counter, a customer—any customer—is a welcome diversion. I give the shorter one my reservation number, and he starts punching away at a keyboard. His taller coworker watches him type.

"So, where you going?" the short one asks.

"Clovis."

The two look sideways at each other.

"Have you been there?" I ask.

"Once," the tall one answers.

"What did you think?"

Silence. He is unsure how frank he can be with me, for I am on one hand also relatively young and friendly, but on the other hand a customer.

"You don't have to answer that," I say.

He wrinkles his nose. "It smells like cows."

The shorter guy hands me my paperwork and keys, and the taller one leads me through a door to my car. They upgraded me to a convertible, probably to be nice but possibly as a cruel joke, given my smelly destination.

"Have fun!" He waves goodbye.

———

Interstate 40 heading east out of Albuquerque is a fast track into one of those vacant pockets of the desert West, where you're more likely to see a beef cow than a person, where radio and telephone reception fade out and the only communication for travelers is through billboards.

MEET JESUS AT THE GOOD SHEPHERD CHURCH

SUN 'N' SAND RESTAURANT & MOTEL

BEGIN A CHALLENGING NEW CAREER IN . . . CORRECTIONS

Stretched across about twenty miles is a series of signs advertising the massive truck stop/food court/shopping emporium at Cline's Corner. Each one offers some new attraction to appeal to a separate demographic of highway travelers. Playgrounds, ice cream, souvenirs, clean bathrooms. Billboard number twelve or so reads: CLINE'S CORNER: SHOT GLASSES & ROADKILL. Plastic bags have collected at the base.

Cline's Corner comes and goes, but the barrage of billboards for other places and things continues endlessly. Then, unexpectedly, comes a message of pure beauty, of beautiful purity. It is a billboard with nothing to sell, just a royal blue background and a pretty blond woman in a crisp, white shirt. It's Miss America. In her hand is a glass of pure white liquid. MILK. THE ONLY THING I WORRY ABOUT IS RUNNING OUT. In this parched desert land, where the only birds are crows, the drink looks like a miracle. Her face is a beacon, growing bigger, brighter, shining—and then it's gone. I turn off the interstate and head southeast on Highway 84, to Clovis.

Immediately the mood of the land changes. No more billboards. The road's punctuation is now the occasional iron arch that announces the entrance to a ranch but leads only to a long, dusty road across the range. The land is flat, beige, open. Far off there are plantations of windmills, harvesting the energy that sweeps unimpeded across this high plain. Closer to the road there is one old-time windmill, rusted arms sitting still. Cactus and sage. Rattlesnakes and quail. More crows.

I slide through Fort Sumner, final resting place of Billy the Kid. I put the top down on the car and the blue sky above me triples in size. On the radio Emmylou Harris sings a train song, and I race a yellow-and-brown locomotive from the Burlington Northern Santa Fe, whose tracks run parallel to the road. My mother's husband is a native of New Mexico. When she told him I was going to Clovis, he pictured it in his mind. "Ah, cowboy country."

At 3:55 in the afternoon I cross the line into Curry County, heading straight east. By four o'clock, driving in front of me is a flatbed piled with huge bales of alfalfa—four feet high and six feet wide. From behind I see just the butt: two across, two high, a stack so tall I can't see any of the rest of the truck. I pull up alongside to pass it and count the bales. The load is seventeen long, which means there are sixty-eight bales total, or about 6,500 square feet of alfalfa. It smells green and fresh, like from some other world.

More houses now, and the first industrial buildings since Albuquerque. The road doubles into four lanes, then divides down the middle into a nominal highway. Irrigation pivots spring up in the fields alongside the road. A crop reveals itself. Billboards. Traffic. And then, like a shot to the head, the first dairy.

It reeks of cows just as the rental car guy promised, except the effect is less like a steaming cow pie in a meadow and more like a gas station bathroom—less a smell than a stench. At first the odor is disembodied; here in the eastbound lane all I can see is a dense row of evergreen trees running perpendicular to the highway. Seconds later they whiz past like a curtain opened, revealing land that is black, barren, and crowded by hundreds of black-and-white cows whose filth has turned them to black-and-gray. No trees, no grass, no humans in sight, just cows and dirt. The whole scene comes across like a charcoal line smudged across a piece of blank paper. Within a moment it's gone, and a sign welcomes to me to Clovis, New Mexico.

———•———

How did we get from Harry's place to this place, from godly pasture to bare dirt and concrete? The story begins in an unlikely spot: Southern California. In the period before and just after World War II, the nation's top dairy-producing county was Los Angeles. At that time, limited refrigeration, processing, and transportation required the source of fluid milk to be as close as possible to its final destination, so all cities grew local milksheds. The bigger the city, the more dairies were needed to support it. I know a farmer in California whose great grandfather had a dairy on land that is now part of Los Angeles Harbor, and whose great uncle raised cows in Compton.

Paramount, he says, was once the hay capital of the world. To this day, the Los Angeles County seal includes an image of a cow named Pearlette, her udder hanging in silhouette.

After World War II, Los Angeles quickly became the most populous county in the United States. More people meant an increased demand for milk, but an even greater demand for real estate. Dairy farmers there sold their ten- or twenty-acre spreads for incredible profit—in some cases from thirty- to ninety-thousand dollars an acre. They didn't spend the rest of their days golfing, however. With these huge sums they moved east and north of Los Angeles and built dairies of a scale the world had never seen.

Some accredit the choice to the farmers' ancestry. Most were relatively recent immigrants from Holland, and for them dairying was not something to graduate out of; it was life itself. The chance to build huge dairies was both a dream come true and a way to stay in business. Others say the decision came because reinvesting their windfall real estate profits in agriculture greatly reduced the capital gains taxes they would pay. Either way, what resulted were operations with three to five hundred milk cows at a time when, across the country, the vast majority of farms had fewer than thirty.

In the communities that grew around the farms—Dairy Valley, Dairy City, Dairyland—cows vastly outnumbered people. That is until the mid-1960s, when the population of Los Angeles needed more room and spilled over into what had seemed far-away lands just a decade before. Dairy Valley became Cerritos, Dairy City became Cypress, Dairyland became La Palma. Once again the farmers sold off and moved farther out, this time mostly to the Chino Valley. There they reinvested in even larger farms and built what would be the world's most concentrated dairy region for the next three decades. In time they would move beyond the Los Angeles market to sell their milk across the country.

Roger Harjes, a lifetime farmer in Green Isle, Minnesota, remembers seeing the change. "I was twenty-one," he told me. "Minnesota was in the Rose Bowl, so five of us got in a car and drove to California. Other people went to Disneyland on the days before the game but we went to the Chino Valley. It was the first I'd seen of that sort of thing. I mean, I'd seen pictures in magazines: hundreds of cows, and they each got on a conveyor belt, a machine attached to them and milked them, and when they got to the end of the carousel the machine came off. And I thought well, I guess that's California. I never thought that sort of thing would come to Minnesota."

Of course dairies were growing throughout the country—it was part of the evolution of agriculture. The difference with the growth of the Southern California dairies was one of magnitude. Their numbers had gone off the charts.

Until then dairying had existed on a human scale. As on the Lewis farm, capital investment served either for careful upgrades of considerable benefit—the milking machines, the bulk tanks—or to fill out what the farm could not provide for itself, things like machinery, supplementary feed, genetics to improve breeding. Otherwise, the farm was treated as a whole, mostly closed system. Its limits were determined by how much the family and its land could provide. Judging from census numbers, the maximum number of cows a family farm could support fell between fifty and a hundred. More than that and the system couldn't support it—they ran out of pasture, they ran out of labor, they couldn't afford to feed all the animals. It didn't make sense to get bigger.

These new operations in Southern California changed the scale of dairy farming by building a system that had no natural limits. The first step was to cease running a whole farm, and instead specialize solely in housing, feeding, and milking cows. As a dairy increased the number of cows into the hundreds and then thousands, the owner simply brought in whatever was necessary to accommodate the expansion. If they required more resources such as feed or water, they bought them. If they needed more humans, they hired them. Having transcended the family scale, limitation was merely a matter of money.

While the smaller farms in traditional dairy regions like the Lake States and New England were juggling the pros and cons of capitalization—while Harry Lewis's father was questioning the salesman on whether or not that new pipeline for the milk barn was worth the money—the new "Los Angeles–style" dairies were being built on the very philosophy of capitalization. Investing in larger operations meant the owner could employ the economy of scale; the larger the operation, the greater that economy. Not only was there no natural limit to size, the business actually worked better the more it grew. As a writer for the Texas ag newspaper *Country World* put it years later, "More cows means more milk, and more milk means more money." Done. The dairy industry never looked back.

It couldn't, really, because the spike in production from the industrial-scale operations unavoidably changed the dairy economy. As the supply of milk goes way up, the value goes down. To make the same net income, a farmer must buy more cows and produce more milk—which of course makes for more milk, which drives the value down further. Economics is too hard a tide for any one farmer to paddle against. With the advent of industrial-scale dairying, dairy farms of all sizes had two choices: adopt the philosophy of capitalization or be swept away. Forget godliness and pasture; efficiency was the new gospel.

Fast forward to the twenty-first century. The small dairy is not gone. As of 2006, three out of four farms in this country that have milk cows have fewer than one hundred of them. That's fifty-seven thousand farms. What matters more, though, is that three out of four milk cows in the United States are on farms with more than one hundred cows; 20 percent are on farms with two thousand–plus cows. And in 2007, the USDA reported that investment in dairies with one to three thousand animals had slackened; investors had moved their interests to those with three thousand to ten thousand.

In the new system, the lush climate that most people associate with a dairy farm—the very thing that made Hopkins County the Dairy Capital of Texas—is a liability. Moisture leads to disease and rainfall means manure running off the concrete lots where cows reside. And to support those lots where milk cows spend their days, you need hard, firm soil, not the pliable loam that grows good grass. With the exponential growth in the size of dairy herds, what's desirable now is a desert climate where rain is minimal; when water is needed, it is pumped in. For this reason, beginning in the 1990s, longtime leading dairy states like Wisconsin and New York were increasingly supplanted by regions in the arid West. Inland California. Southern Idaho. Clovis, New Mexico.

"There are dairies everywhere here," an extension agent with New Mexico State University told me while I was visiting Clovis. "You can't hide them—there are no trees."

He delivered the statement without irony or regret. He was not suggesting that you would want to hide the dairies, only that you couldn't. That's because they are a boon for New Mexico, particularly the destitute high desert communities on the state's border with Texas. Dairy has become New Mexico's top agricultural commodity, thanks to through-the-ceiling growth—a 104 percent increase in the past ten years. Indeed, the university is proud of exactly what I would think they'd want to hide. While they are only seventh in milk production in the country and seventh in number of cows, the University boasts that they are first in number of cows per operation—the average herd has 2,088 animals. Curry County, with Clovis at its center, has the largest average herds in the state, at 2,750 cows apiece.

———

Probably there are happy people, strong families, and pride of ownership in Clovis, as in any town, but from my vantage point I can't see it. A two-block strip of old-time downtown remains, with classic Western storefronts on a brick street. Around it, though, has grown a grid of box stores and mini malls that provide the town's new landmarks. A gas station attendant gives me directions: "Go nine lights and turn right at Wal-Mart. You can't miss it."

Between here and there are countless tacquerias, churches, and discount stores interspersed with little houses beleaguered by decades of wind, protected only by chain-link fences. Above each building, tall, lighted signs call out the occupants below: K-BOB STEAK HOUSE AND SALAD WAGON. CHINA BUFFET. MOTEL 6 and MO-TEL 7. #1 VALUE INN. DAIRY QUEEN. Above the Bison RV Center is a repeat of the Miss America billboard advertising MILK. One block down, another billboard with a woman on it, this time a Latina in a blue hardhat and yellow apron, standing in a meat locker look-ing happy. I CHOOSE OPPORTUNITIES. JOIN OUR MEAT SOLUTIONS TEAM. CARGILL.

Along the south side of town runs four-lane Highway 60, and alongside it run the railroad tracks. All day and all night, trains and big rigs come and go, bringing loads of one thing and carrying away another. Alfalfa hay, cottonseed meal, distiller's grains; milk, meat, heifers, and calves. At dusk I join them heading east out of town and quickly we're all back in the wide open, the sprawl of town blurred in the waning light. The road leads to the Texas border and into what's known as the High Plains, a land similar to here but long ago tamed for cotton fields. A green highway sign announces the upcoming destinations:

TEXICO 8

BOVINA 20

MULESHOE 30

While I'm headed for Muleshoe tonight, when I see a sign for County Road E, I make a quick turn off the highway. There's noth-ing at the intersection, but I see lights maybe a mile down the road, radiant pink in the twilight. I have a hunch.

I pass a couple of houses and a rusty windmill. Then, a po-lite distance beyond them, the cattle business begins. On the first lot is a massive colony of long, low wooden sheds, each divided in compartments about two and a half feet wide. The top half of each compartment is open, a pail hanging from each door. Row after row, for a hundred yards, then another hundred yards, then another. They seem to be vacant, but why would someone give this much real estate to an abandoned operation? Maybe land is really that cheap out here. No, wait. Sticking out of one compartment I see the head of a calf, and I get it. It's a veal calf. There's one in each of these stalls.

Behind the sheds is an open building that's two-stories tall and crammed with hay bales. Beside it, a sign in block letters: TULS CUSTOM CATTLE RAISING. Rather than the dairy I expected to find, this operation raises animals in conjunction with the industry. This first section is feeding animals for slaughter: veal calves, but also spent milk cows that will become hamburger and dog food. Just after the hay is a row of evergreens planted along the road. Through the branches you can glimpse the feedlot behind, where old dairy cows by the thousand mingle with brown beef cows and a random assortment of others destined to become low-grade meat. A sign planted in the evergreens: NO TRESPASSING.

Just driving down the county road I feel like I've crossed into a place that is off-limits, like I could get shot if I slow down or look for too long. I'm more repelled by this than anything I can think of, and at the same time I'm mesmerized. I roll along at three miles an hour, almost gawking. Just past another big hay barn the road ends in a T, but looking forward, I realize the drive has only just begun.

As far as I can see before me, there are Holstein cows. I could throw a wet napkin at the nearest one, and the lots beside it extend a third of a mile down the road heading east. Connected to the backsides of those lots are more lots, and behind them even more, stretching north. Imagine yourself on a boat at sea, where the wind-swept blue carpet extends to the horizon. Now replace each white-cap with a black-and-gray spotted cow, and all the water between with dirt. If there's a sunset in your imagination, replace it with a gray smear in the sky. Welcome to TULS.

This part of the operation is raising females that will replenish and expand the surrounding dairies. Each lot has a different age group—calves, young heifers, full-grown cows ready to sell. The work is basically feeding them high-protein rations until they're ready for market, and the lots are designed accordingly. A feed trough runs the length of each lot, and above it the fence is made of loose metal bars through which the cows stick their heads to eat. Between the troughs is an alley just wide enough to accommodate a feed truck. Driving along, I stop at the top of an alley and look down the row: a hundred heads lift their eyes from the trough and look at me. A second more and they look back down. No slot in the fence is empty.

The lots themselves are abjectly flat and featureless, the bare, brown ground delineated only with metal fencing. Within them the cows mostly stand in random distribution—being here with two others is no different from being over there alone. It looks odd, but isn't that just what cows do, stand around all the time? Not until later does it dawn on me: cows don't just stand around, they eat. In fact, pretty much all we ever see them do is stand in the pasture and chomp grass. With the grass removed, this is what they look like: purposeless.

There is one exception, one attraction. The dried manure and dirt has been plowed into a mound just taller than a cow, one in each lot. Some cows cluster around it to claim territory on the slight incline, to stand there still and tight around the single animal that owns the summit. King of the Mountain. Driving along, I imagine the ones at the top are trying to get a look at what's beyond this place. In reality, though, each one has that same empty look on her face. Eventually she, too, will get hungry and relinquish her post.

Earlier today I had the rather optimistic idea of coming out here in the dark and putting down the convertible top. I imagined occupying my eyes with the night sky and thus allowing my other senses to take over, to gain a more complex experience of this place. Turns out it's too cold, so I settle for just rolling down my window. When I do, a wave that is putrid and diarrheal rolls in. As I breathe it the only sound is the clinking of metal made by necks rattling the spaces in the iron gates above the troughs. I roll my window back up.

And then it all ends. Over the last fence the land turns to red dirt, plowed and ready to be planted next spring, probably with corn that will end up in the steel troughs. Panning the view, it's the same: road of packed, red dirt, then more red dirt cropland on the south side. Looking back over the feeding lots, I see the lights at the far end have turned into distant, dirty stars in the milky dusk. I cannot help myself. I take another drive by the lots, then turn back past the beef cows and veal calves. I follow County Road E back to the highway and rejoin the other travelers heading west toward Muleshoe.

No sooner do I hit the pavement than an orange light starts flashing in the rental car's console. I pull into a gas station and get out to inspect. Flat tire. It's hard not to think that TULS cursed me for meddling. Five minutes later I'm bundled up against the cold and on my knees under the floodlight of the parking lot, positioning the jack. An old, low pickup pulls up and stops, and the man inside gets out. Between drags of his cigarette he begins helping me, and with insistent chivalry he finally commandeers the tools, leaving me to stand by and make conversation.

He swears a lot, but he's nice. Tells me he doesn't mind helping, it's better than being at home, where he was just drinking beer and watching *Spiderman* with his nephews. Tells me he's looking after them for his sister and they were driving him crazy, all jacked up on Halloween candy. Tried to bribe them with the movie, but they just started watching and kept on with the candy, which made them a double pain in the ass. He ran out of cigarettes so he came down here to buy more, but really (I infer), to talk to the girl behind the counter, whom he says is his "friend."

"Your girlfriend?"

"Man, who even knows? She's damn twenty years younger than I am."

"Oh."

"I'm Javier," he says, holding his now second cigarette between his lips and sticking out his hand.

I tell him my name and ask if he works in Texico, the cleverly named border town that's the closest place to here.

"No. I just collect unemployment and fuck around."

"How long do you think that'll last?"

"Another couple months, probably. 'Til my unemployment runs out and my lawsuit settles."

"What's your lawsuit?"

"I worked at the Excel plant but they fucking fired me," he says. Excel is the meatpacking plant in Texico, where TULS's slaughter cows will likely end up. It is run by Cargill Meat Solutions, the place of opportunity advertised on the billboard with the happy, hard-hatted woman in a meat locker. Javier is not their poster boy. "I got hurt on the job and then some guys started talking, saying I was fuckin around, so they fired me. They had no reason to. I mean, it was total bullshit. So now I'm suing them."

He spins the nuts back onto the bolts that hold my new tire in place. "But shit, Cargill? They're a big corporation, they don't give a shit."

He leaves the tire iron and the jack on the ground and stands up. I thank him and we say goodbye as he gets in his truck. He pulls out of the light and onto the highway screeching. Within seconds he, too, becomes just another set of lights in the murky desert night.

5

Since early this morning, people have been lining up their lawn chairs along the sidewalks of Sulphur Springs. Where there are no houses, pickups are parked up on the curb and filled with whole families intent on getting a good view of this year's parade. Every child in town has a plastic bag furnished by Wal-Mart, and as the morning progresses they cluster in the middle of the closed-down streets, waiting with increasing restlessness. Finally, just after eleven o'clock, a seven-foot-tall toy train decorated with Christmas lights and tinsel chugs out of the fairgrounds and onto Connally Street. When the people riding it begin tossing candy canes to the crowd, the waiting children snap into action like aquarium fish that have just been fed. The forty-eighth Hopkins County Dairy Festival has officially begun.

The Christmas theme strikes me as slightly odd, given that it's the ninth of June and sweltering even on tree-lined Connally Street. But I learn there's a reason. The festival began in 1959 during Hopkins County's heyday as the dairy capital of Texas, and for decades the center of the celebration was the farmers themselves. In

1985, for the talent portion of the Dairy Festival Queen pageant, Miss Francie Bell performed a skit entitled "A Day on the Dairy From a City Girl's Eyes." It culminated in a tribute to the county's farmers, accompanied by the song "We Are the World."

The industry has dried up considerably since then—roughly four hundred local dairies have left the business since its height. Still, the festival makes a point of honoring those who remain. Thus the tinsel-draped train: This year's parade marshals are the Screws family, dairy farmers who are locally famous for decorating their house as "The North Pole of Texas" every December. They build a winter wonderland complete with nativity scene and thirty thousand colored lights, and give rides through it all on this train. You wouldn't know they were farmers if it hadn't been announced, but that's okay. It's no secret that elves and candy canes are more fun than milk cows, and so this parade begins with a flurry of tinsel.

The festival pamphlet explains that this year's theme is "Moo-niversities," or simply Moo U, a concept that comes with no explanation aside from an illustration of a leaping Holstein cheerleader with pompoms. The most diligently theme-loyal float offers a complete bovine college: On the front half a cow-costumed professor lectures to a group of cow students seated at desks, while "outside" a group of cow football players scrimmages beside a crepe-paper–covered goalpost. For the float entitled "Moo U Spring Break," the flatbed floor has been transformed into a beach with bed sheets the color of sand and ocean. On the shore a woman in a floppy, zip-up Holstein suit lies under a sun umbrella on a beach chair, sipping a tropical drink through a straw.

Most other floats make only a nominal nod to the dairy theme—girls throwing gumballs wear white t-shirts with black spots attached; someone has repurposed a worn choo-choo train by taping a cow windsock to the back. The float representing Cocina Maria Authentic Mexican Food Restaurant doesn't bother at all, instead the drivers blast Miami Sound Machine while a gaggle of little girls in the back do a wild conga dance and huck lollipops in every direction. The truth is, it doesn't really matter what's on the floats. As long as the candy keeps coming, the crowd is content.

From way down the street I see the head of a fiberglass cow, about twelve feet high. Aside from the size the likeness is quite realistic, and as it rolls closer I can see the udder, bigger than a hay bale and decorated with bulging veins painted Pepto-Bismol pink. With the cow comes a trolley whose banner reads "Hopkins County Dairy Families," under which sit ten adults and twice as many children. Some of the kids are excited about throwing candy, but for the most part the group is less than animated. Frankly, they just look hot, and tired.

Perhaps it's because I don't know anyone here, but from the sliver of sidewalk I've claimed the event passing by feels slightly hollow. One woman points out to me what she thinks is the problem: no music. The festival used to be held in May, but now that it's in June, the high school kids are already out for the summer and can't be bothered to get their instruments out. One year the festival organizers tried blaring country music from a loudspeaker attached to the courthouse downtown. Today, though, the closest thing to a marching band is Miami Sound Machine.

And yet I can't help but think it's not that simple. As I stand here I'm reminded of a story I once heard from a Native American man named Enrique: The young men in his community were re-learning the tribe's ancestral rain dance, hoping to save it from being lost to modernity. They spent weeks making elaborate traditional costumes and rehearsing their dance steps and singing, but no matter how much effort they gave something was always missing. Enrique watched them and knew. The purpose of the rain dance was to call on the heavens to bring water for crops in the field, but these young men didn't farm—nobody did anymore. Even if all their actions were perfect, they would never *feel* the dance. The meaning had dissolved.

Here on Connally Street, people from a dairy promotion group are handing out bottles of chocolate milk. A flatbed lined with hay bales carries employees of the dairy processing plant, all wearing matching T-shirts with the company logo. Three gray-haired men putt-putt by on antique tractors. And the nine girls competing to be Dairy Festival Queen ride past us, each waving from the backseat of a convertible. Later today, when they compete in a contest that involves milking a cow, most will be unsure how to work the udder, reluctant to wrap their hands around the soft, pink teats and squeeze.

What life the parade did have drains out as it heads south from downtown and onto the fast food and chain store strip that leads to the highway. The procession that filled tree-lined Connally Street feels diluted on this five-lane road, where two whole lanes are empty aside from the candy thrown into it and the kids scrambling about. By the time I arrive on the strip things have backed up, as each piece of the parade waits to enter the supermarket parking lot where the whole thing ends. I sit down on the curb in front of a Ford dealership, and it feels like I'm watching a traffic jam. This is the tail end of the parade, so no more floats. A string of antique cars and shiny new Corvettes passes by, then a series of enormous new tractors and combines from the implement dealer in town. Now comes a convoy of tractor-trailer trucks, undecorated except for the names of their companies written permanently on their sides: Brookside Farms Ice Cream, Winburn Milk Company, Grocery Suppliers of Sulphur Springs.

The trucks come to a standstill, and I look toward the parking lot to see what's behind the bottleneck. It's the enormous fiberglass Holstein, so precariously top-heavy that it can't make the tight turn into the supermarket parking lot. It can be solved—there are five lanes to work with—but that entails a slow process of backing up, which requires all nearby floats and trucks to back up, too. Some smaller entries are able to pass the whole mess and head to the next driveway into the parking lot, relieving the congestion somewhat, but the trucks in front of me are too far back to capitalize on the relief. Instead they just idle their engines and throw the last of their candy to the few tenacious kids still waiting with plastic bags below. When the candy is gone the truck drivers roll up their windows to keep the a/c in. Every once in a while they honk their horns, as festively as they can.

———◆———

By the time Harry returned to the family farm in 1980, the national strategy of farm growth and consolidation—"get big or get out"— was in full swing, nowhere more than in the dairy business. Of course as farmers increased their production, they only fueled the same old vicious cycle of supply going up and prices going down. In attempts to control the oversupply, the USDA sponsored programs that would buy out a farm's herd and exterminate it, just to keep their milk out of the market. At the same time, they offered guaranteed loans to desperate farmers, but only on the condition that the farmer have at least two hundred cows and that each one produce forty pounds of milk each day. They figured that with production any less than that, the farm wouldn't be able to survive long enough to pay back the loan.

"So the government sat up in a lab somewhere and decided it takes two hundred head of cows to make a living," Harry told me, his face contorting to underscore the offense. "Well, I don't *want* to milk no two hundred head of cows! And forty pounds of milk? As my brother said before he passed"—and here Harry starts to snicker—"if I can get forty pounds, I don't need your money in the first place! But what happened? Here in Hopkins County we have lost four hundred family farms to the idea of getting bigger, bigger, bigger."

At the end of 2007, 147 dairies remained in the county.

More than once Texas has been considered a nation unto itself, and what happened among dairies across the country was mirrored within state lines. After more than fifty years as the state's dairy capital, Hopkins County took a backseat to Erath County in 1989. In the middle of the state, an hour southwest of Fort Worth,

Erath's drier climate and cheaper land was better suited to larger, industrial-style farms. In time, even some Hopkins County dairies moved their operations there so they could expand. Then production shifted further west. In October 2007, for the first time in recorded history, Hopkins found itself in fifth place, bumped out by Deaf Smith, Parmer, and Castro. These three counties, along with Bailey and Lamb, comprise a dairy region known as the Panhandle. It's in bone-dry West Texas, just over the state line from Clovis, New Mexico.

The whole region, Panhandle and New Mexico counties combined, is called the High Plains. The Texas portion hardly existed as a dairy region at the turn of the twenty-first century. Today it's booming, in part because New Mexico has toughened its environmental regulations and so new operations are jumping state lines. Between 2001 and 2007, the Panhandle went from twenty thousand cows to one hundred and forty thousand and it's predicted to add another hundred thousand by 2012. As the *Southwest Farm Press* reported in 2007, "About the only thing slowing up the expansion of the dairy industry into the New Mexico and Texas High Plains is a shortage of cows." Because it's all new, the Panhandle is resetting standards the way the dairies east of Los Angeles did in the twentieth century. Here, one-thousand-cow dairies are old news; the area is now being defined by three- to five-thousand-cow operations. As each new one comes online, smaller dairies across the state can feel it.

Sulphur Springs historian and former dairyman Bobby MacDonald was one of the hundreds of farms lost in Hopkins County. As a young man, dairy had been his certain future. He graduated college in July 1977, and on the first of August he bought seventy-two milk cows and a bull. "'Course, my story was no different than anybody else's here," he told me. "Nearly everybody here was in some way associated with a dairy farm. We thought it would never end, you know? It was a thriving deal."

He grew the herd to one hundred and fifty cows, but eventually got rid of them all. I asked him what finally made him get out of the business. "I didn't want to go into debt by borrowing the money to milk eight hundred cows," he said. "Once you get over about two hundred cows they all jumble together and become a big number. Instead of working with your own cows, you're more a personnel manager, and that was not my bent on the dairy business. That's a big change, a real big change."

In 1992 he sold his herd and opened an accounting office, where his main work was helping the remaining dairies get loans to expand.

Bobby's brother-in-law, David Lawrence, took the opposite track. From the start, it seems, he was primed for the business of it all. In January 1980, at eighteen years old, he married his wife, Jan, and bought forty cows. Nine months later, he bought another twenty. He leased a barn until, at twenty-five, he bought his own, in the now mixed-race community of East Caney. By 1998, the thirty-six-year-old was milking five hundred cows and itching to move to the High Plains so he could grow more.

David and Jan are friendly and warm, the kind of people who exude honesty. As a couple, they complete each other. He is tall and thin with clipped hair just starting to gray. She is soft and bosomy, her wavy brown hair streaked with the colors of autumn leaves. Jan is the talker, friendly and easy with her stories and her smile. David chooses words more carefully, but when he does talk he is sure of what he's saying. He looks you straight in the eye from first word to last. He doesn't like to fight—when the topic is controversial, he fiddles with a pen, his lips even quiver sometimes. Still, when something needs to be said he will say it, and firmly.

Their corner of the High Plains is a sort of cross between Clovis and Hopkins County. The climate is definitely High Plains. They get only fourteen inches of precipitation in a year, compared to Hopkins County's forty-four. Wherever the landscape is not currently being irrigated, it is bleached by sun. The dirt road that leads up to their dairy is desiccated white, and each tractor-trailer truck that passes through stirs up a thick cloud of dust. Throughout the area, trees are in short supply. Still, the community has little of the industrial air that pervades Clovis. Especially around the Lawrences' dairy just outside of Muleshoe, the landscape is rural in a familiar way: open, agricultural, quiet but alive, like Hopkins County.

The farm itself is decidedly High Plains. The main facility is a series of concrete lots that house the milk cows, beside which acres of feed grow under irrigation pivots. When they first started out, the Lawrences thought if they could ever milk a hundred cows they would be a success. Now they milk three thousand, six hundred and fifty cows and raise another three thousand replacement heifers. On a dry, hot day in October, I met them in the back room of the dairy's main office, a new brown brick building with a star-shaped window above the main entrance. As we talked they took turns cradling their infant granddaughter in their arms.

"In the beginning, I wasn't a very good dairyman," David said. "But I did know how to work, and that's what made the business succeed. What I've done is what's made this country great. I mean, not what I've done personally, but this type of thing: the type of person who starts with nothing and builds it into something. This business now creates *forty-five* jobs."

David is told where his milk goes each day in the trucks that come to pick it up, and the day before I visited it broke down like this: first shipment to the cheese plant in Clovis, second to New Orleans, third to Hattiesburg, Mississippi, fourth to Birmingham, fifth to Little Rock. He's proud of how many people the farm feeds, and suggests no reservations about the scale at which it's operating.

"We focused our business on being able to compete in the marketplace. The market said it wanted clean, high quality milk, at a low price. So that's what we set up to produce." He paused after saying this. "It's not that my goal when I was eighteen was to milk thirty-seven hundred cows, but I knew that if I was going to continue in this business, I needed to grow and compete."

It goes without saying that David no longer milks cows himself. On paper he is still the farmer, but his work is largely making the business run as a whole. To help with that, he and two other dairymen in the area formed a company to manage the work done on their three farms, which altogether have fifteen thousand head of cattle. In charge of the company is a young man with a business degree, who figures out how the three businesses can band together to run more efficiently. They buy as a group to reduce prices for feed and veterinary services. At the end of each month they look over spreadsheets and compare numbers, looking for weak links and new possibilities.

As David talked, Jan was watching him, nodding, looking at the baby in her arms. When he finished, she explained that a big reason why they moved to the High Plains was their kids: they had always known their oldest son, Michael, wanted to stay in the business, but they also knew the operation in East Caney couldn't support two families. Out here, Michael does the farming—growing corn and alfalfa—and their daughter Abbie's husband runs the feedlot they've rented to raise their replacement heifers. *That the dairy here can support three families is a blessing*, Jan said. She repeated it more than once.

As she talked David flipped a pen back and forth. Finally, he interjected. "A lot of people get a misconception that if it's a large farming operation that it's corporate farming, and that's not true. With most all of these dairies out here, the big investor-type dairies have been the exception to the rule. Most of these are family farms."

"I've heard people refer to the Wal-Mart dairy," Jan said, smiling. "But for us—and for a lot of people here—it's not that. It's still the family farm. It just grew."

6

THE NIGHT BEFORE the annual meeting of Harry's milk cooperative, there is a banquet for the farmers. Most people wear their good clothes, but it's not a fancy event. Takes place in the basement cafeteria of the co-op's headquarters in LaFarge, Wisconsin, and about the only thing that changes is the tables get tablecloths and a whole lot of extra chairs are pulled in. Farmers have come from all over the country for the meeting tomorrow, and by six o'clock in the evening the room is packed with close to two hundred of them.

If you are imagining a room full of men in flannel shirts and worn caps, stop. Replace that image instead with this: To the far right is a table of Mennonite couples, the women wearing homemade dresses and kerchiefs on their hair. To the far left is a rowdy crowd of young, bearded guys from Vermont, wearing Farm Aid T-shirts and drinking beer. In between is a crowd that includes a former Fulbright scholar who's breeding high-altitude cows for her dairy in the Rocky Mountain foothills, a couple in head-to-toe motorcycle leathers who have forty cows on their farm outside Sheboygan, and a cattleman from South Dakota, dressed up in a tweed sport-coat and Western hat. There are also a fair number of those classic-looking Midwestern farmers in button-down shirts and blue jeans. But their caps don't have patches from John Deere or the local feed dealer; instead they're embroidered with the words ORGANIC VALLEY, FAMILY OF FARMS. Below the words is a picture: a red barn, with green pasture below and blue sky above.

Tonight is the awards banquet preceding the annual meeting of the Cooperative Regions of Organic Producer Pools, or CROPP, best known for their brand of dairy products called Organic Valley. Harry and Billye are there in sweaters and slick leather jackets, sitting with a Mennonite farmer named Aaron. He and Harry are trading stories, hooting and slapping their knees. The Lewises joined the cooperative in 2004, after being inspired by an informational session at the Best Western in Sulphur Springs. Harry admits he was skeptical at first, caught off guard by the longhaired hippie guy leading the meeting. But the co-op had come to Hopkins County specifically seeking out its small family dairies, and that said something in itself. When the longhaired guy spoke, his words echoed the gospel Harry believed in: freedom, independence, pasture. Harry wasn't necessarily even looking for a premium price, he mostly wanted a basic stability that was impossible to find in the conventional dairy industry. "I figured, we been in fifty years," he told me. "This is what I was gonna do, what I was gonna retire on. I was just looking for something I could stay in on."

That sentiment is the same for more or less all of the more than one thousand farmers who made up the cooperative in 2007. Of those I have spoken with over the years, not all were as colorful as Harry, but nearly every one of them talked like a burst water main, stories and opinions and hopes and fears flooding out. They spoke about the good times, of doing chores with their kids before school in the morning and of lying on the grass with their cows in the evening. They spoke about the bad times, of groveling with bankers and watching their neighbors sell out and waking up every morning at four o'clock only to work sixteen hours and wonder the whole time *Why the hell am I still doing this?*

One man from near where I live in Northern California recounted how when his family talked about selling their dairy he contracted an unidentifiable illness. "I was so stressed out it caused an ulcer. I was dizzy all the time, and my stomach hurt so bad—like someone had tied it in a knot. I wasn't even twenty-five years old and my wife thought I was gonna die," he said. "I would come out here in the evening and I would sit out in the pasture and just cry. To think of losing this place—I mean, I was born here. I had so many ideas for it, so many dreams. Finally I decided that I would buy the place myself, somehow. It caused a big family controversy, but what drove me was to know that I never wanted that feeling again. If you're a farmer, what else do you have but your land? It's *me*."

All the stories were different, but they had a common thread: these people were dead-set on saving their farms, and knew that in order to do so they had to escape the conventional market. They simply could not compete in a system that calculated value only by numbers. They were drawn to the cooperative because its core goal was to create just such an alternative market in which farmers and their careful work were valued and rewarded. To the prevailing industry belief that farmers must get big or get out, they offered a third option: stay small, stay in. It makes sense, then, to learn that CROPP was founded by six organic dairy farmers. Even to this day, their farms are not far from the co-op's headquarters.

Among the original six was the longhaired hippie guy from the meeting in Texas. His name is George Siemons, and for years he has sported long blond hair parted in the middle and a wardrobe that rarely rises beyond T-shirts in summer and baggy sweaters in winter. He has an easy, almost drowsy manner, hands in his back pockets as he gives an interview or a speech. The company refers to him not as the chief executive, but as the C-E-I-E-I-O.

Tonight at the awards banquet he is the first speaker, and he approaches the front of the room with a bottle of dark beer in his hand. On the table beside him is a row of small trophies. They are merits for quality, to be awarded to outstanding dairy farmers in each of their four regions or "pools," as well as to the best members of the pools for other products—beef, pork, eggs, and produce. Each award will be bestowed by the head farmer of the pool, who will first be introduced by a cooperative employee, making for a long string of small speeches by big personalities. Before that, though, George explains the inscription on each trophy.

"It's a Japanese proverb, which says, 'None of us is as smart as all of us are.'" Everyone smiles. The Vermont guys raise their beers. "But, um"—and this George says with a little smile that is four parts amusement and one part chagrin—"the whole proverb was too long to engrave on the plaques, so we just had them do an acronym: N.O.U.I.A.S.A.A.O.U.A." The room breaks out laughing.

I once heard George say that CROPP is a social experiment disguised as a business. People in the town of La Farge would quip that that's putting it lightly. Word on the streets is that the co-op's employees go barefoot in the office and the founders are members of a commune. The accuracy of those statements varies depending on who you talk to. It is true, however, that at the end of the co-op's first year in business they wrote their annual report by hand. The ad-hoc accountant was a man named Jerome, whose hair is longer than George's and who does in fact go barefoot a fair amount of the time. He was an original member of CROPP, though these days he has transitioned to the unofficial position of spiritual adviser to the co-op.

Despite the sometimes eccentric image they project, the co-op is composed largely of straightlaced farmers. What's radical about them is their effort to create a sort of agricultural democracy, its core principle governance of, by, and for farmers. Harry explains with great satisfaction, "It's one farm, one vote." While there is a sizable staff at the La Farge headquarters and elsewhere, the farmers make the final decisions. They are the board of directors and the executive committee. They do much of their own marketing, too, which consists mainly of setting up booths at trade shows, conferences and fairs and talking to passersby. One farmer in Washington watches shoppers at the grocery store buying milk. When he sees one pick up a carton of Organic Valley he walks over, shakes the person's hand, and says, "I'm the guy who made that."

The greatest benefit of the system they've created is the stability that Harry talked about. In the conventional system, farmers have no idea what they'll be paid from month to month. Good times can be flush, but in what is commonly referred to as a rollercoaster ride, prices can fall so fast it makes their stomachs drop. The reason is that the dairy industry is dominated by corporations such as Dean Foods and Kraft, which run like any other publicly traded business: costs of production are juggled to create maximum profits, which are then paid to shareholders; farmers are treated as part of the production system, and the prices they are paid fluctuate with the market. CROPP turns the system upside-down. The farmers collectively set their own prices in the beginning of the year, according to what they need to make a decent living. They pay themselves before anything else. If there is a profit at the end of the year, it's divided into a bonus they all share—a "thirteenth check" on top of their monthly earnings. In high times their conventional neighbors might make more, but most CROPP farmers aren't tempted to go back. Harry explained his feelings about it: "What I'm looking for is to be able to do what I do because I'm in love with it. If I know my expenses for the next three years, and the money I'm going to make, that's a lifetime of value for what I've had to deal with."

Harry had belonged to other co-ops before. In fact, for decades most American dairy farmers have belonged to one. The problem is that most eventually have their self-government diluted or are taken over by outside interests. When Harry heard about CROPP, it impressed him that it was founded and run by people who had faced the same problems he had, and they were committed to making sure those things wouldn't happen again.

"A long time ago I stopped listening to so-called experts and decided it was time for me to become my own expert," Harry told me. "I go and do my own research and say, *Hey, uh, that don't jive*. Well, it's the same way with the people up there at Organic Valley. They say, *Hey, wait a minute* . . . and then they make their own way. We as a co-op are not intimidated. And when you're not intimidated, you're not to be fooled with. What we're doing? It's like David telling Go-liath, go to *hellll*. And I have picked up my first rock."

———

This is not the first time that David has tried to throw a rock at Goliath. For as long as there have been farmers in this country, there have been movements for them to get their fair share. They have gone on strike, by not delivering their grain or livestock to market. They have poured milk down the drains rather than sell it for too low a price. They have marched and petitioned and organized into political parties. "There were physical clashes with District of Columbia policemen," the *New York Times* reported in 1979, "when farmers chained their tractors together to block the entrance to the Agriculture Department's administration building and then set fire to an old tractor they had stalled in the middle of Independence Avenue." When a few days later the editors of the *Washington Post* admonished the farmers for holding "the wrong kind of protest," the farmers headed to the newspaper's headquarters and burned stacks of the paper on the front steps. After meeting with the editors, a Georgia farmer named Tommy Fulford told reporters, "They agreed they don't know a hell of a lot about agriculture. They know a lot more now."

With every movement or public action, farmers have had more or less the same demand of being paid fairly. Milo Reno, president of the National Farmers' Holiday Association wrote it down in 1932: "We are simply demanding the same consideration for our industry that is cheerfully conceded to every other industry. We assume for ourselves the right to obtain this consideration in the same way other institutions obtain theirs; that is, to refuse to deliver the products of our farms for less than production costs."

And yet no matter how many headlines they generate, the farmers have more or less failed every time. As one observer wrote in 1962, the concept that farmers would set their own prices and get them through collective bargaining is "as revolutionary as peace and as impractical as a bridge of butterfly wings." That's because agriculture isn't organized like other industries. Rather than being workers united, farmers are independent operators within an international marketplace. Even if ten thousand refuse to sell their grain or livestock, there will be another hundred thousand who will sell theirs. In 1961, when asked if he feared the impact of an impending strike organized by the National Farmers Organization, an executive from the meatpacker Swift & Co. replied, "It wouldn't be a drop in the bucket."

Another obstacle is that agriculture can't be put on hold the way assembly lines can. Livestock must be cared for and fed. Milk and produce spoil. Grain can be stored, but most farmers are under such tremendous financial pressure they can't afford to sit on their holdings while accruing more interest on their debts. Farmers have threatened to strike by not planting their crops, at times chanting *Hell no! We won't grow!* But for most it's an empty threat: they're so beholden to the banks that they don't have the option to forego a season. By nature of their business, farmers are captive to the prices the market decides for them—price-takers rather than price-makers.

The reason Harry believed in CROPP was that their vision went beyond simply becoming price-makers. In the past, farmer groups had asked only to be paid fairly, but never to have their role in the system change. CROPP wanted to create a whole new system, in which the farmer counted. It runs parallel to the original idea behind the organic farming movement: create a new set of priorities based on more than maximum production for minimum cost. In conventional agriculture, the farmer is a passive laborer, often more like an employee of agribusiness than an independent operator. But in a system that values health and ecology and community, farmers are essential; indeed, they are the only ones who can lead.

Harry is hopeful that the combination of organics and the CROPP system might finally bring back the small dairies in Hopkins County. He also sees it as a chance for young people across the country who want to become farmers but are stymied by the colossal investment it takes to get a foothold in the conventional system. It would be extreme to compare modern dairy farming to slavery, but it's not a stretch to compare the possibility that Harry sees in this new way of farming to the opportunity embodied by communities like East Caney and Smith Bottom. In its purest form, this new system is about the same things: independence, freedom—pasture.

Now it is Saturday morning in La Farge, and overnight the downstairs cafeteria has transformed from banquet hall to jam-packed boardroom. At this annual meeting, the members have mud on their boots and babies on their laps. While the CFO gives a PowerPoint presentation, someone's ten-year-old daughter plays along, recording the numbers in a notebook with kittens on the cover. Before lunch, a dairyman from Iowa blesses the meal with words from Saint Francis of Assisi.

After lunch, George stands up to give his executive report. Such necessary acts bring out the Eeyore in him, and he drags his feet through his own PowerPoint, replete with graphs and charts mapping sales and growth. Finally there is one slide that makes him smile. It shows how the number of farmer-members has increased since the first year in 1988. The co-op is growing so quickly that they haven't had time to update the slide for the meeting. Instead, George announces that CROPP just added its seven hundredth dairy farmer, a woman from Tennessee. She stands up from her seat in the back and the crowd applauds. As she sits back down, George's gaze falls on a couple seated at a nearby table. "Man! Meg and Arden, I remember when you guys were number *five* hundred," he says to them. "It's just so amazing." And he looks, if a bit sleepy, also truly amazed.

Despite the family atmosphere, the farmers listen as intently as they would at any business meeting. On paper the co-op seems solid and its growth entirely positive. The spreadsheets and graphs projected on the screen at the front of the room indicate over and over just how big CROPP has become. In 2006, their nearly seven hundred dairy farmers produced forty percent of the country's organic dairy supply—more than any other company, including Dean Foods' subsidiary Horizon. The unspoken part of the report is that with each expansion and every new member, the collective interpretation of what it means to be organic becomes less clear. Most members are too mild-mannered to say anything controversial at the meeting, but every vote this afternoon assumes the air of a referendum on which direction the co-op will go. Behind closed doors, there are even some fierce arguments taking place.

Most of the disagreement is about pasture, specifically how much each cow should get and for how much of the year. The debate is raging throughout the organic dairy industry, especially as larger companies get involved. But in a way all of the disagreement within the co-op is about the larger sense of the word pasture, the one Harry is so passionate about: pasture as a principle and a code, which guides farmers toward doing what is deep-down right. With seven hundred farmers come seven hundred different personal histories, financial equations, and philosophies. If CROPP is a social experiment, one of the preliminary findings is this: it is one thing for an individual farmer to take a stand and farm in the way he feels is correct, but it is another thing completely for a whole community of farmers—much less an entire nation—to do so.

7

To SUPPLEMENT HIS milk checks, Harry cuts and bales hay for people who don't own the equipment themselves. This fall he's doing a late cut of a field that belongs to a couple who retired from dairying when it ceased to be worth it. Fifty-three acres of pasture had been all but forgotten, taken for dead from drought over the past few years. Then the rains came this summer and woke up the sleeping Bermuda grass. Now, in late October, the grass is resting again, this time exhausted by the ecstatic growth of summer. It is thick and long, two feet tall in places but mostly lying in heavy, dun clumps. The tips have turned to seed, the green bleached out of everything but the layer closest to the earth.

A friend of Harry's has leased the pasture and Harry is haying it for him. The work is straightforward. Today, he's cutting the grass and after it dries for a few days he'll bale it. For today's work he's driving the hulking orange tractor that Wynton uses to round up the cattle for milking. The forklift on the front is raised above the tractor's cab like a person's arms above his head, making room for a flat, cutter attachment that is low to the ground and sticks out eight feet beyond the right side of the tractor. Inside is a circular chain lined with blades. The tractor pulls the cutter over the bumpy ground, and whatever falls within its strict horizontal grasp is cut. It's not a very nuanced machine—some low grass slips under, some anthills are leveled—but it works well enough.

Untended for years, the meadow is less perfectly geometric than most farmers would like. The northern edge of what used to be a rectangle has been surrendered to some old trees with tire swings hanging from the limbs and a couple of tents pitched in their shade. Just beyond their branches a gully splits the top half of the meadow in two. The dip is not too deep to be impassable but it is filled with trash: the rusted body of a washing machine, old planks bleached by the sun, a rusted gray-blue Aerostar van with the bumper sticker DRIVER CARRIES NO CASH—HE'S MARRIED.

Harry doesn't need perfect geometry. He steers the tractor and hay cutter in concentric rings around the meadow's perimeter, gradually closing in on the center. From above, his path would look like a topo map, the rounded lines accommodating, almost fanciful. When the tractor meets a young mesquite tree in the middle of the field, Harry steers a loose circle around it and then another, getting as much grass as he can. When he comes to the big old trees on the meadow's north side, he tucks in under them and lets the forklift crash through the branches above. Turkey vultures circle in the sky. Somewhere in the grass, the cicadas are peeping.

The final side of the meadow is straight, and here Harry hits the gas to make up time. As we buzz along, he points to a gray building just over the fence. "That's a Grade-A dairy barn," he says. He explains how you can tell but I can't hear over the roar of the tractor.

All I see is a low, humble building, maybe thirty feet by forty, with a row of white-silled windows and a blue tin roof being consumed by rust. A wall of prickly pear cactus has grown up around it. It's in sight of another barn, the one that belongs to the owners of this meadow. "That's how small they were when we had hundreds of dairies," Harry says.

"But they're both out of use now, right?"

"Yeah," he says. "Now they're just part of history." Silent again, he rides on to the end of the first lap and steers seamlessly into the second.

I ask Harry how the summer was.

"Good for hay. Bad for milk."

Try as he may, it seems Harry cannot insulate himself from the cold mathematics of the dairy industry—even as an organic farmer, and even as a farmer-owner of the great cooperative. At the CROPP annual meeting in March, marketing director Theresa Marquez called the previous twelve months "The Year of the Milk Diet," in which demand was so high in relation to supply that the co-op turned away prospective buyers. But in the next sentence she warned of what lay immediately ahead: "The Year of the Milk Bath." Whereas 2006 had been known among farmers as The Year of the Thirteenth Check, in 2007 the co-op had to drop the price farmers got by fifty cents, something they had never done before.

What happened is, basically, this: as organic food surged in popularity early in the decade, larger and less principled interests were attracted by the smell of money. Because the new players cared less about creating an agricultural revolution and more about winning market share, through them the conventional mindset crept back in. On this day that Harry mows the pasture, the front page of *Country World* newspaper reads: "Lawsuits announced against nation's largest organic dairy; Class Action suits seek damages from sale of fraudulent milk." The dairy corporation in question drew the certified organic milk from five farms in Colorado and Texas, each with thousands of cows. One of the main contentions is that the animals are raised on dry lots, without access to genuine pasture.

Within a year the management of CROPP will get busted for a similar violation, buying from a farm with upward of three thousand, five hundred cows and replacement animals supplied by massive feedlots in Missouri and Nebraska. To boot, the farm will be in the Texas Panhandle, not far from Clovis and Muleshoe. In their own defense, the people from CROPP headquarters will argue that the cows there were truly grazing, but the farmer-members will slam down their fists and stop the conversation there. For whatever disagreement still exists among CROPP's own farmers, they will roundly agree that the farm in question does not hold the pasture principle.

But what happened to make the summer of 2007 bad for milk, as Harry said, started before all that. It began in 2004, when a blueberry farmer in Maine named Arthur Harvey sued the USDA, saying that organic regulations should be both tighter and more tightly enforced. He contended that the process for converting a dairy farm to being certified organic was not stringent enough. In 2005, Harvey won enough of a victory that the regulations were tightened.

All this seems good for Harry in the long run, since it would seem to strengthen the integrity of the organic dairy industry. But first, in the summer of 2007, it meant a chain of events that felt uncomfortably familiar. In advance of the new, stricter regulations going into effect, droves of dairy farmers who had been considering converting to organic did it—all at once. The organic milk supply went way up, and relative demand plummeted. And with all the newly converted farmers, the price of organic feed skyrocketed.

The standard measure for milk production is the "hundred-weight," denoted as "cwt" and meaning one hundred pounds of milk. Harry tells me that over the summer he was getting twenty-five dollars a hundredweight, but for every hundredweight he was spending twenty-three dollars on feed. "You know what that is?" he says, turning sideways to look at me on the tractor. "That's two dollars."

The banker's suggestion: buy more cows.

"That. Don't. Work," Harry says to me, bobbing his head with each word. "It's like swimmin in the sea. You got the minnows, you got the tuna, and you got the great white shark." He stiffens his arms and sticks them out in front of him, above the steering wheel, one on top of the other, like jaws. He claps them together, palms slapping, flashes his own great white teeth, and snaps his jaw shut in one big bite. "That great white? Gonna eat em alllll up."

At the same time that the organic market was swelling, conventional dairy farmers in the area were on the tip-top of the milk price rollercoaster, getting an almost unheard-of twenty-three dollars a hundredweight. By Harry's calculations, they were paying only nine dollars for feed, which is to say making fourteen dollars to Harry's two. Friends have been telling Harry to go back to the conventional market, where he could run his farm the same but buy the cheap, non-organic feed and get that fourteen in profit. He tells them to forget it.

"They'll crash," he says, "and they always crash *harder* and *faster* than they rise up. Sure, it's temptin. But I got into this for the long haul—make it or break it. I got to use what I have and make it work. If I went back to conventional, maybe it'd be good this year, but next year it'd be back down. If I went conventional"—he throws his head toward the abandoned Grade-A dairy barn surrounded by prickly pear—"I'd end up like them."

Harry tells me that instead of buying more cows or switching markets, he plans to stretch the feed he buys and feed the cows more on hay while he waits out the winter for spring. When the grass returns to the growing stage, he'll see what happens then. A brown rabbit takes off through the hay, just escaping the cutter's sweep. A yellow butterfly bounces along in the air. The conversation drifts into other topics—how our nation got lazy as it got efficient, how we should spend money on education instead of incarceration, how the Queen of England is a parasite of the poor, and how the Pope is, when you really think about it, nothing to worship. "Hell," Harry says, "he's unemployed!"

Harry turns to me. "You know what I saw?" His eyebrows lift to let his eyes widen. "I wouldn't even believe it but another guy saw it, too. There was a little thing in the field, think it was a field mouse. Hawk came down and *grabbed* it. He was eatin it right there, had it like that"—Harry takes his hand from the steering wheel and gnarls his fingers into a claw, puts them in front of his mouth—"and just like that two buzzards swooped down, one on either side a him. They challenged him for it! Buzzards! I couldn't believe it." Harry shakes his head, lets out a soft laugh. "I thought, *Man! Times is getting hard.*"

———•———

The most famous proponent of the great-white-shark-eats-em-all-up approach to agriculture was Earl Butz, Richard Nixon's Secretary of Agriculture, originator of the motto "get big or get out." But a full decade before Butz, there emerged a version of the consolidation gospel that was more nuanced but equally hostile to smaller farmers. It portrayed consolidation as being pre-destined, paving the way for what we now commonly hold as the inevitable truth that any farmer who does not grow sufficiently must eventually die off. The report was called "An Adaptive Program for Agriculture." It was written in 1962 by the Committee for Economic Development, an influential group of businessmen and educators chaired by the president of Ford Motors and including leaders of companies like AT&T and Sears, Roebuck & Co. The report's authors sought to solve "the farm problem," which meant stopping the government programs that supported agriculture and instead releasing it to a free-market system. The primary obstacle, the problem behind the farm problem, was what they called a "persistent excess of resources." In other words: too many farmers.

"Rapid technological advances, and increasing capital investment, have made it possible for fewer and fewer American farmers to supply the food and fiber needs of larger and larger numbers of people," they wrote. "American farmers have shown great initiative and competence in responding to the opportunity thus created. They have taken up the latest production methods with a speed that amazes the administrators of agriculture in planned economies."

However, the excess of resources remained. "Although the exodus from agriculture in the past decade or longer has been large by almost any standards," they wrote, "it has not been large enough." The report recommended the "retraining and movement" of two million of the nation's five and a half million farmers.

Farmers were outraged. After the report was presented to the House Agriculture Committee in the late summer of 1962, the National Farmers Organization called a strike and had members take their hogs, cattle, sheep, corn, and soybeans off the market. In Nebraska, mobs of farmers went to Sears outlets and Ford dealerships, insisting the managers explain why the corporations' leaders would espouse such policy. Of course we know the end of the story, even before knowing it specifically. The strike ended weeks later— on September 25, the *New York Times* ran the headline "Wide Selling Hits at Farm 'Strike.'" Sears and Ford stayed in business, while two thousand farms disappeared from Nebraska in 1962. The world went on predictably, inevitably.

And yet so, too, did the farmers. Despite what could be called either attrition or extinction, many farmers continued to believe deeply that they were the indispensable heart of American society. Leader of the National Grange Nahum J. Bachelder had said it well in 1908, at the annual meeting in Washington, D.C.: "The prosperity of other industries is not the basis of prosperity in agriculture, but the prosperity of agriculture is the basis of prosperity in other industries . . . Immense manufacturing plants and great transportation companies are dependent upon agriculture for business and prosperity. Great standing armies and formidable navies may protect the farmers in common with other people of a nation, but their support comes from the tillers of the soil."

One hundred years later, Harry is saying it to me in Sulphur Springs, Texas, as he fixes a hay rake on the lawn outside his barn. He sits on a folding chair and wields a wrench against the rusty bolts that hold the rake together, twisting off the broken tines and replacing them with others that are burnished by use but still sturdy. He speaks of Manhattan, how that whole, gigantic city started from a little teepee in the woods; how the bright lights of the twenty-first-century city cannot deny their origin as the light of a campfire started by a flint rock, a flint rock held by an Indian, an Indian who was a farmer.

"Don't tell us that we need you," he says, pointing his wrench at me severely, solidly. "You need us. You need us because we still got our flint rock totin in our hip pocket."

His grandchildren are drawn in by the seriousness of his voice and the cool of the shade. They put their arms around Harry and look with curiosity at the bolts in his lap. Wynton is returning from lunch, gearing up the tractor to head back out to the hay meadow.

"You can't get away from the campfire even if you're walkin on Times Square. If you lose all the flint, you can't have your neon lights." Harry shakes the wrench at me. He is wrapped in grandchildren's arms, yet his eyes are straight ahead. "I don't need Donald Trump. Trump needs *me*. He can sell all the real estate he wants, but if he can't buy food, he can't do nothin."

The birds above go quiet. Harry talks about the great civilizations of the Western Hemisphere—the Maya, the Aztecs, the Inca—about how it was the success of agriculture that enabled their societies; and how when they vanished it was because they allowed their agriculture to collapse. "The rest of us take our food for granted," he says, his near eye squinted shut and the other looking over and up at me. "But you know what's gonna happen. The rest of us are comin up on Judgment Day, and it's comin up soon. Might not be fire and brimstone, but the judgment day is gonna come."

Harry draws a deep breath and spins the last bolts into place on the hay rake. As he works he tells me how he'd like to go to Washington and address Congress. He's mentioned this before. He has it all planned out in his mind. He'd wear his coveralls and his boots and before even sitting down he'd have everyone else stand up to honor the past, present, and future farmers of the United States. He'd answer questions first, to get a sense of where the people on the other side of the table were coming from. Then he would lay out his own list of priorities, starting with pasture.

"I'd tell them my side of the story," he says, "the real American side of the story. Falwell can talk about the moral majority, but I represent the *real* moral majority, of homegrown people in America that's from these little no-name towns. If what I said stuck, fine. If it didn't, I know that when I left at least they would remember Harry Lewis, Texas."

He stands up, and grandchildren scatter across the lawn. Wynton drives the orange tractor up to the rake and begins attaching it, while Harry walks me over to my rental car in the driveway. No convertible this time. I'm driving a little, tin-can kind of thing and Harry teases me about it, says I should get a truck and move to the countryside. I tell him I'll think about it.

"We're proud of who we are out here," he says as I climb in to the driver's seat. "It's not like in the city where everything's designed to reach into your pocket. You get out here, and it's real." He thumps his chest once with his fist. He's thinking about it, getting excited. "Someday, we're gonna riiise up and take back the country. Heh!" He's smiling now, on a roll. "Yeah! Robin Hood is here!"

I turn on the gas and Harry starts walking away. The grandchildren have piled onto the tractor with Wynton, and he fires up the engine and starts chugging out to the hay meadow. As I head down the dirt road, I beep my horn and look over my shoulder. Harry doesn't turn around, but he does lift his fist in a loose salute. "Ya-hoooo!" he calls out, and heads back to the barn.

Abiquiu, New Mexico

The American disease—and I'm quoting someone I can't recall—
is forgetfulness. A person or people who cannot recollect their
past have little point beyond mere animal existence: it is memory
that makes things matter.

—William Least-Heat Moon,
Prairyerth

1

At FIVE O'CLOCK on Saturday evening, sun is still baking the dusty grounds of the Rio Arriba County Fair. This is the fair's final night, and nearly everything has already shut down. The 4H exhibit hall is locked. The cafeteria window that sold hot dogs and posole is closed. After the bull-riding contest ended two hours ago, at least half the fairgoers left, probably to go somewhere with air-conditioning. But I was surprised to see that nearly as many people stayed. They found slivers of shade or sat in front of the big fans in the livestock arena, all waiting. For them the last event, the livestock auction, is the main event.

The auction is the final step of an annual ritual performed by kids in 4H and Future Farmers of America (FFA). Each year they raise animals from infancy to sale weight in a sort of scale-model of what their parents do for a living. The process is part practical how-to, part life lesson in values like responsibility and hard work. Months of caring for these animals culminates in this fair, where over the past three days the kids have been acknowledged for their efforts and judged on their achievements. Tonight, they cash in.

In the final hour before the sale begins, the arena becomes a livestock beauty parlor. Goats are shorn and blown dry, chickens combed and sponged. One brown sow is showered with green glitter. In a designated wet area lined with pebbles, three little girls wash two big lambs: they pour Woolite onto their bare hands, slap their palms on the wet animals, and furiously rub their sides into thick white coats of foam. Next to them is a lamb that has been shorn slick everywhere except for the wool below its knees, which now reads as fluffy legwarmers. Above it a big man—no doubt a father—wields a carwash-style vacuum hose that extends from the wall of the arena. Over and over, he runs the hose from knee to hoof, sucking the wool out to downy perfection.

By six o'clock, the stands are packed fanny-to-fanny with grandfathers in glasses and feed caps, moms chatting with other moms. Most kids are parked on a thin strip of sawdust on the ground between the stands and the show ring, their chins resting on the metal fence bars. The only ones not sitting are the fathers. In their plaid shirts and white cowboy hats, they cluster in the back or along the perimeter of the ring. Wherever they are they stand shoulder-to-shoulder, eyes looking straight ahead to the rest of the world while they talk sideways to one another.

Over the loudspeaker a voice brings the arena to order with the announcement of three children who will recite the Pledge of Allegiance. Everyone stands. Hats come off, hands go to hearts. The children crowd around a microphone and deliver the pledge with more or less accuracy and absolute pride. The audience sits.

Next, three teenage girls enter the ring, one in a green, checked shirt, the other two in blue corduroy FFA jackets and brown ponytails. The emcee announces that they will read the 4H pledge and the FFA creed. Again, the crowd stands, and all hats come off. As the two ponytailed girls recite the FFA creed, some of the older men put their hands on their hearts.

"I believe in the future of agriculture," the girls read, "with a faith born not of words but of deeds—achievements won by the present and past generations of agriculturists; in the promise of better days through better ways, even as the better things we now enjoy have come to us from the struggles of former years."

The crowd cheers. The crows of roosters bounce off the steel ceiling. The emcee comes over the loudspeaker. "I see a lot of you at the basketball games, but I'm really glad to see you here tonight. Before we begin, I want to remind buyers that this auction is really about supporting our kids. It's better to spend money on them at this age than to spend money on bail bondsmen and lawyers when they're twenty-five. *Muchisimas gracias.*"

Just inside the big open doorway next to the show ring, a crowd of fathers watches the proceedings intently, their hats lit by the setting sun. The first animal enters the ring, a meat goat with green ribbons tied around its ankles and GRAND CHAMPION painted on its side. Around its neck is a chain, by which the girl who raised it proudly leads it around the ring. The auction's bid takers, three fathers from the community, spread out toward the stands and focus their stare on the crowd.

"She has written on it GRAND CHAMPION," the emcee calls out. "And you can see clearly that that is a quality animal. Yooooou BET!"

Without a pause between voices, the auctioneer calls out the first challenge:

"Who'll

give

a hundred

dollar

bill?!"

It's on.

"Now I need a hundreddollah bill—"

HO! Calls one bid-taker, shooting his arm up but never taking his eyes off the stands.

"Now a twohundreddollah bill, got a twohundreddollah b—"

HA!

"Three hundred—"

HO!

"Four hundred, I need a fourhundreddollah—"

HA!

"Five hundred dollar bill—"

HEH!

The goat is stopping and starting, leading the girl around the ring in loops. The bid-takers have crazy, excited looks on their faces as they watch for the next hand to go up.

"Six hundred dollar bill, got a sixhundreddollahbill on the money."

HO!

"Seven hundred dollar bill, I need a seven hundred—"

HAW!

"EIGHT hundreddollahbill—"

HAI!

"Ninehundreddollahbillninehundreddollahbill—"

HO!

The auctioneer takes a breath, as if he's starting a song's second verse. His voice has a new lift to it.

"A thousand dollar bill, folks! I need a thousand dollar bill a thousanddollahbill thousanddollahbill thousanddollahbill well you bet Ri-o Ar-ri-ba County!"

The crowd spontaneously starts clapping out a beat.

"We need a thousand dollar bill for this goat! I need a thou—"

HO!

"I need eleven hundred, Amen!"

Thunderous clapping.

His voice tilts up and then down: "Now elevenhundreddollah-bill, elevenhundreddollahbill."

HA!

"Twelve hundred dollar, I need a twelve hundred dollar bill on the money."

The clapping softens as people watch intently, craning their necks to see who's still in the bidding.

"A *mil ciento cincuenta dólares*—

HO!

"Alllll rrright! That's eleven-fifty. Now I need a twelve hundred. I need a twelve hundreddollahbill, all *over* again, twelve hundreddollahbill, lookin for a twelve hundreddollahbill, twelve hundreddollahbill. Call-ing A-ONCE! Sell it your way, José. Eleven hundred and fifty whopping dollars for the champion goat of Rio Arriba County!"

The crowd goes wild.

Next up is the fair's overall grand champion, a 1,095-pound black steer with full shoulders and a broad back. It belongs to one of the two girls who read the FFA creed. She's tall and pretty, now wearing a pink plaid shirt and white coral necklace. "Let's take a moment of silence to admire," says the voice over the loudspeaker. "That's the best piece of meat you can get in Rio Arriba County!" The steer's coat is fluffy from blow-drying and glistening with glitter. Around his neck is a red bandana and atop his head a tiny straw hat with a chinstrap looped under his thick neck. Gold bells are tied to the middle of his tail, and they jingle as the girl tours him around the ring.

Cattle are auctioned by the pound, and almost no sooner does the bidding start than it's at five dollars. One of the bid-takers has jumped onto the railing of the bleachers and is wiggling six fingers at the woman who bid four dollars just seconds earlier. The auctioneer paces.

"Ladies and gentlemen, I guarantee that for only six dollars a pound you're getting TOP Choice Beef. You can't get any better than this. Ieee need a six-dollah-bill-six-dollah-bill-six-dollah-bill-six-dollah-bill—"

HO! The bid-taker launches off the railing.

They go for seven but the bidding ends at six. Still, the girl with the grand champion steer is beaming. At 1,095 pounds, that's $6,570. On the wholesale market the price for steers is hovering around a dollar a pound.

The auction continues down the list, from grand champion to first and second places. A red-ribbon lamb decorated with red heart-shaped stickers is sold. The beglittered pig enters the ring, now wearing a tiara, and one of the county commissioners buys it for six dollars a pound. I slip out of the stands and into the gray-blue twilight, where the wind is picking up. In the animal washing area, a kindergartner in a tall hat ties a stiff rope into a lasso. The sunset has been swallowed by thick clouds piling up in the south. The fathers stand by the door, watching the clouds with one eye, hoping for rain.

Moving through the men is Virgil Trujillo, a rancher from the nearest town. He's taller than most, about six two in boots and a cowboy hat. His shirt is a rich orange, with long sleeves buttoned at the cuffs. Black jeans and black, wraparound sunglasses hooked into his belt. By day you would never see Virgil without the glasses. Indeed, he has a tan line from them, a band of paler skin from his nose to his sideburns. In the middle are his dark eyes, which look directly at you when he speaks. Get on the right subject and they will drill holes.

The skin below Virgil's cheekbones is reddened by the high desert sun, and pocked in spots. Every day he goes over this skin with a razor, shaving and shaping the corners of his thick moustache and the upper limit of his goatee—fastidious grooming that I suspect comes less from vanity than propriety. Thick, dark hair peeks out from under his hat, with just a few strands of gray in his sideburns. Two weeks ago, he turned forty-seven.

Virgil has been at the fair since noon. This morning he watched his daughter Chavela ride her horse in the barrel jumping contest and win second place. This afternoon at the rodeo he sat in the last row of the bleachers in the blazing sun, holding a white umbrella over himself and his wife, Isabel. Since the auction began he has slid along the periphery, talking with men by the pens, by the door.

From afar you'd think he was just like the rest of the men. In many ways he is. He has cattle like so many of them have cattle. He knows more or less everyone here, is even related to a good number of them. What sets him apart is his willingness to break with convention in order to pursue his calling: the land. That might not sound very unique, untamable individuality being the very core of the cowboy archetype. But in fact the worlds where Virgil exists find their strength in sameness, constancy, known quantities—and that becomes even truer as those worlds shrink. In their midst, Virgil comes up with ideas nobody has heard of and asks questions nobody wants to answer. He places his bets on creativity rather than custom. He's willing to talk to anyone, including me. And more than just talk; he's willing to let me in. Ranchers these days have lots of reasons to harden themselves to the outside world, but Virgil opens his door.

I catch up with him in the wide, dusty area behind the bleachers. No sooner have we shaken hands than a girl of thirteen in a plaid shirt and green Mardi Gras beads around her neck walks up and inserts her plea to Virgil. "Wanna buy my goat?"

Turns out that as the top tier animals are sold on the auction's main stage, there's a secondary market happening back in the pens for all the animals that didn't win ribbons.

"Oh, I don't know," Virgil says to her, hands in his pockets. "I just don't know."

"C'mon, buy my goat."

"How much is it?"

"I don't know yet."

"Well, find out how much it is and then we'll talk."

The girl runs off and we stand there, looking back toward the auction ring. "It's a pretty great turnout," I say.

"It could be so much better." I'm surprised by his answer.

HO!

A lamb sells for six hundred dollars.

"I mean, this is the core," he says, "the people who really care. But it isn't even a *fraction* of the community." For such a bull of a man, his words come out soft, each syllable distinct from the next. Important words are stretched out and enunciated extra. "Imagine what it would look like if twice as many people were here? This place would be *boom*ing. We wouldn't even be able to hear each other."

It's true that the arena is a fraction of the county population. What's more, the kids' hometowns that the announcer is calling out are primarily up north, close to the Colorado border, towns like Tierra Amarilla and Chama. Ranching and agriculture in general remain a mainstay of the community up there, whereas down here they are rarer each year. And these things are self-perpetuating: if you have a strong agricultural base, the veterinarians and feed stores stay in business, even grow, and the buyers keep coming back; but if ranchers are selling out every year, the services disappear, the buyers stop showing up, and each season a few more are forced to give up.

The girl with the goat returns, breathless. "Two hundred," she says. "And there're two of 'em."

"Oh, I can't do it," Virgil says.

"One seventy-five!"

"Really, I just can't." It pains him to say the words. "But you know what? I bet I know someone who would want them. How about Wilbur? Do you know Wilbur?"

The girl's head falls a bit. "Yeah, I know him. He already bought my brother's pig."

"I'm sorry. I'm *really* sorry."

She just stands there for a second, then turns around and walks back to the pen.

Virgil's eyes look straight ahead at the ring. "Man, I hate to say no," he says, "but I already bought a goat *and* a pig. I'm already maybe a thousand bucks in the hole."

He bought the pig because his son is getting married in two weeks. He and Isabel promised to provide the *carne adovada,* a New Mexican dish of pork slow-cooked in red chile. They have one hog at home, but the guest list keeps growing and Virgil wants to make sure they have enough.

"Congratulations," I say, "y'know, on your son getting married."

"Well, they're still pretty young." Hands in his pockets. He takes a deep breath. "He and his wife are nineteen and they had a baby last year. Just turned a year old, week before last. He was born on my birthday, which is really cool—to *me*. When it happened I thought, *Maybe it's another little miracle.*"

The unspoken story is that Virgil's son and eldest daughter have yet to show any interest in raising cattle like he does. "Do I wish they would?" Virgil once said. "Oh, I *wish*." Virgil bought his son a black-and-white horse named Estrella, but it's mostly Virgil who rides her. His eldest daughter is heading to college next year. His third and youngest child, though, seven-year-old Chavela of the barrel-riding contest, is locked in, at least so far. When I asked her if she wanted to have cattle when she grows up, her reply was: "I already do."

"Really?"

"Yeah, I go out on my horse with my dad and I pick them. For the ones I pick, he still puts his brand on them, but on the ear tags he puts my initials—'CT' instead of 'VT.'"

"How do you choose them? By their color? By their faces?"

"I like the big ones," she said. "They live for longer. The little ones can die off."

The new grandson, Isaias—named for the prophet, in Spanish— he's an additional possibility. Virgil acknowledges the risk that his son and his son's wife will have too many children while they're young, potentially limiting their opportunities and options. "But I say, *Hey, don't worry about it. Bring them all to me.*" He lets out a little laugh. "I need as many chances as I can get."

Outside, lightning cracks the dark sky open and reveals the jagged horizon of mountains. Another second and it's flat black again. People are starting to empty the bleachers. The thirty-fifth animal comes up for sale, a black steer that's foaming at the mouth, moving slowly. They get one dollar a pound then one fifty, then two. *Two and a quarter, two and a quarter.* The audience claps out a beat, but it's soft, due to attrition. They close the bid at two even.

When the last animal finally sells, the whole arena sets into a different, leaving motion. The rodeo queen has been pertly posing for pictures with the auction's kids in a makeshift photo booth;

now she closes up shop like a barmaid at two o'clock in the morning. The green glitter pig is nosing through the slats of its pen to drink from a neighbor's water pan. The grand champion steer's hat and bandana have been taken off, and white wood chips now hang from his fluffy fur.

The animals that haven't been sold carry a quiet air of desperation, their young owners having given up and drifted off with friends. Hanging from the pen of a black-faced lamb is a sign with a photo of the boy who raised it and a line from the 4H handbook: A BLUE RIBBON BOY WITH A RED RIBBON PIG IS MORE DESIRABLE THAN A RED RIBBON BOY WITH A BLUE RIBBON PIG. Next door are two lambs, one with $ LAMBCHOPS $ on its side in green paint, another with a simple BUY ME written in oil stick. From the front of their pen hangs a miniature license plate decorated with a stylized Stars and Stripes. Below the waving flag, in thick block letters, the license plate reads GOD BLESS AMERICA.

2

FROM THE AIR, the land of northern New Mexico looks skeletal, like brown skin shrunken down over the bones of the earth. The mountains push up through the surface like the sharp points of elbows and knees, skin stretched tight. The dry mesas break off like empty ribcages, suddenly dropping into canyons, into the cavity where the soft organs once were.

What makes it this way is water. There's so little of it, the soil here is reduced to survival mode, hugging itself against the ground just to hold on. What water does come comes fiercely, in sudden thunderstorms and surging rivers that carve away the stony earth into these canyons and cliffs. Last night lightning lit up the black sky over and over, and this morning the Chama River is running thick and red with clay, more like lava than water. Ten miles north, the storm never hit. In the arroyos there, water exists only as the negative space of rivulets, carved into the sandy bottoms by the last torrent that came through.

Virgil once said to me, "You know how east of the Mississippi, you say, *Rain, rain, go away?* We don't have that poem here."

"Has there ever been too much rain?" I asked.

His voice was hushed, reverent as he answered. "Never."

This is particularly true of Abiquiu (aah-bih-kew, pronounced like *barbecue*), the town where he lives, forty-five miles northwest of Santa Fe. An outsider might lump all the towns in Rio Arriba County together as dry, but El Vado with its fourteen inches of rain and Chama with twenty seem rich compared to Abiquiu and its ten. The result is that life here happens low to the ground—creeping animals, thrifty plants, cautious people. Nothing too cocky survives.

To the world outside, this place is known as "Georgia O'Keefe country." The artist lived here for nearly forty years, until two years before her death in 1986. Her signature paintings of a barren yet deeply sensual desert landscape are depictions of this place. "Wonderful emptiness," she called it. One year she sent her husband in New York a package full of bones she had found here. Later she would write, "The bones seem to cut sharply to the center of something that is keenly alive on the desert even though it is vast and empty and untouchable—and knows no kindness with all its beauty."

Every summer a stream of cars comes up Highway 84 in search of the enchantment that O'Keefe found here. Most drive out of Santa Fe, leaving behind its endless displays of turquoise jewelry and kachina dolls. They pass the Indian casino at Tesuque pueblo, then go through the commercial city of Española, with its burger joints and tire stores. Continuing west, Highway 84 quickly leads into mostly uninhabited country, hills tinted red and dotted with juniper trees. As the miles count down to where Abiquiu should be, the number of houses and mobile homes increases, but the town itself appears to be just a general store on the right and a post office on the left. Most people get gas or a drink then drive on, disappointed.

Those who follow the narrow road up behind the post office and into the village find a pretty, quiet plaza, but hardly a sightseeing jackpot. One day I watched a man with a sunburn and a camera around his neck enter the library, looking hopeful. He walked the perimeter of the room, inspecting the black-and-white photographs that lined the wall above the bookcases. Without turning from the images he called out to the young woman behind the desk. "Is this a historic pueblo?" Without taking her own eyes off the papers in front of her, she answered blankly, "Yes." He looked for a moment more, then walked out, took a few photos, and got in his car.

The plaza does have a nice adobe church like those in postcard images of New Mexico, but otherwise it's lined with small, "regular" houses, some sweet with blue trim, some not. On one lot ringed with chain-link fence, all that remains is a chimney and a pile of crumbled brick. Aside from a few hand-lettered signs offering tours or maps, there are no accommodations made for visitors, no reason given for outsiders to stay. Georgia O'Keefe lived just off this plaza, but there's little indication she was ever here. Most people drive on.

But the road continues beyond the plaza, now as dirt, rising slowly past a few homes and on into hills that are scrubby and wild. Occasionally cottonwoods bud in the opportunity of a creek, but mostly the unmarked land is inhabited by prickly pear and cholla cactus, patient plants built to go thirsty. Here and there, in the distance, the hills are planted with wooden crosses.

Less than a mile up the road is the local cemetery. The original boundary is marked by an ancient adobe wall whose smooth exterior has disappeared, revealing a mound that looks like a giant swallow's nest, just bits of mud and straw. Closer to the road is a replacement fence, built more recently than the first but still some time ago. Its posts are straight, rough limbs from a skinny tree, linked by wires woven into a diamond pattern—a handmade chain-link. No gate, just a wooden cattle guard. The instant I entered, I felt that I was trespassing.

In the very back of the cemetery there are newer headstones, engraved by machines and decorated with plastic roses or occasionally an American flag. But the majority of this place is inhabited by simple wooden crosses: two planks nailed together, now warped by weather and bleached to gray by the sun. From the backside the cemetery looks like a forest of tiny, wizened trees, the arms of the crosses their only branches.

"Oh, these people knew hunger," Virgil tells me. "Guaranteed, they knew hunger."

I never discussed the cemetery with him, it never felt quite right. But he did tell me about that life, that time. He can't tell his own story without it. He has lived in Abiquiu more or less his entire life. Before that his roots here go back ten generations, to a time of Spanish colonists and Native Americans. His recognition of his ancestors and their forbearance is deep—he brings them up with reverence even in casual conversation. And yet when he talks about this place, two hundred and fifty years get compressed into one moment. He and they become we. At times the past slips into present tense. The hunger they knew informs his understanding of today.

"Well, we're so far away from anything. There's no industry—there's no huge logs to cut, there's no coal to mine, there's no gold. No huge rivers to irrigate thousands of acres. There's *nothing*. Just the land."

"Then what was the economy built on?"

"What economy?"

"Was there ever an economy?"

"Not in Abiquiu. The economy was basically, if you can get food on the table, that's the economy. Abiquiu is a poor community. It always was."

In recent years that has begun to change. Every so often, one of those people who journeyed up here seeking the Georgia O'Keefe landscape makes the decision to stay. In the surrounding mountains live a handful of movie stars and an oil heiress. In the valley are painters and aspiring vintners and retired stockbrokers. Along the dirt roads between are signs for Sotheby's real estate, behind them modern adobe homes with skylights and solar panels.

At Bode's, the general store that visitors take for the whole of town, the new dichotomy is on bizarre display. The shelves offer books on Georgia O'Keefe and organic beer alongside Welch's grape juice and tubs of Bueno brand red chiles. Organic Gourmet brand chicken citron frozen dinner. Frozen tamales. One day, the man in line in front of me was wearing head-to-toe camo and buying a cold four-pack of Chelada tall boys—that is, Clamato and Budweiser in a can. The man behind me was stocking up on Pellegrino.

It's a familiar story. Even if the rural economy worked at some point, at least to get food on the table, now it's broken. If the community is lucky tourism will come along, but really how lucky is that? In Abiquiu the economic benefits have not trickled down. The tourism industry is run largely by newcomers, and the influx of dollars spent on things like real estate and shopping end up in Española or farther away. In the twenty-first century, Abiquiu has two classes: one that made its money somewhere else and came here to live out a dream; the other, people who are from here and are trying to make a living. The latter is still the majority, but the migration out continues as fast as the new arrive. At times, a complete transformation seems likely. As Virgil said, there is simply no economy in Abiquiu, just land.

And I suppose this simple piece gets to the heart of what makes Virgil different from the people around him. For him, what Abiquiu has is enough. As long as there is food on the table, the land is all he needs.

3

When visitors leave Abiquiu they generally head west on Highway 84, following the Chama River. The road is at about six thousand feet elevation but it feels low, unremarkable, tucked into a valley of small fields and red cliffs. Then, just as passengers begin dialing the radio or checking for cell service, without warning the road climbs a steep hill and turns a corner and suddenly the landscape cracks open. To the left are blue peaks and to the right sharp cliffs. In the middle a huge grass-covered plain stretches across a valley ten miles wide and more than ten miles long—a miracle of land. Finding it there feels as if you've discovered the secret heart of this jagged landscape.

Since the Spanish arrived here this place has been known as El Valle de la Piedra Lumbre, the Valley of Shining Stone. It was formed in the same fashion as the Grand Canyon, with a river washing away the bottom of the land at the same time that earth muscled its way up and out, breaking through the crust. The cliffs ringing the valley are cross sections of geologic evolution, stacked layers of rock that were once swamp, beach, lake, now stripes of white, mossy green, brick red, sandy gray. Some of them have been whittled by wind into precarious-looking spires; others have eroded into what look like giant piles of red dirt or green sand. Then there are the cliff faces that give this place its name, which stand straight up, living records of the earth's seismic thrust. In bright sun, they truly shine.

Those passing through are taken aback by the stark beauty. In fact, this place is what Georgia O'Keefe came for; she built the house in Abiquiu only when she could no longer handle winters in the remote valley. Virgil loves the Piedra Lumbre, too, but he admits he hardly even notices the cliffs anymore. What draws him is instead the grassy plain between them, locally called a llano. To understand the attraction, a person would have to first consider the surrounding hills and mountains, with their steep slopes and rocky paths. That land seems to gasp for a drink for much of the year, and fights gravity to keep what little water it does get. This place, though, is milk and honey. To begin with, it's gloriously flat. It's also about fifteen hundred feet lower in elevation than most other local grazing land, which means it has a longer growing season and a greater variety of plants. Unlike in most tracts of land in the area, cattle can graze here year-round and stay well fed. For a long time, northern New Mexico was divided into *patrónes*—grand owners of land with vast herds of livestock—and *peónes*—farmers who subsisted on communally owned land and, for a wage, herded the grand landowners' animals. This place is *patrón* land.

Early in the twentieth century Virgil's maternal great-grandfather Manuel Salazar bought two-thirds of the Piedra Lumbre, forty-two thousand acres. The Salazar family had come from Portugal in the eighteenth century and Manuel was wealthy by local standards, a *patrón* with thousands of sheep and more than five hundred cattle. But he was not invulnerable. The 1930s brought several years of drought and hard winters, the decline of the wool industry, and of course the Depression. Salazar went broke and had to sell twenty-five thousand acres of the ranch.

He sold the land to Arthur Pack, a wealthy Easterner with an MBA from Harvard. Pack had fallen in love with the Piedra Lumbre and moved here from Princeton a couple years earlier. In time he came to own half of the Piedra Lumbre, calling the whole thing Ghost Ranch. Under his ownership the land transformed. Primarily it became a dude ranch geared toward trail rides for adventurous blue bloods and intellectuals. Pack and his partner did run livestock, but their Piedra Lumbre Cattle Company failed after two seasons. He then restored the thousands of acres of range to wild land. In his most flamboyant act of conservation, he flew in baby antelope from Wyoming to restart the wild herds that had once roamed the valley.

Before his death Pack donated his land to the Presbyterian Church. Today the church operates Ghost Ranch as a retreat. The place has a loose spiritual tradition that seems to be as much Christian as it is vaguely New Age. It attracts a crowd that you might find raking the Zen garden or placing photos on the altar behind the dining hall. Ghost Ranch is also just a nice place for families to have a relatively inexpensive nature vacation. During summer, it has the air of an all-ages summer camp.

Virgil has worked at Ghost Ranch since he was twelve, full-time for twenty years and part-time for fifteen. His father worked here for thirty-four years before retiring in 1995. Every day at work Virgil wears a beige nametag that reads "Ghost Ranch, Virgil Trujillo, Ranchlands." His full title is Ranchlands Manager, which means he is in charge of maintaining all the property's lands. This includes the lawns around the headquarters and the paths to the campgrounds, but more importantly—to Virgil, at least—it includes the twenty-one thousand acres of rangeland that lie mostly across the highway from all the buildings. Not since Manuel Salazar sold his land has this place been a working ranch, but in winter local ranchers are allowed to graze their cattle there, in a program that Virgil oversees. It's one of the primary reasons he sticks with this job.

When I once asked him if it stung to be an employee here, given that his family used to own this land, he shrugged off the question.

"Sometimes it will cross my mind that some of this was my great-grandfather's ranch. For me, it's been kind of an opportunity. It's a nice thing, y'know, that at least I can be on the land. The hard thing is you're not always in control of your destiny. I think when you own your land, you're much more . . ." His voice trailed off in search of the word, then came back to explain, almost apologize. "That's just the independence part of me. Part of me has been very independent since I was very small."

"Just part of you?" I said, teasing. Even the first time I met Virgil it was evident he was not the kind to follow orders from someone else.

"It kills me here at the ranch that I cannot do whatever I want to do. They give me quite a list to do, and most of the time I'm pretty good at getting the list done. I think they're always checking up on me." He laughed, then paused. He turned contemplative, hesitant to say what he thought out loud. "But then there's also a nostalgia—to the rancher, to the cowboy, to the stockman. Lots of people kinda wish they were involved. So there's a lot of jealousy here at the ranch, too."

"Because you're actually doing it?"

"Oh yeah, my supervisor kills me."

"He wishes he were a cowboy?"

"I don't know." Virgil laughed. "I can't say he wishes he was a cowboy. Sometimes he just wishes I wasn't."

Virgil's office at Ghost Ranch is in the back of the shop building, one half of a concrete-floored room that was split in two but never sealed off with a proper door. It is the office of a person who has been there a long time, perhaps too long. Towers of paper and folders on top of folders cover every flat surface. There's a tin can with an ancient bottle of bug spray in it, boards and rope and rolled-up maps that hang from hooks in the ceiling. A blackboard next to the desk is scrawled with reminders. A mud-covered wheel from the front of a wheelbarrow leans against a beige file cabinet bearing bumper stickers that read: NEW MEXICO AGRICULTURE and BEEF, IT'S WHAT'S FOR DINNER. The walls are decorated with bones of all sizes, including a pair of antlers with two rodent skulls looped onto them through the eye sockets.

When I arrive Virgil is seated in front of his computer, trying to unlock it. The screen is asking for his domain name, user name, and password, and he has no idea what they are, just keeps trying different combinations that get rejected. Apparently he's in the doghouse for not responding to emails, and silently I wonder if he has ever responded to one. Get the man face-to-face and on a subject he likes, and he will talk for hours. Try to reach him remotely, though, and you're probably wasting your time. Setting up this visit to Ghost Ranch took me twenty calls over two months' time; I caught him twice. I even sent an email three months ago, but looking at the dusty computer I have a feeling it's still in there.

He gives up. As I wait for him to collect his things so we can leave, I notice a painting crooked against the wall next to the doorway—either it is propped up on a stack of papers, or it was hung there so long ago that the papers have risen to meet it. The faded watercolor shows two cowboys loading up their horses. They seem to be leaving the old-time building in the near background, heading into the wild land that makes up the rest of the image. It reminds me that I want a picture of Virgil, and I ask if I may photograph him today.

"Yes," he says. "But not here."

Virgil is wearing the same outfit as every time I have and will see him at Ghost Ranch: Blue denim shirt tucked into blue jeans, both worn and patched with pieces of denim clothes that came before. He wears his white cowboy hat, of course, and under it a bandana that has been cut and refashioned into a black skullcap. He says he must wear it during the summer, presumably for sweat. I respond that I can't believe he wears this whole long-sleeved outfit on days like today when it will get into the dry, blistering nineties. "Well sure, I'm more comfortable in a T-shirt. But I'm never sure what situation I'm going to get into out here. I don't like the bugs, y'know, or getting scratched up." He reflects for a second on the fact that I think it's strange. "This is just what I do, y'know? This is what I've done."

Before we're even out the door Virgil slips on his customary black shield sunglasses. They have a tiny picture of a cowboy in the top left corner, emblem of the Winchester firearms company. Really they are a big part of why he comes off as disarming: you can just barely see him looking at you, his dark pupils behind the black wall of lenses. Mostly you see your own reflection.

To and from work Virgil drives his own truck, a burly, black, double-cab Dodge Ram 2500 4x4 with tinted windows. If that vehicle is the Lone Ranger, the truck he drives at Ghost Ranch is an aging Frankenstein, a green 1960s Chevy Suburban with a deep well in the foam of the driver's seat and a tailgate that is permanently open. (When someone we meet on the road later tells Virgil a phone number, he takes out a pen and writes it on the cracked dashboard.) We get in and he starts the engine rumbling.

His work this morning is laying out the site for a meditative walking path called a labyrinth. It will be made of flagstones laid into the earth on their sides, so that just enough sticks out of the ground to mark a subtle, spiral course. An older labyrinth behind the mess hall will serve as the model, so we go to take its measurements. Virgil drives the dusty roads at a snail's pace, holding the steering wheel with one hand and a plastic cup filled with coffee in the other. At significant bumps he nearly stops, to avoid spilling. We pass seven donkeys in a pasture, which he tells me do no work aside from modeling for photographs. A woman in airy white garments with diamonds on her fingers flags us down, and asks Virgil for some duct tape to patch her tent with. I comment that this isn't exactly the work you'd expect of a "ranchlands manager."

He laughs a little laugh. "Yeah, I spend most of my time in the 'et cetera' part of my job description." He thinks for a second. "What was it, y'know, Darwin—the strongest survive?"

"The survival of the fittest?"

"Exactly, survival of the fittest. What it's really about is adaptation, that's what fitness is. Being able to adapt to your situation, that's how you survive."

Leaving headquarters we drive a mile down a gated road, toward the Casa del Sol, where Ghost Ranch's director lives. The new labyrinth will go behind the house, in a wild, open area of red earth, black rocks, and gray plants. In winter, the cattle graze there.

We park and walk to the area where little blue surveying flags have been stuck in the ground. Virgil stands in the center of the space with the tip of the tape measure between his fingers. He has me stretch the orange strip out to twenty-five feet and walk in a circle around him, moving the flags to reflect this new radius. He tells me to look out for rattlesnakes.

As I pull the tape across rocks and over juniper bushes, Virgil begins without prelude to explain why he is who he is.

"Okay, so when I was seven or eight was when they built the community center in Abiquiu. The first thing they had in there was roller skating on Saturdays. All the other kids would go roller skating, but my dad would take me up to the mountains to check on the cattle. I would complain to my mother, y'know, that we always go to the same place and the cows are always right there and they're always fine. Then it would rain up there and it would get muddy and we'd get stuck and everything would take much more time than I thought and we'd get back late. In the end I did learn to roller skate, but not that well. But all those bits and pieces of being with my dad in the mountains, those are what made me what I am today."

He can't pinpoint the moment, but in time Virgil went from resenting those trips to loving them. The first part he loved was the horses. He remembers riding on the saddle behind his dad when he was little, but as soon as they put him on alone he never rode with anyone again. He got his first horse when he was seven, like Chavela, and from then on rode it anytime he could. After school and all summer long he would ride along the rivers, in the mountains—anywhere he wanted.

"I always knew I wanted to be a rancher," he tells me. "At an early age, before I could really even think about anything, I already knew exactly who I wanted to be like—what I wanted to be. I grew up looking at my great-uncles, my uncles, my grandfather, my dad for sure, all of them as my heroes. I just wanted to be like them."

Virgil comes from a big extended family—it feels like half the people you meet in Abiquiu are Trujillos or Salazars. When Virgil was a kid, every Sunday after Mass his family, which is to say thirty or forty people at a time, would gather for breakfast. While the women cooked, the men would tell stories. All recounted living life as ranchers and farmers, mostly right there in the Chama River Valley. He says it was the highlight of his week, sitting at their knees, listening intently. For him there were no boring stories.

His grandfather Jacobo told the best ones, always with a great punch line, but you can tell from Virgil's stories that his dearest grandfather was Benjamin. (Virgil uses the Spanish pronunciation, Ben-ha-meen.) He worked as a sheepherder, which meant he would leave for four or five months at a time to tend other people's flocks by himself in the mountains of Colorado and Utah. He would come home for some holidays and for plowing in spring, but then he would leave again. In the right weather, his wife would visit. Virgil remembers going to church as a child and seeing the old men there, wondering which one Benjamin would look like when he saw him next.

Benjamin herded sheep for fifty-two years, from when he was twenty until he was seventy-two. After coming home for good, he became effectively blind, losing sight in one eye from glaucoma, and in the other eye from a wood chip that flew up while he was chopping firewood. When his wife died, he asked Virgil, then twenty-four and newly married to Isabel, to leave his job in Los Alamos and come home to Abiquiu to take care of him. They went immediately. Among the first things Virgil did when he arrived was to build a chain-link fence that stretched from their house to the one next door, which allowed his blind grandfather to go walking.

"He loves to walk, he's walked his whole life," Virgil explained. "He's walked for countless years herding. He had horses and everything, but he always preferred to walk. So he walks from one house to the other, back and forth. I had a chair right there at the end of the fence where he can sit down. He did it for five years, every day the weather would allow. To me it was inspirational, because in no way was my grandfather ever gonna give up."

When Virgil was a boy he had wanted to be exactly like Benjamin. "I would tell him, *You know, I'm going to be a sheepherder when I grow up.* And he would look back at me and say, *Mijito, they don't make men like that anymore.*"

Still, through grade school and high school Virgil always assumed he would be able to live the life that his father and grandfathers had. "I guess I thought life was always going to be the same," he told me. "Then two months before I graduated high school, it dawned on me that it wasn't."

After graduation Virgil took vocational training, first learning auto mechanics, then carpentry, and finally landing a good job doing construction. When he moved back to Abiquiu to look after Benjamin, people told him he was wasting his life. But in Virgil's mind the chance to spend time with his grandfather was an incredible opportunity. "He was my hero! He was ninety-three years old, and there was no limit to what he could tell me about the world. When I said that I left my job to take care of him, it was more like him taking care of me."

Benjamin told Virgil stories for hours on end, in some cases the same one for the fifth or sixth time, but always with different details. Just like the Sunday morning stories he had been told as a child, they were simply about life in Abiquiu or out herding—how people lived and grew food, the natural world around them, the history. Virgil came to know the stories as if he had experienced them himself, and he talks about them now with longing in his voice. In the same breath that he speaks of the difficulty of hunger and a subsistence economy in Abiquiu, he recalls a tightly bound community where people collaborated and supported one another as a matter of course. Work was physical and life was hard, but they made it.

As a child, those Sunday morning stories had built in Virgil a faith that the life they described was the one to aspire to. When he returned to take care of Benjamin, he remembered that was all he had ever wanted. It was less about being a rancher or a sheepherder per se. Those were just means of doing what really mattered: being on the land, and through that, being free.

"I realized how great my life was in Abiquiu around my family," he said, "how I was always happy and comfortable, how when I got out into the world I started worrying about financial success and professional success and all those other things that you get caught up in. I figured out that life was actually pretty basic, and that the real work was just gonna be keeping it that way."

———

After a slow drive back to the Ghost Ranch headquarters, we find that we've talked so long over the measuring tape that lunch has come and gone at the mess hall. Virgil lets us in the back door and a cook friend of his points us to the counter holding what remains of today's meal, cold pepperoni pizza and a dish of jalapeño peppers. We fill our plates, pour drinks, and move to a table in the dining hall, where a few stragglers are still eating. Virgil removes his sunglasses but not his hat. He pours a mound of sugar into his palm and flips it over into his iced tea. He pops a whole jalapeño in his mouth. Behind him an old man struggles with the levers of the cafeteria's milk dispenser.

As we eat, the conversation comes into the present. Technically, Virgil is not now a rancher. He does own cows, currently a herd of eighty and he's hoping to almost double that soon. He does own some property, but not a ranch. If you use the term *rancher* he'll go along with it, but more often he refers to himself as a stockman, meaning he raises livestock, which graze on various pieces of land that are mostly owned by other people.

Changing that technicality is at the top of his list—literally. In his shirt pocket he keeps a slip of paper with a handwritten inventory of his goals, which he periodically looks at and adds to. Having a ranch of his own has been on his mind since before he ever had the list, practically since he was a kid listening to those Sunday morning stories. In terms of the land economy, buying that ranch is only getting harder. Subdivisions are making properties abundant but land scarce, especially the big tract that he would like. Rangeland that could support a viable ranch is nearly impossible to find, and even if he did find it, Virgil guesses the price at a thousand bucks an acre. Still, he looks at the For Sale ads regularly. I ask him if any of the listings tempt him.

"All of them do."

He does buy real estate, mostly old residential properties in Abiquiu that people inherit but can't afford to keep. He prefers low-key, owner-financing deals—can't stand paying interest to the banks. Says he's been buying property since he was sixteen, and since then he's never been without a handful of mortgages. Currently he has three, and he just signed on to buy another because it was too good a deal to pass up.

Virgil buys cattle, too, when guys can't afford to stay in the business or someone dies and leaves the herd to a child who isn't interested. It's how he has built what is a relatively large herd. While most guys around him have five or ten cows, Virgil has had as many as two hundred. He says he'll buy anything and everything if he sees in it a value that can be leveraged. "I call it aggressive savings."

As a result of his financial planning, he's unpopular with some people in town. They think of him as greedy, a small-time but ruthless cattle and land baron. This is one of those topics that raises his voice, puts him on the defensive attack. Virgil figures they're jealous. Or that, in the case of selling their cattle, they feel ashamed that they can't or don't want to maintain the agricultural tradition of their forebears.

The whole thing strikes a chord with him, but he has no intention of stopping. These properties, even these cattle, are means to an end—sub-goals on the way to the top of the list. He would mortgage them all in a heartbeat, even sell them, should he find the dream ranch for sale. And even that would be a means to an end. In his vision, having land would allow him to do the things he enjoys. He fantasizes about being financially self-sufficient, his only work that of raising cattle and horses.

"My goal is to be independent and to do as I darn well please." He spaces the words out like a kid stomping his foot, then laughs. "And *when* I darn well please. It always has been! My mom told me that when I was three, four, five years old."

As we make our way through the cold pizza, Virgil eventually tells me that he probably, maybe could already do exactly what he dreams—perhaps not a thousand-acre spread, but something. "But I keep making excuses," he says.

"Why?"

"Well, there's flaws in everything." He tips back in his chair. He speaks the next sentence gingerly, as if tiptoeing through the words. "One of my flaws is that I guess I'm afraid to take the jump. Meaning . . . Right now I have three kids. My older daughter is going to college. This job keeps me secure. Maybe that's it, or that's part of it."

Perhaps if his kids were entering the cattle business it would be different. Or if he lived somewhere else there would be less risk. He mentions that there's a nice parcel of three hundred acres available, but it's a little too far away. So for the time being the dream will remain an entity unto itself. He will continue giving his paychecks to Isabel, who pays the bills and makes sure life proceeds smoothly. The other investments will stay separate, his alone. Any profits from the properties and the cattle will be recycled into more of the same, making up for losses and in good times buying more. Probably his neighbors' jealousy will grow, especially as more tourists come to Abiquiu and fall in love with the place and decide not to leave. In turn it will grow harder to buy land, and the ranch will become more elusive. But then reality seems to be something that Virgil can keep in check. There is a time for putting food on the table, but that does not have to impose on time spent dreaming.

By now the kitchen staff have finished eating and begun to clean the dining room. Virgil's cook friend is vacuuming the rug under the salad bar when two young girls walk in and ask him a question. He points them to Virgil. The girls approach the table nervously and ask if it's okay to pick some alfalfa and feed it to the donkeys. "Yeah," Virgil tells them blandly. "Sure." He pushes his empty plastic plate forward, puts on his sunglasses, and goes back to work.

4

In the movie *City Slickers*, Billy Crystal plays Mitch Robbins, a schmuck from New Jersey on the brink of a mid-life crisis. After a party for his thirty-ninth birthday, he is totally depressed, so much so that his wife asks him not to join her and the kids on their trip to visit her parents in Florida. She urges him to instead go away with his two buddies on the adventure they planned for him as a surprise gift—she tells him to go "find his smile."

And so Mitch and his buddies go to Ghost Ranch. In the movie it's called Stone Ranch, and the set designers have remade a corner of the llano into a working ranch, complete with old-fashioned corral and picturesque wooden barn. Still, it's unmistakable as the Piedra Lumbre—every other shot is framed against the cliffs of shining stone. Mitch and his New Yorker friends are there for a dude ranch vacation, during which they'll help the real cowboys drive their cattle to Colorado for the winter. In a slapsticky montage, they and the other hopelessly urban guests learn to ride horses and rope cattle in a couple of long, hard days. At sunrise on the third day they set out on the trail, riding metaphorically toward renewal and self-discovery.

Leading them is a mythic man named Curly, played by Jack Palance. He is the cowboy archetype, clad in leather vest and chaps, bandana around his neck and a cigarette hanging from his lips. In a seminal moment along the ride, he commands Mitch to roll up his sleeves and deliver a calf from a sick cow. When the mother dies moments later, Mitch adopts the calf, naming it Norman. Back on their horses, Mitch having proven himself, Curly bestows the key to personal enlightenment. He holds up his index finger, gloved in black leather. "The secret of life is this one thing. Nothing else means shit."

"But what is that one thing?" Mitch asks.

"That's what you have to figure out."

Virgil figured it out a long time ago. For him, that one thing is the land—that's what makes him Curly in this story. Still, the first few times we met I couldn't help but see the Mitch side of his life: the part where he's stuck in a workaday existence that is less than fulfilling.

It's a common story among people in agriculture, that the life they watched their parents and grandparents live is simply unavailable to them. At the time of the last U.S. Census of Agriculture, more than half of all farmers and ranchers worked "off farm," most of them full-time. For them agriculture becomes an activity for weekends and evenings rather than an occupation. The vast majority of the time, the reason is money.

It's not news that being a farmer or a rancher doesn't pay well. Things improve if you can work the economies of scale and draw on a force of cheap laborers, the way a nineteenth-century plantation owner would have. In the twenty-first century, add in vertical integration, government subsidies, and a deft hand for the commodities market, and you can have a highly profitable farming corporation. But for individuals who do the work themselves and sell to someone else, agriculture is virtually never big-money business. The primary reason is that in our economy, human labor is too valuable in relation to the food and fiber it produces—or, said another way, the food and fiber is too *de*valued, too cheap. Work the same number of hours "making" insurance policies or software, and the labor is rewarded much better. This is a primary reason why we have come to believe it's inevitable that the American agriculturist is a dying breed; the numbers don't work.

The relative values of food and the humans producing it have gone off-balance for a variety of reasons, everything from the Industrial Revolution to immigration policy. At the top of that list is the application of fossil fuel power, particularly petroleum, to agriculture.

Journalist Richard Heinberg aptly put it in perspective in his 2006 lecture to the E. F. Schumaker Society, titled "Fifty Million Farmers":

> Think about it. Have you ever run out of gas along the highway and had to push your car two or three yards to get it off to the side of the road? You know that's hard work. Imagine pushing your car twenty or thirty miles. That's the energy equivalent of roughly six to eight weeks of hard human labor. It's what we get from a single gallon of gasoline for which we're paying less than $2.25 right now. Imagine getting six to eight weeks of human labor for $2.25. You can't do that even in China.

What was for decades a relatively cheap source of energy allowed us to defy the basic laws of thermodynamics, at least temporarily, and build systems that consume far more usable energy than they produce. In the case of agriculture, that meant that food production became overall less expensive, and in turn the relative price of food fell radically. The upside has been, of course, a mostly stable and affordable supply of calories and nutrition for everyone; now when hunger comes, it is the result of social inequity, not lack of food. And because Americans spend less of their income on food than any country in the world we have had a greater portion available for other things. Since World War II the percentage of our incomes given to buying food has steadily dropped—from more than 20 percent in the 1940s to less than 10 percent now.

Through all this, what has not changed is that the humans involved in agriculture still must survive in the same economy as the rest of society. They pay for electricity and health care and new clothes at the same rates the rest of us do, but the product they have to trade has steadily depreciated.

This is compounded by the fact that as the food system has moved toward more processing and greater centralization, farmers and ranchers have received an ever-smaller fraction of the ever-smaller retail price for their product. Whereas in 1950 farmers received forty-one cents of every retail dollar spent on food, today their cut averages out to nineteen cents. Even that number is high, for it factors in foods like fresh produce and milk, which are minimally processed after they leave the farm and therefore leave more of the final price for the farmer. The person who grows wheat for Wonder Bread receives less than three cents of the dollar; the one who grows corn for Cheerios gets about a penny and a half. The rest goes to processing, packaging, marketing, distribution, whole-saling, and retailing.

In the case of beef, it works like this: The supply chain begins with the rancher, who owns a herd of cows. Each year each cow gives birth to a calf. In the conventional market, the calf is raised for approximately six to ten months and then sold—the rancher's sole income for the year. The calf is bought by a stocker, who fattens it to maturity, then sold to a feedlot, where it is fattened on grain to a final weight, then sold again to a packinghouse, where it is slaughtered and processed into parts. The meat is sold to a whole-saler and in turn to a retailer, then finally to the consumer. For the $7.29 per pound that you would pay at Safeway for a mid-range cut like tri-tip steak, Virgil would receive just ninety-one cents. Or eighty-three cents. Or, on the best of days, a dollar and a quarter. The price fluctuates according to market elements like supply and demand, and the prices of diesel and corn. It is also adjusted by companies along the chain to benefit their bottom lines. A million different factors shift the price per pound that a calf will bring, and yet there is one part of the commodity chain that has no influence whatsoever: the individual rancher. Whatever price is offered when he sells his calves, that's the price he gets. The ranching business, it's said, is like playing a poker game in which the other players control the cards and make your bets for you.

———•———

In the end of *City Slickers*, Mitch and his two buddies do find re-demption in the land. Curly dies and the rest of the group desert, leaving the gang of three to drive the herd on their own. Without maps or compasses they find their way through the treacherous wilderness and bring the cattle safely home. The journey is half Saint Francis of Assisi, half John Wayne. In a slow-motion sequence, we see the three triumphantly enter the corral on horseback, transformed. They are strong, capable, proud. Finally, they are men.

And then they go back to New Jersey. Mitch brings Norman the calf home, saving him from being sold to "the meat company." But when Mitch's wife sees the animal at the airport's curbside pickup, Mitch promises he'll find it a nice home in a petting zoo. With that, they all pile into the minivan and drive off into the Newark sunset, the calf's head sticking out the window.

Probably the movie did not intend to comment on the state of the American agricultural economy—it was not a very *complex* movie—but the statement is there nonetheless. As the minivan drives off we realize Mitch has identified the secret of life, the one thing that matters. It is his family. To provide for them, he will return to his unrewarding spot in the industrial economy with a smile on his face. He will pay his mortgage, his kids will go to college, and then they will follow in his dragging footsteps. Even if he could convince his family to move from New Jersey to New Mexico, the numbers just wouldn't work. His brief time on the land was sweet, even a dream come true, but staying there was never an option.

What's striking about Virgil is that for him just the opposite is true: *not* staying on the land was never an option. He cannot ignore the economic reality of his current life, but he could no sooner abandon his determination to have a different life, on the land. I once broached the subject with him, suggesting that most people

142

would think his dream was unrealistic in this day and age, even nostalgic. His reply: "I would imagine for most people it is."

For a long time I didn't get it. For such a hopeful figure, Virgil had goals that seemed impossible, at times even sad. Then one day he told me the story of where he comes from, and at last I began to understand.

———•———

The first time I met Virgil, he referred to himself as Spanish, which I incorrectly took to mean descended from the conquistadores and their progeny. I later learned that New Mexicans use that word where people elsewhere might say Hispanic or Latino, but it turns out neither of those is accurate either. To understand who Virgil is I had to learn a word that even most people in New Mexico don't know: genízaro.

Virgil learned the story behind the word from his grandfather Benjamin, but today he tells it as his own. When the Spanish arrived in New Mexico, it was inhabited by both pueblo Indians who had been there for millennia and nomadic tribes who had migrated there from the Plains. During intertribal conflicts among the nomadics it was common practice to kidnap members of another tribe and sell them as slaves. With the Spanish colonists as customers, a lucrative market arose.

The Catholic Church forbade outright slavery, but the Spanish devised a way around it: they paid a "ransom" for the Indian servants, raised them as Spanish-speaking Christians, and released them when they reached adulthood. But released them into what?

These people had no money or assets and had mostly lost their families and languages. As Virgil puts it, they couldn't just buy a bus ticket home. So they stayed, some under the wing of their former owners, and many under the general protection that came through assimilating with the Spanish. "They were a new people," one historian wrote, "completely Native American yet belonging to no tribe; they were familiar with Hispanic culture yet were not Spanish." By 1776, these new people were thought to comprise one third of New Mexico's population.

The name they were given was genízaro. It's a Spanish take on the word *janissary* (in Turkish *yeniceri*). Dating from the fourteenth century, janissary refers to prisoners of war and Christian youth who were forcibly converted to Islam and charged with helping defend the Ottoman Empire. Beginning in the 1740s, the genízaros of New Mexico played a similar role, being placed in Spanish settlements throughout the territory to help bolster those communities against attacks by nomadic tribes. In the short term they would bring the fierce fighting skills that came as part of their nomadic heritage. More importantly, the Spanish hoped the genízaros would stay and help grow the settlements for the long term. In this turf war, lasting communities were the ultimate weapon.

Virgil's home of Abiquiu was modeled on this premise, except there was no existing settlement for the genízaros to bolster. Abiquiu was the northernmost point in the Spanish empire, ten miles from what was known as La Tierra de Guerra, the Land of War, which was ruled by nomadics. (The unofficial entrance to that land was the southern edge of the Piedra Lumbre, right about where

Highway 84 crests the hill and drivers see the valley revealed.) Over time there had been numerous Spanish and Indian settlements in the area, but none that could withstand the constant assault from surrounding tribes. So in 1754, Spanish authorities bestowed the land grant called El Merced del Pueblo Abiquiu. A tract of more than seventeen thousand acres was granted to thirty-four genízaro families, in hopes they could make the pueblo of Abiquiu last. It was a challenging proposition, but consider the circumstances: these were people whose recent history had been one of violence, slavery, and ethnic homelessness. The chance to put down roots again and create a community of their own would have been a compelling reason to play the odds of this place.

The logic of settling this frontier was akin to the United States' Homesteading Act that would come a century later. Throughout what would later become the state of New Mexico the Spanish granted land to civilians in exchange for their claiming and holding the territory in the name of the crown—same as the American government did. In practice, though, there was a fundamental difference. The Homesteading Act deeded land to individuals. The Spanish did as well, but more common were land grants like the one in Abiquiu, which were given communally to a group of people. While small sections of it were subdivided into individual plots of farmland along the irrigation ditch, the vast majority of the land was owned in common by the community. Called the *ejido*, it was the source of their subsistence livelihood, a place for livestock grazing, fishing and hunting, and collecting firewood and rocks. That part of the land grant could not legally be sold. The *ejido* was not an asset to be leveraged, it was life itself.

Over the years the Spanish gave way to the Mexicans, and the Mexicans in turn to the Americans. Through it all Abiquiu centered itself inward, keeping its political affiliations loose and focusing instead on sheer survival in this land of ten-inch rainfall. After the Americans set up a garrison here in the 1840s, Abiqueño men joined their military forces in fighting off Indian attacks. And yet those same men continued to trade with the Utes, even as the tribe warred with the Americans. Abiquiu's loyalty was, ultimately, to itself.

The Mexican-American War ended in 1848 with the Treaty of Guadalupe Hidalgo, which made New Mexico part of the United States. In the years following, the Americans set out to determine what parts of their new territory belonged to whom—or more accurately, what of it belonged to the U.S. government. In the end, the majority of land grants were never ratified. The land became federal property or ended up in private hands, often with Anglos who had never lived there and never would.

The reasons were numerous. The regional administration was perennially understaffed and ill-equipped to deal with what ended up being hundreds of claims covering millions of acres of effectively wild land. At the same time, the American bureaucracy was a foreign concept to the people holding the land grants, many of them subsistence farmers with little or no education, and whose native language was Spanish. Individual land speculators exploited the grant holders' weaknesses and swindled them out of their land. Locals of northern New Mexico will tell you the land-hungry U.S. government was no better, setting up official policies with the express purpose of appropriating the grants. Also at play was plain old bureaucratic ennui. As the hundreds of claims piled up most were dismissed on minor technical grounds.

More than anything, though, the land fell out of "Spanish" hands because of the difference between how the two clashing cultures defined land ownership. For the grantees, land was less a possession than it was a right to make one's livelihood in a place. El Merced del Pueblo Abiquiu and other community land grants were not given so they could be sold; they were meant to connect people to a place in perpetuity. It followed that validating ownership took an experiential form. New Mexico State Historian Robert J. Torrez wrote this description of Mayor Bartholome Fernandes officiating a grant in 1769:

> After going through a number of preliminary procedures in which he described the boundaries of the grant and reviewed a number of conditions for the settlement and defense of the proposed community, he proceeded with the actual act of possession, noting . . . they all said they understood . . . [so] I took them by the hand and walked them through the said lands, they pulled up grass, threw stones, and shouted to the four winds three times in strong voices, "Long live the King and may God Guard Him," all as a sign of true possession. This marvelous procedure demonstrates that in order to own property under the Spanish and Mexican land grant system, you had to physically step on the land, run your fingers through the soil, and make a public commitment to live on it, cultivate it, and, if necessary, defend it with your life. This was an important part of the land grant process. If this was not done, or done incorrectly, the settlers' legal claim to the grant could be called into question.

In great contrast, the American mindset toward property was more or less as we know it today: land may have meaning to an individual, but for official purposes it is a precise entity that is bought and sold. The Spanish had determined boundaries organically; for instance, the banks of a river would form a shifting border. But the Americans saw the world as a two-dimensional grid. All ownership was defined by measurements of points on that grid, calculations that left nothing to interpretation. The benefit of this system was that land could be bought and sold easily, on paper, even without ever seeing the place. Land could be a commodity, and therefore a source of capital.

Imagine then, when American rule came to a place like Abiquiu, the new officials asking for proper documentation of people's ownership of the land. If the grantees did have papers they likely couldn't read them, leaving interpretation in the hands of the government. But the papers didn't matter to the grantees in the first place. In most cases, their primary documentation was that they had been living and farming there for a century or more. They must have thought, *What better proof is there?*

This proof allowed some grantees to keep at least their individual homesteads—private property that the Americans could understand. But the *ejidos*, the vast tracts of common land that they depended on for sustenance, were a concept unfamiliar to the assessors. Except in a very few cases, this land simply became public, which is to say U.S. government property. This was what happened to the land grant of San Antonio de Vallecito, of which Virgil's father's family was part. They were allowed to keep their homesteads, but the rest of the land went to the U.S. Forest Service. Today,

Virgil pays the federal government a fee for the right to graze his cattle there.

"The issue has *never* been laid to rest," Virgil told me. "We're still fighting for those land grants. We still know what their borders are. For half of them we still have the documentation, which they should have honored and they didn't. They destroyed countless communities."

When Virgil talks about this his voice rises and his shoulders come forward. Should he be driving he will grip the steering wheel as if to choke it. The first time I met him we got on the subject within ten minutes of shaking hands, and I, green to New Mexican land politics, was startled by his fury. As he talked, the years seemed to collapse together, so that these wrongs of one hundred and fifty years ago were his current events. It was his livelihood that had been taken away.

"My cattle that are up there, they're merely a privilege? Bullshit." (This, the only time I've ever heard him swear.) "We were there since 1807. The reason that not a shot was fired when the Southwest lands were ceded to the Americans is that they promised and guaranteed us all these rights *that we already had*. We would have gone to war in a second if someone would've told us that we were all going to end up in low-income housing divisions."

Look at a map of New Mexico and you'll see a giant green area along the west side of Highway 84. What used to be dozens of land grants, including the one that was partly owned by Virgil's father's family, is now National Forest. There is a bright side to this story, though, at least for Virgil. Within this green area on the map there are two significant blocks of white, representing private property.

One is the location of Ghost Ranch, the Piedra Lumbre, and includes land that belongs to Virgil's grandmother. She still owns more than twenty thousand acres on the valley's south side, what was left after her father, Manuel Salazar, had to sell out to Arthur Pack during the Depression. But no piece of that will come to Virgil for decades yet, if ever. There are too many heirs, and even in this day and age Virgil is at a disadvantage because he comes to the land through his mother, a female. However, the other stretch of private property on the map—and this part of the story Virgil tells with almost breathless words—is El Merced del Pueblo Abiquiu. The land granted to Virgil's ancestors in 1754 was one of the very few that was ratified by the American government against all odds. Today, all 16,708.16 acres of the grant are still theirs, owned in common by Virgil and seventy-two others.

How did they keep it? They got lucky, Virgil says. "Of all the papers and testimonies that had to be presented to the court, it was the very last sentence that saved us. It says, *These people have lived continuously on this land since 1754, when the King of Spain made the grant.* And by the grace of God—some things really make you believe in God—they accept it. That was it." He shakes his head. "It is a *miracle* that this is our land."

5

Across the street from the pretty adobe church on the Abiquiu plaza is a gray brick building that no tourists notice. It is the José Ferran Gym, the community center where Virgil learned to roller skate four decades ago. On a Sunday in August 2007, just after church and lunch, it is the site of the annual meeting of El Merced del Pueblo Abiquiu, known here as "the Merced" or simply "the grant."

Even after the U.S. government ratified the grant's claim in 1894, the community has had a challenging time holding on to the land. Into the 1920s the land grant was still owned communally by the descendents of the original genízaros. While these people had never fit neatly into a single ethnic category, the government had erred on their native side and designated Abiquiu an Indian pueblo—an entity separate from the state but also subject to its caretaking and direction. After years of watching the poor treatment of their full-blooded Native American neighbors, in 1928 the community voted to give up their pueblo status and become a village of the state of New Mexico.

In Virgil's explanation the decision was coerced by land speculators. These vulturous outsiders knew that when the pueblo became a village it would have to begin paying taxes. They hoped
that a combination of ignorance and poverty would cause the community to default on those payments, at which time the state would
take possession of the land, and in turn the speculators could buy
it. It nearly happened in the 1930s: taxes had been paid on private
holdings within Abiquiu, but the monies for the *ejido* mysteriously
never made it to the state. When the government moved to seize the
land, the community wrangled an extension. In 1942, they formed
a cooperative to govern the grant, the membership dues of which
paid off the delinquent taxes. Disaster was averted.

By and large it was a victory for the community. They got
to keep their land and have ever since—that's why there's an annual meeting today. The downside was that when the cooperative was formed, membership was opened to anyone who lived
in Abiquiu and had twenty dollars cash to join. This let in people
who weren't descendants of the original grantees—according to
Virgil, even some of the speculators themselves. It also shut out
a number of true descendants who were too poor to pay. Today
there are seventy-three members, only about 60 percent of them
original descendants.

Despite the change in structure, in most hearts the grant is
still the grant it always was. Membership is inherited and can be
passed to only one person, most often a blood relative. (Virgil's
father, descended from one of the original grantee families, still
retains his membership; Virgil received his from his grandfather
Benjamin.) While most of the grant members still live in town, some

have traveled here for this meeting from Española, Albuquerque, or farther afield. Beforehand there's the air of an extended family reunion, with women hugging and kissing on the steps of the gym, men shaking hands.

Inside the gym there is a bathroom and a kitchen, but otherwise it is a single room with corrugated tin walls and old, wooden floors, most of it marked as a basketball court. A heavy fan in the wall rattles hard, churning the hot afternoon air. Fifty folding chairs have been set up, and they're filling from the back; the front row is empty. Facing the audience is a line of folding tables with five chairs behind them, where the board members will sit.

Virgil is on the board, holding the position of range manager, which means he is in charge of the *ejido*. There's a briefcase at his chair, but right now he's standing by the entrance, greeting and talking. He's up for reelection today. (When I asked him last night at the auction if there would be any campaigning, he said no. They either like you or they don't.) He's talking with a younger, skater-looking guy who's wearing a black T-shirt that reads HIGH SOCIETY against a picture of a green marijuana leaf. Next, he talks to an older man, the only one aside from him who is dressed in rancher uniform.

Surveying the room, I find it odd that the crowd here looks nothing like the cowboy crowd at the county fair. Virgil is dressed as usual, in boots, black jeans, and white hat. He wears a long-sleeved, collared shirt with a Southwest design on top and along the bottom; across the middle is an image of a man on horseback, looking over the range and toward white mountains. The board members all wear boots and jeans, but otherwise people here might as well be from Iowa or New Jersey for the way they dress: shorts and T-shirts, khakis and sneakers.

The grant's meetings use parliamentary procedure, which begins with a smack of the gavel and a roll call. *Present. Presente. Sí. Right here.* Forty-six members in attendance; the secretary enters it into the logbook. Two more people walk in and he changes it to forty-eight. The president reads aloud the minutes from last year.

When he finishes he calls for a perfunctory motion to approve the minutes as read. Instead people start standing up and letting bullets fly. One woman is furious about the limitless water rights she believes are being given to the man in the row in front of her, who will use them to build a hotel on the highway. She has a letter to prove her assumption, and has made copies for everyone in attendance. Another woman is demanding that the board—and if not them then a mutiny of the members—reverse the injustice that has taken place with her sister's death, which passed membership in the land grant to her sister's husband rather than to her, which was what was directed by their mother's will. Others stand to defend the speakers or defend themselves, and before long it's a free-for-all— people formally address the group or just call out from their seats or whisper loudly to their neighbors. The bottle has been corked for twelve months and finally, suddenly, it is exploding. Thunder rolls above. The president patiently, tiredly, explains that there will be time to discuss all of this, but first they just need to get a motion to accept the minutes from last year as they were read. *Yea?* A lackluster chorus sounds. *Nay?* The two women with the original grievances dig in their heels.

The next six hours is a marble cake of chaos and order, with dozens of motions and votes to approve the proceedings and a record of it all written in careful longhand by the secretary. They debate whether the road through town should get pavement or speed bumps, discuss how to disburse permits for elk hunting on the grant, argue whether the final word on who inherits a membership lies with the grant members or the Rio Arriba County probate court. Rain beats down on the roof, and thirty minutes later sun scorches the yard outside. The fan is turned off because it's too noisy to hear with it on, then it's turned back on because the stuffy heat is unbearable. Some members make impassioned pleas for family and land, others read magazines and eventually wander outside. When things go bad there are a handful of nasty comments but mostly the result is just plain communication breakdown. At one point an eloquent man in a sleeveless gray T-shirt rises and suggests that because the communication is so poor, perhaps they should discuss implementing a system that can better disseminate information between meetings, so that when they do meet it feels less like a firing range.

No outsider could untangle the disputes that take place at this meeting, saddled as they are with layers of history both public and private. What is clear to even the newest of newcomers, though, is that owning this land together is not as obvious a task as it once was. No doubt the forefathers that Virgil invokes did their share of bickering, but at least they had a common vision of what the land was for. They all needed it to survive, so they had to work together in using it. Today, Virgil is one of just five people who still graze cattle on the *ejido*. He puts as many of his cows on the grant as he is allowed; it's an essential part of how he keeps his herd of eighty cattle alive. But he's the sole person with a significant economic interest in the land. The others with cows have no more than ten apiece, as a hobby. For the rest of the people in the grant, the original meaning of the land has become abstract. Or worse, Virgil fears, it has been forgotten.

The community's transition away from the land began before anyone who is alive today can remember. Many northern New Mexico historians date it to the very end of the nineteenth century and the arrival of American capitalists, who introduced a new style of land use based in extraction. They saw the land as a sum of its resources, "virgin and almost unoccupied territory ripe for capitalizing." They brought a whole new set of business practices and technologies, most notably the railroad, which allowed minerals, lumber, and livestock to be shipped to industrial centers back East.

The profits went back East as well. Take the sheep industry, for instance. Most locals had a lifetime of experience raising sheep, but in small quantities. The new economy dealt in the tens of thousands. Because they didn't have the money to invest in big herds, locals instead sharecropped livestock owned by investors. Or they were hired as herders, the way Virgil's grandfather Benjamin was. "I guess you could say there was some money in Abiquiu during that period," Virgil told me, "but it's the well-to-dos who have all the sheep. It's the same as it is now: you have the well-to-dos and you have everyone else. There's not really a middle class."

Whereas survival before had been based on sourcing the raw materials of life, the new capitalist economy required cash. Families continued to raise gardens and livestock to feed themselves, but increasingly they moved away from subsistence agriculture and became dependent on incomes from jobs in the mining and logging industries, as well as in commodity agriculture. By the 1920s, up to 85 percent of men in a northern New Mexico village would leave to work elsewhere for six months of the year. In tiny Abiquiu, that was more than one hundred men, gone.

In many ways, Abiquiu's story is the story of rural America. The particular details of the community are unique; the early history of its capitalization brings to mind a tropical colony rather than a region of the United States. But in terms of Abiquiu's fate as a traditionally agricultural community, the story has parallels from Georgia to Montana. After World War II, people started leaving and not coming back. In many cases it was a matter of necessity; Abiquiu was too poor to support them, even as part-time residents. At the same time there was so much growth elsewhere—Salt Lake City, Sacramento, even just over the mountains at Los Alamos National Laboratory—that it was hard to pass up the opportunity.

For those who stayed, agriculture increasingly lost its importance. Partly it was practical: it's hard to work a forty-hour week and still be on the land. But in addition to that, food production, once the daily existence of this community, was evaluated differently in the new cash economy. Considering all the labor that goes into growing a garden or raising livestock, the risk that weather and insects pose, it no longer seemed worth it. In the eyes of each new generation, there was no longer reason to struggle with the ten-inch rainfall. Virgil puts it plainly: "Why bother? There's food at Bode's."

As people ceased to care about agriculture individually, the community aspects fell away as well. Every year fewer cattle graze on the grant's land. People stopped hunting there, stopped using it for much of anything other than collecting firewood. With individual jobs that take them to separate places each day, there's less reason to collaborate, less incentive to care for the land as a group. I'd guess at least half the members in that annual meeting haven't even been to the *ejido* in years.

This practical and emotional separation from the land is just the sort of transition that the Committee for Economic Development (CED) recommended in "An Adaptive Program for Agriculture," its report from 1962 that argued there was an "excess of resources" in agriculture; that the exodus from agriculture had been large, but not large enough. The CED advocated a facilitated migration of two million farmers out of agriculture, partly in the name of giving those people a chance at the "attainment and maintenance of high and secure standards of living" that the industrial system enabled. The problem is, nothing ever replaced agriculture in Abiquiu. As wage labor has become ever more scarce, only welfare has filled in.

This story of rural decline is particularly familiar in the interior West, where the wide-open spaces between cities make it less likely that former agricultural communities will fall under the suburban wing of an urban neighbor. Instead, towns shrivel up or they metastasize with the infections that poverty brings: alcoholism, drug abuse, despair. On one day while I was visiting Virgil, the front-page stories in the Rio Arriba County newspaper included a string of robberies, a stabbing, a suicide—and a shortage of police officers. Inside: major layoffs at Los Alamos; a park ranger shot; a woman busted for bringing her boyfriend in jail a green chile hamburger from McDonald's with a baggy of heroin inside. For years, Rio Arriba has earned the dubious distinction of having the most drug-related deaths per capita of any county in the United States.

Ben Tafoya, who runs a nonprofit addiction recovery organization based in Española, traces the county's drug use directly to people's separation from the land. He begins by explaining that drug use nearly always stems from a personal loss. In a healthy grief process, a person goes through stages that include denial, anger, and eventually acceptance. The problem comes when a person gets stuck in one of those stages and turns to drugs or alcohol to medicate the bad feelings.

"In northern New Mexico, what you have is entire communities that got stuck in one stage of grief," he told me. "And those feelings have been passed through generations now." As he sees it, the loss began with communities being robbed of their land grants after the Treaty of Guadalupe Hidalgo, resulting in a sense of disenfranchisement and disillusionment with the new system in power. The loss continued when people were further disconnected from agricultural life in the twentieth century. In the past few decades the loss has multiplied, in part because of its own cure: as agriculture has become an untenable occupation, many people have turned to the state. But in order to qualify for general assistance in New Mexico, a person cannot own more than two thousand dollars' worth of land or other "non-liquid real property." In other words, if a person has managed somehow to hold on to some land, it's likely that to be eligible for welfare he or she will have to sell it. The cycle of loss and despair becomes self-perpetuating.

Most of the local newspaper's stories of drugs and violence take place in Española and involve players from the more heavily populated towns on the south side of the county. Abiquiu and other towns in more rural areas do seem more intact and secure, although according to Tafoya drug abuse is no less prevalent there, it's just less visible. Either way, Virgil, in any conversation about Abiquiu's woes, is sure to stress that goodness still prevails. "We have peace of mind and peace of heart," he says. "We don't have big money here, but we have big people."

Still, for those people in town who want to create better lives for themselves—the promise of the "Adaptive Plan for Agriculture" that was never delivered—every day is a struggle to pull Abiquiu away from the cliff over which so many rural communities have fallen. There has even been talk of Abiquiu regaining its designation as an Indian pueblo. Virgil explained that as a pueblo Abiquiu could build a casino like the one down the highway in Tesuque. Some like the idea of the fast dollar, he thinks, the "put in a nickel, pull out a million bucks" approach to life. But Virgil reminds them that becoming a pueblo means becoming a ward of the state; that back when Abiquiu was a pueblo, his grandfather—and probably theirs, too—was sent to Indian school. He believes it would be a step toward further dependence, and that is a step in the wrong direction.

Virgil has a solution of his own: the land. It is the one great resource they have in Abiquiu. Yes, it is dry, even desiccated in years of drought. In only two of the last ten years did the area get its ten inches of precipitation; in 2000 it had less than seven. And yet for two centuries the land sustained this community, with food as well as something more. "It was only on government paper that Abiquiu and its extended community was called poor," one historian wrote. "Abiqueños never thought of themselves as destitute or anything resembling poor, even in the Depression years." Because they had land, they were independent and proud—they were in charge of their own destiny.

Virgil insists that this could be true again. As range manager of the land grant, he is trying to implement all kinds of new actions that would get agriculture back on its feet and make it worthwhile to people again. He'd like to improve the land's yield by planting more native grazing plants, like shrubby green winter fat, which offers cows something to eat even when snow covers the ground. He'd like the board to dip into its funds and buy fifty cattle, which could then be given to grant members who lost their cattle during the drought but want to get back in the game. And with more cows on the grant, he'd like to implement progressive land management techniques to get maximum production from the land.

"I'm just concerned that there aren't enough people up on the grant," he told me. "I'd like for people even to just ride their horses up there and say, *That's the boundary, this is my land*. Take their kids and say, *This is going to be your land*. What if every year we get everyone up there and go to the four corners of our property. Or do a ceremony like they used to do when the King would give them land, *Oh, thank you, King! Oh, God, thank you*." His eyes light up with the idea. "And why just once a year? Why not every month?"

It's not about food—Virgil isn't envisioning a return to subsistence farming. It's about the deeper rewards the land offers:

Independence. Purpose. Continuity. The notion is so clear to him he can't believe no one else seems to feel this way.

"It's our *home*," he said, his voice straining. "You have to take care of your home, because if you don't pretty soon it's just a place. In Spanish we say, *At least you have somewhere to drop dead. Ni siquiera tienes donde caerte muerto.* Meaning, at least you have a home, a place to call your own. Just imagine when your generations come after you, and they're struggling like heck. Think of when they're having to bow to somebody else because they don't have a home. Those are the days when we're gonna be really sad."

At the annual meeting, Virgil mostly sat patiently in his chair in front of the room, raising his hand to be called on in the midst of the chaos. When it came his turn to report as range manager, he stood before the members and made a plea in both English and Spanish, hands clasped before his chest. It ended with these words: "We're so small now, and the concerns are so big. I would encourage anyone to participate." He put out a legal pad and asked people to sign up for a committee that would take action toward using the *ejido* to its full potential.

The crowd responded with a spray of bullets. Some of the shots Virgil may have deserved, some not—again, the dealings of a community this tightly woven are too intimate for an outsider to judge. Though no one said it overtly, it seemed clear that people saw Virgil's initiative as self-serving: invest in the land at the grant's expense so that his herd—huge, to their eyes—could get even bigger. When the members voted to reelect or replace the board members, Virgil lost his seat. At the end of the meeting, his sign-up sheet was blank.

The next day, Virgil was right back in the groove, coming up with new ideas and wishing people would get involved. "You know, I had a good upbringing. A lot of seeds were planted, so I feel like I have to keep them going. That's why I have the cattle. Could I be doing something else? Could I be going home on the weekend and relaxing and watching TV all day long, resting, so I can actually be my best at work when I come back on Monday? I could." He takes a long pause. "But I can't. I could, but I just can't."

6

It's the first Saturday in November, and Ghost Ranch is waking up from its summer sleep. That is, the rangeland at Ghost Ranch. The visitor center's busy season is June through August, but the tens of thousands of acres of open land have been vacant since May. Today, the cattle return.

In 1967, Ghost Ranch started a program that allowed local stockmen to graze their cattle on the llano for the winter at subsidized rates. The program was a boon for small producers in the region. Nearly everyone grazes their cows on Forest Service land during summer, but those who don't own irrigated land had always had to search for a place for their cattle between October and May. Ghost Ranch quickly became an integral part of their survival as cattlemen.

The program has had up to fifty-five ranchers at a time, but there are fewer people in the business now, especially since the drought. In the worst years, 2002 and 2003, the Forest Service mandated that they take their animals off the summer grazing allotments up to a month earlier than usual, the first in a chain of drought-related events that made it so nearly everyone in the area had to sell off animals. Some ranchers went out of business completely. This winter there will be about forty stockmen in the program, mostly with fewer than fifteen animals. For the season all of their cattle live as one herd of six hundred.

As rangeland manager at Ghost Ranch, Virgil runs the program. When he took the full-time job at Ghost Ranch, he agreed to a wage that was less than he would have liked on the condition that they support his education about rangeland management. He wanted to administer the grazing program as best he could, as well as care for and even improve the rangeland. Through seminars and workshops he studied Holistic Resource Management (HRM), a decision-making method that, when applied to ranching, refocuses attention on the entire system—land, water, grass—rather than just the cattle. One of the first steps is to see the ranching system as based on solar energy: the sun's energy grows plants, then cows harvest that energy and transform it into protein that is edible for humans. HRM ranchers still make their money by harvesting the cattle, but their strategy for success is to take care of the land that grows the plants.

The most basic application of HRM is a system of rotational grazing. It is meant to make cows replicate herds of heavy ruminants such as bison, whose symbiotic relationship with the flora was an integral part of grasslands ecosystems for millennia. The herds would concentrate in one area, eat its plants down to the ground, then move on and not return until the forage was sufficiently regrown. Had they returned sooner, they would have compromised the plants that they depended on for survival.

Cattle, on the other hand, if left in one big open space, eat only the best plants, trimming them repeatedly without regard for their recovery. To counter this, the HRM rancher divides the open range into fenced pastures and moves the animals through at intervals of a few days or weeks. With this orchestrated migration, a smaller area is grazed hard for a short period of time, then left to rest until the plants have grown back—just like with the bison. HRM practitioners swear (and some research confirms) that the range ecosystem profits substantially, in some cases becoming healthier than if there were no cattle at all.

Virgil's predecessor at Ghost Ranch instituted an HRM approach in 1986, and when Virgil took over he continued the process. Under his direction the llano has been divided into permanently fenced pastures of four hundred to thirty-five hundred acres, each grazed for two weeks at a time. The benefits are huge, Virgil says, particularly the reduction of labor. Traditional ranchers use the "Columbus method," which means turning the cows out in fall and then riding out to the far corners of the range in spring to "discover" them again. Should they want to check on the herd or give them supplemental feed in hard weather, the search can be arduous. At Ghost Ranch, ranchers know where their cattle are every day.

That is not to say the program was a hit from the start. "We had our socks laughed off when we put up the first electric fences," Virgil told me.

"Who laughed at you?"

"Pretty much everybody. They were just used to seeing the cattle all over the place, because that's the way it's always been."

"Have they changed their tune?"

"Oh yeah, of course. Big time. Now, in two hours they see all their cows rather than spending the whole day looking for them. In a way it's actually a mixed blessing, because I really want guys to spend more time out there. But what do you do after two hours? You're just sitting there watching them graze."

In a way, Virgil applies HRM to the ranchers as well. Under his direction the grazing program will not simply board people's cattle; anyone who has his cattle there is required to be an active part of the system. Every two weeks throughout the season, everyone must make the drive to Ghost Ranch, get on their horses, ride out on the range, and help move the cattle to new ground, even in the bitter cold. Once the group of forty riders is out there the process takes twenty minutes tops. The truth is that one person could do it alone with a truck and some hay, just honk and the cows would come running into the new pasture for the feed.

"Sometimes I feel guilty," Virgil says, "like I'm wasting their time, gas, energy. But if I do it for them, they'll never show up again. That's the thing I worry about. They'll become less and less in tune with what's happening out there."

He says he also fears that the next generation is not out on the land and therefore not learning how to do all this—or learning to want to do it in the first place. To him it's tragic that kids don't have grandparents showing them the way forward as his did. So he has put in place programs at Ghost Ranch that mandate it. There have been times that if a stockman wanted to increase the number of cattle he grazed there, for every new cow he had to also provide one for his child.

Skeptics could write off Virgil's enthusiasm for getting people of all ages involved as self-serving: the stronger the overall ranching community, the more there will be businesses to serve it and buyers drawn in to patronize it, and the more he will succeed. Probably there is an element of self-interest at play, but it's undeniable that Virgil is also serving something larger. You can hear it in his voice. Virgil gets worked up telling the story of one boy who would excitedly make lunch the night before the bi-weekly ride at Ghost Ranch, then wake his groaning father at five o'clock in the morning to be sure they arrived with their horses by eight. "It's just one or two kids like that, but that's exactly what I wanted," he told me. "Who knows? It may be one of them who ends up taking my job when I decide to move on."

—————

Over the course of the winter the cows will fan out across the llano. But first they all must enter through one spot on the east side of Ghost Ranch, where they are processed and examined. You'd never notice the place if you weren't looking for it. All you can see from the highway is a wooden archway marking a dirt road. Up a slight hill, out of sight, is a series of dusty pens enclosed by basic metal rails, with enough separate spaces to work a dozen groups of cattle without mixing them up. Today, scattered around the periphery are pickups and cattle trailers, and three semis off to one side. Other than that there are two sheds and a little building made of concrete blocks painted pink, and that's it. There isn't even a bathroom on site. The scrubby rangeland creeps in on all sides.

The pink building does grant shade from the high desert sun, but otherwise it feels more outside than inside. The doors are open and sun is streaming in. The windows are spattered with mud but also slid open; one perfectly frames a view of Cerro Pedernal, the magnificent flat-topped peak that Georgia O'Keefe painted over and over. The floor linoleum has a decorative pattern of rocks, and it's covered with a layer of crumbly dirt, once the dried mud of boots. The accoutrements are minimal: a low desk with the veneer peeling off, four ancient folding chairs, a garbage can with no bag, two light switches marked INSIDE BUILDING and OUTSIDE BUILD-ING. Beside the door a box made of plywood has been turned over to serve as a stool.

Inside I find Virgil, wearing the same thing as ever at Ghost Ranch, though this time with a thin black sweatshirt under his den-im shirt. At his side is his youngest daughter, Chavela, her long, brown hair in a high ponytail. In her hands is a weathered wooden cane whose ground end has frayed into a point, and she leans her forehead against its curved handle. When I approach she turns to nest her face in Virgil's stomach, and the hairs from the top of her head stand up fuzzily with static from his shirt.

Standing near them, at the veneer desk, is a stout, decidedly Anglo woman in her mid-fifties. By comparison to the 99 percent male crowd here she is feminine, in stretchy dark pants and a short-sleeved shirt embroidered with flowers. Every thirty seconds her two little, fluffy, grungy white dogs tear in one door, past her an-kles, and out the other door.

I introduce myself and the woman explains that she is the cat-tle buyer, down from the Four Corners area. This is what happens on weekends in the fall, at the end of the season: while the mothers go onto the range at Ghost Ranch to graze for the winter, their calves are sold. This place doubles as the sort of outdoor showroom for that sale, but really there's not much selective about it. This woman and her husband run a feedlot where the calves will be fed up to slaughter weight, and they're taking everything they can get.

She and Virgil stand before the big open windows, watching the view directly in front of them: a narrow, fifty-foot-long cattle pen. Its floor is a scale, and every ten minutes a new group of calves is corralled through a series of gates and into the pen. Immediately they run to the far end and squish into the corner, then run back, each time passing in front of the windows. As they go, the buyer woman watches with total concentration, counting and inspecting, making notes in a ledger book before her. Her husband, a similarly stout, older man in a vest and a sweatshirt, works the outside, calling on guys to bring their calves up to be weighed.

Meanwhile, Virgil reads the weight on the scale with a giant steel measuring beam so worn it looks antique. The design is the same as what you'd find in an old-fashioned store or a doctor's office, a long arm with sliding blocks. The difference is that this scale registers in thousands of pounds, and details to hundreds and tens. When the weights balance the beam, Virgil pulls a lever that stamps a slip of paper to record the number. He hands the slip to the buyer, and to his side Chavela sticks a blank slip in the slot, ready for the next stamp.

Virgil is the only one here who can work the scales. They are the property of the New Mexico Producers and Marketing

Cooperative, and he is the designated rep. Members of the co-op are stockmen of the sort who graze their cattle at Ghost Ranch, and as such the lots of calves they're selling are small—seven heifers, twelve steers. After the woman inspects them and Virgil hands her the weight slip, the calves are herded to a holding pen and a new group moves into position.

During a break between lots, Virgil's eyes drift over to where mother cows are being processed to go onto the range for winter. Seeing some commotion, he excuses himself, takes the weathered cane in his hand, and walks off. Chavela follows him.

The people processing the cows are the guys who own them. They are all men, all dressed to work, in jeans and boots and work shirts; a few sport cowboy hats but most wear ball caps. They don't look like cowboys the way the men at the county fair did. Outside this context you might not even know they had cattle, but they know what they're doing, working in groups of six or eight to process their herds and their neighbors'. Some use crops to move the cattle but mostly they have sticks akin to Virgil's cane; some guys just wave their arms. Their kids are there, playing or hanging on the rails watching. So are their dogs, scruffy herding breeds that are running as a pack for the day. Their trucks and cattle trailers are parked at random in the open spaces. Some are old and rusty, others sleek like Airstreams.

The work happens in a building that's a cross between a barn and a shed, with tall, corrugated tin walls, open on the ends, and a peaked roof. Leading into the building from the holding pens is what's called a crowding pen, a steel-walled enclosure that is the shape of a pie with one piece missing. It works like a big turnstile:

cattle are let in through the missing pie piece, and then a door like a radius, hinged to the center, swings behind them and crowds them through the circle. From there they enter a straight, narrow chute, exactly wide enough for the cows to go forward in a single file line. On the outside of the crowding pen are welded steel rods, which support old planks of wood, making a circular catwalk. As the cattle enter the enclosure, men on the planks reach down to prod the animals as necessary. Most times they don't need much prodding. It's a relatively orderly process; if you can get the cows going in one direction they'll just keep moving forward, nudged by the cow behind.

The commotion Virgil spotted is that the guys processing cattle right now have loaded nine cows into the pen, which is too crowded even for the crowding pen. The cows are spooked and confused, and in turn guys are pushing the revolving door against the resistant mass to force them into compliance, spooking them more. Two guys are up on the catwalk, poking and pushing with sticks. The cows are lowing. Before Virgil is even quite there he calls out in a steady voice, "Hey, only put four in there, otherwise you'll never get any of them in the chute." The men stop what they're doing. "And just keep calm," he says, arriving at the steel wall. "That's the way this will work." The men back five cows out into the holding pen, and the other four settle down and line up.

At the end of the straight chute is the final destination, the contraption that will hold the cow in place while it is processed. Called a working chute, it has two sides made of green metal bars that are angled downward to make a V shape, from the height of the cow's shoulders to its belly. In the rear is an improvised back flap made from a metal sign that once advertised Chamisa Realty, its phone number now covered in crusted manure. The instant the cow walks in the chute someone pulls a lever and the chute clangs shut: curved bars close around the cow's neck, the sides clamp in, and the back flap swings shut. The cow is sandwiched into place and, for the most part, immobilized.

Aside from the working chute there's little in the shed. There's a table made from two-by-fours and plywood; a faucet stuck through a hole in the wall and a sink under it whose drain is open to the concrete floor; a worn pink cooler and a shovel. Virgil has his toolbox open on the table, offering its clamps and punches and markers to those who don't have their own. Leaning against the wall, watching the cows come through, Virgil says to me, "I had hoped we would have new equipment by now," but offers no further explanation. I'm not sure if he's excusing the makeshift conditions for my sake, or voicing some true longing of his own.

The purpose of processing the cows is to ensure that they are healthy enough to live unattended over the winter. First the man taking notes records the number off the cow's ear tag and gets a physical description so the animal can be identified by anyone out on the range. The cow gets a shot with a broad-spectrum vaccine against things like Icterohaemorrhagiae and Bovine Rhinotracheitis. Then she is sprayed down the middle of her back with blue liquid parasiticide. Virgil tells me he wants this to be the last year they do this, as the liquid is a pesticide that's probably doing more bad than good. "It's just one of those things, you've been doing it so long, you know?" If the cow has horns they are removed in an unsympathetic procedure involving a hacksaw.

And finally the cow's teeth are checked, to make sure they are fit to chew the tough plants that enable survival on the range in winter. The issue is that so many of these animals are older—some ten or twelve years old. If these ranchers were rich they might have culled them for younger, stronger animals, but these guys are willing to stay loyal to an animal that has consistently given them a calf every year for a decade or more. That and it's expensive to replace them. Virgil once told me it breaks his heart when he finds a cow whose teeth aren't good enough to make it, but he knows he has to reject her from the program; if she went out on the range she would surely die.

Once the animal is cleared, the working chute releases and she walks forward into the sunny corral. When the rest of her owner's herd has been processed, they'll all be loaded into a trailer. Later today, they'll be driven out to the llano, and there they'll stay until the first of May. Aside from the wildlife, they are the most permanent residents of the Piedra Lumbre.

I'm standing back from the action now, watching the whole place work, and up walks a man who introduces himself as Julio. He wears a green sweatshirt, dark jeans, a white cowboy hat, and rimless, mirrored sunglasses. Down his back is a thin black ponytail, and his gray beard is cut into a sharp line that follows the contours of his jawbone. When he smiles and laughs, which is often, he shows the big gap between his front teeth. As we talk, he stands next to me like the guys at the county fair: talking sideways to each other while looking straight ahead. I ask him where he's from and he points to the west, to the dip between two mountain ridges. "There," he says.

Today Julio and his nephew brought a combined total of sixty-five cows, which were processed early this morning and are now waiting to go out to the range. That's more cows than most people have here, but it's still fewer than his average. Like most other local stockmen, during the drought he had to sell off many of his cows. It's a lose-lose situation when that happens. If they had kept the cows they'd have had nowhere to graze them, but selling during a drought means prices are rock-bottom because everybody else is selling, plus nobody wants them because it's dry all over.

"Then when you get some rain," he says, "the price goes up, and you gotta buy em all back. You can't win."

This year was better because it wasn't as dry as in recent years, but a lot of guys lost cows to a mysterious respiratory illness. He and his nephew lost six, and he knows a guy who had fifteen die. "At six hundred dollars apiece," he says, counting on his fingers, "that's about nine thousand dollars."

Julio has been bringing his cattle to Ghost Ranch to graze winters for twenty-five years. He was also part of a similar program a few years back, started by a millionaire oil-fortune heiress who moved here from Texas and wanted to do something good with her ranch. It lasted only a few seasons, though, before it went bankrupt. The ranch, that is.

"Not her whole thing. I mean, you'd really have to screw up for her whole thing to go bankrupt." He laughs. "I read this article about her brother. He was the owner of the Kansas City Chiefs, and this was during a time when they were really bad. He was losing something like a million dollars a day on the team, and this reporter asked him how long he could afford to lose like that. *For the rest of my life.* That's what he said. I'll never forget that."

Julio lifts his hat and runs his hand over his black hair, damp with sweat and flat against his skull. "But you know, who needs it? I'm happy." He opens his hands to the land around him. "I'm here."

I see Virgil walking up from the processing shed, slowly, the cane in his hand. Chavela walks purposefully at his side. He sees a shiny wrapper littered on the ground and stops to pick it up, then continues on to the building of pink concrete. The scale pen has been loaded with calves again.

I ask Julio, "Are there people here who make a living from their cattle?"

"Oh, yeah. Sure."

"Their whole living?"

"Oh, no." Now he gets what I mean. "Not anymore. No, you gotta find other work. I do backhoe work most of the year. I sell all my calves at the end of the season, and if I can pay my bills and make maybe twenty grand, I'm happy."

Julio thinks for a second then speaks again. "There's a guy I know in Chama, a rancher. He won the lottery, twenty-nine million dollars. You know what he said? *I wish I'd won the week before, because the jackpot was double.* Can you believe that? I mean, what do you even do with all that money?"

"What *is* he going do with it?" I ask.

"Beats me. Well, you know the old story: A rancher wins the lottery and someone asks him what he's gonna do with the money? He says I'm gonna keep ranching until it's all gone." Julio shakes his head and chuckles. "Money is just . . ." He doesn't finish the sentence. Instead he looks at me, smiles and says, "As long as you have your health, right?"

———•———

It's past one o'clock now and the sun is beating down. All the cattle for Ghost Ranch have been processed and the empty shed has been taken over by a swarm of kids playing a Star Wars–themed make-believe game. The guys who have had their calves weighed are all leaning against the rails of the pens, sometimes talking with their eyes trained down on their hands, sometimes silent and looking into the distance. Once in a while a truck drives up and unloads some calves to sell. The men shake hands with the new arrival and then return to leaning against the rails, looking back over their shoulders to check out the new lot. Virgil stands on the far side of the pink building, talking business to this man and that. While he talks he scratches lines in the dirt with the sharp end of the cane, over and over, one horizontal, one vertical, in the shape of a cross. They are all just waiting. The issue is that in order for the sales of the calves to be official and legal, a state inspector must certify them—mostly to ensure that no one is selling stolen livestock. People have been waiting since ten this morning for the inspector to show up, and no one knows where he is.

The buyer remains at her table by the window, hands clasped behind her back, counting calves. When the scales are empty, she is sorting through the white receipts before her. Her husband comes in often and they confer in quiet voices, she punching figures into the calculator and he writing names and numbers in his notepad. There is a whole crew of workers who will be necessary once the calves are officially sold, but until then they are just sitting around outside. It's easy to tell who's who out there. The ranchers are exclusively Spanish men, all wearing long sleeves and standing in groups. The buyers' crew don't wear hats or boots. They have sunburns and smoke cigarettes, and sit on the ground at times. One driver has a slick, red ponytail and wears a muscle shirt. The short, wide woman next to him wears a T-shirt with the slogan: YOU'RE NOT YOURSELF TODAY—I NOTICED THE IMPROVEMENT IMMEDIATELY.

An hour later everybody is still waiting. It turns out that nobody ever called the inspector—whoever Virgil gave that job to forgot. Now they're trying to coax a different inspector out of his Saturday afternoon and up here into the hills to check the boxes and sign the papers so they can all get on with their own days. The guys who were leaning are now sitting on the railings, their feet hooked under the middle bar. Some people have gone back to their trucks and are eating lunch on the tailgates, others are drinking beer. Chavela is munching on a piece of Halloween candy and drawing in the dirt with the cane. One of the drivers throws an old cow horn for the grungy white dogs to fetch. Without explanation, there is a hog running around the parking area.

I see the emcee from the county fair livestock auction, dressed today in a camo vest over a plaid shirt. He's here selling his calves and, like the rest, is just waiting around for the process to move forward. I ask him how he did this year and he shrugs. "I don't know yet," he says. "Until they get us in that little room we don't know."

What he means is the little back room in the pink building, where the buyer couple are now setting up shop. They've pulled the table and chairs in there but otherwise it is empty: wood veneer walls and a single lightbulb overhead, no window. The inspector finally arrives and starts certifying the sales, which sends a stream of signed papers into the back room. Starting then, the woman leans out the doorway and calls out the sellers' names, one at a time: Salazar. Martinez. Chacon. One by one guys jump off the railing and go in to sit down at the table. The buyers tell him how much his cattle weighed, how much money that became, and they write him a check. That's what it all amounts to. All the grazing and breeding, the droughts and respiratory diseases, the judgments made and time spent driving out to take care of the herd after work and on weekends, all that becomes calves, and each calf, pound by pound, becomes this check. The rancher walks out, and the woman calls another name.

Meanwhile, the buyers' crew has started to work. They've backed up one of the double-decker semis they brought here so that its loading end is flush with the pens. Using bright yellow paddles to prod the calves, they move each group from their holding pen, through a series of corrals and finally into the narrow chute that leads them single-file onto a ramp and into the truck. There are two guys in the chute with the calves and two guys on planks like at the processing shed, reaching down into the chute and slapping the rumps with their paddles.

Because the chute and the ramp have solid walls, it's an odd sight. From across the yard you can see nothing but the guys on the planks and the heads and shoulders of the guys in the chutes, all swatting at unseen things with those yellow paddles. The calves aren't tall enough to be seen until the last second, when they appear at the top of the ramp and disappear into the truck. There are more animals than expected, so calves are crammed in tight. The last few on each deck require a man on the ramp, pushing the animals with his shoulders; the final calf takes two men with all their might.

When she's done in the back room, the buyer woman brings her tally to Virgil. For each calf sold $1.50 has been deducted as dues for the co-op, and she hands him a check for $516. They small talk a bit, Virgil casually networking and encouraging them to come back to buy again. He explains the co-op and tells her sincerely that this is one of those few places left where people still have small operations. He tells her he cares about a buyer who will keep prices fair, and as good as possible. "I just want the small guys to be able to survive," he says. "You know, if they have twenty head, this is one of the highlights of their year." She replies that prices are hard on them, too, that there are no margins for anyone in the business. Then she asks how on earth they own such a prime piece of real estate. "It must be worth millions!"

Virgil explains to her about Ghost Ranch and the Presbyterian Church. "Believe me," he says, "realtors are knocking down our door every day. They say, *Just a hundred-acre tract, you won't even notice it's gone.* Well, I guess the guy *after* me can do that. For now, it's not for sale." She hands him her card, and they shake.

7

DURING THE DAY at the livestock scales I stuck out. In part because I was one of just three women there (and the only one not driving a truck), but more so because I was from the outside—not Spanish, not local, not in the cattle business. The buyer man asked me if I owned the place; it was the only thing he could think of that would explain me. Most of the ranchers there eyed me sideways, and a few approached to ask me point blank who I was.

One of them was Andrew, a short man in the standard working outfit of cap, jeans, and plaid shirt. He had gray at his temples but an otherwise boyish face, pudgy and red with sun. By the time he approached me it was the waiting-around hours, and he was drinking a can of Bud Light. He walked up to the fence where I stood, leaned his arms on the railing, and asked me what I was doing. Friendly, but definitely feeling me out.

Like Julio, he is also from "over there" in the mountains. He's been ranching all his life, had his own herd since he was young. He had sold his calves the previous week; that day he was just helping his cousin. "That's the way we do it," he told me proudly. "You need help anytime, anything, just ask and the family is there."

Immediately—effortlessly—we fell into a familiar conversation of the kind I've had with ranchers all over the West. He told me how the Forest Service is screwing them daily in favor of hunters, wildlife, and bigger ranchers, all of which bring in more money than the small-time grazing permits do. He told me how buyers screw them, too, with contracts that back them into a corner and then penalize them for having an animal that is even one pound off the desired weight of five hundred. He talked indignantly about the damned animal rights activists, and then about the damned environmentalists. "They screwed up their cities so now they want to come and take land that, frankly, isn't theirs. And they have the nerve to say they're saving it." Under his breath, he said more.

At some point during his twenty-minute rant he referred to "us poor ranchers." I stopped him there. "Wait," I said. "Isn't the whole rancher persona one of independence, strength, toughness? *Us poor ranchers* makes it sound like you're helpless."

"No," he said. "We're not helpless. It's just that nobody's on our side."

He took a pull off his beer and then looked me in the eye. "Whose side are you on?" I suspect it was the question he came over to ask me in the first place.

"What do you mean?" I said.

"Are you for or against?"

"For or against what?"

"Ranchers."

The question had never been posed to me so bluntly. I thank him now, for putting it in such plain terms. Either you're for or you're against. That's how it feels these days, especially in the mountains of New Mexico. The most contentious issue in these parts is land management, and more specifically, how, when, what, and where cows graze. Environmental groups have argued that ranchers are ruining fragile Western lands by grazing cattle on them. That many ranchers do use public lands for that grazing is seen as a crime against the common good. When things get heated, environmentalists call the transgressors "welfare ranchers," who in turn call the environmentalists "watermelons"—green on the outside and Red on the inside. Environmentalists cut wire fences that ranchers have erected to contain their animals within the national forests, and ranchers threaten to do worse in retaliation. The "range wars" have been going on for years.

If Andrew has something useful to say in response to the attacks of the outside world, it's unlikely it will ever be heard. Farmers and ranchers are now less than 1 percent of the population—there are more people in prison than there are farmers and ranchers on the land. So deeply are they in the minority that their concerns and priorities rarely make it to the table. Indeed, outside of food-section pieces and postings from the latest drought or flood, the general public usually hears from agriculture only when there's a controversy; more often than not, the farmer/rancher is the bad guy. So instead of talking, Andrew and his people dig in their heels. And when approached, they fight. Ranchers are, before anything else, tough.

I know a rancher named Tony Malmberg who was once part of the range wars in Wyoming but now positions himself outside the conventional ranching world. Tony is wise about these things, and he once gave me his take on the whole digging in of heels that has become an integral part of the modern rancher's stance toward the world. "Yes, you've got to be tough to be a rancher," he said. "But being tough doesn't mean bitching about the damned environmentalists. It means breaking your leg five miles from the ranch and being able to ride home because you have to. It's about being humble and making hard decisions about your life that go against what everyone else is doing. Being tough is about being able to survive."

Virgil does his share of bitching, but more often he does something unusual in these parts: he talks, and listens, and questions himself. He makes hard decisions because what matters to him more than any of it is staying on the land. His strategy is to find whatever system will let him do that.

"Some guys would argue that we've been here for two hundred years, and we're perfectly capable of managing ourselves," Virgil says. "I say that's true, but at some point we're gonna have to prove our management. So I say let's test our beliefs. I mean, if we're wrong, let's realize it and start tweaking what we do so we can stay on the land. And if it's right, well, we'll have bragging rights. But either way we'll have a way to measure how well it's working, instead of just saying we've been here for two hundred years and everything's fine."

When Virgil talks about solving the issues that the ranching community faces, the word that comes back over and over is creativity. He believes that if you have to get somewhere and you find the door in front of you closed, you have to look for another opening—that or find a way to open the door. "Do we have things to learn? Sure we have things to learn. We know not all grazing practices are sound and great. So I step out of that box and try to learn something."

He is taking baby steps with the Ghost Ranch grazing program and trying to do the same with the Merced's land. On his own he has made bigger changes, including switching from winter to spring calving to be more attuned with natural cycles and minimize predators, as well as hiring a herder to live with and tend his cattle during the summer. For all the sense they make, the practices Virgil is implementing are unusual, if not unheard of. In these parts, questioning the status quo is not a popular thing to do. For one, ranchers are such a small group that their unity feels precious; there is no room for dissent within ranks. And though few would admit it, having one of their own scrutinize their tried and true methods suggests they themselves might be in the wrong. "There's a traditional way of ranching and then I come up and change everything," Virgil told me. "They don't like that."

Perhaps Virgil's greatest transgression has been joining a group called Quivira, a coalition of progressive ranchers and damned environmentalists. The group's name is a Spanish colonial term that referred to a mythical city on the horizon, a sort of Shangri-La. The word was used on old maps to mark areas that were uncharted, which is why the organization chose it: the alliance between ranchers and conservationists was unknown territory. The point of the group is to find that elusive common ground, so they can stop bickering and instead join forces to save the land they both love from development and other threats. Virgil says the thing that makes Quivira special is simple: the members are willing to come to the table and talk things out. That is enough to earn him scorn as a sellout in the community.

To be clear, Virgil has not switched over to the other side. Like most Western ranchers he has an allergic reaction to the Sierra Club and reserves a special brand of loathing for the Forest Service. He sees his role in Quivira not as capitulation, but rather as representing his community's interests by bringing the voice of the small-time, northern New Mexico rancher to the table. Virgil might be willing to question the system, but he is as convinced as anyone that, having been there for two hundred years, Spanish ranchers like him are the best people to manage the land.

Virgil tells a story about giving a tour of Ghost Ranch to two environmental activists. As he drove them out to the llano, they told him they planned to request money from Congress to buy out permits for grazing on land that belongs to the state and federal governments. Their goal was to rid all the public lands in the West of cattle—and ranchers.

"One of them told me, *You guys work too much for nothing anyway. You should just sell out, take the money and give yourselves a really good vacation.*" Virgil says the last word like it's dirty. "I told him he should know by now that up in northern New Mexico, we like a good fight more than we like a vacation."

—•—

Every week during summer Virgil gives a tour of Ghost Ranch's rangeland for the ranch guests. He brings them first to a place on the llano called the exclosure, a one-and-a-half-acre patch of range that has been fenced in for at least seventy-five years. (It's believed that the Civilian Conservation Corps put up the fence in the 1930s.) Given all that time, it looks remarkably similar to the rest of the llano surrounding it, a place of grass, shrubs, and sage. The main difference is that the plants inside the fence are shaggier: the clumps of grass are denser, with pointed ends drying out in the sun; the shrubs are a little taller, but woodier. Yet even those differences are slight. By looks, the fence could have been installed last year, just before the cattle came through.

And that's the whole point: the significance of the fence is that the exclosure has not been grazed in seventy-five years, and yet the land seems no better off. Or more importantly, the land that has been grazed seems no worse off. "I'll make the math easy," Virgil said when he showed me the spot. "The grass out here grows six inches to a foot every year. After seventy-five years, do you see that grass inside the fence seventy-five feet high? No. And is the grass outside the fence dead? No. I'm just harvesting it. When I bring people out here, I remind them that they do their own kind of grazing in their front yards, with their lawnmowers. And is the grass there dead? No! In fact, they're sick and tired of mowing the lawn. The only difference between what's inside the fence and what's outside is that we've harvested nothing off the exclosure."

That is to say, no human food has come from the exclosure, and no living has been made from it. Some would applaud the exclosure's symbolic preservation of nature in its wild state, while the land around it is irrevocably changed by human interference. For others, including Virgil, the exclosure represents a sort of zoo mentality in that the fence removes the land from a natural system of which humans are an integral part; what's inside is not an accurate reflection of the world.

Opinions aside, the fact is that even in this modern age we depend on the land for our survival. We must be able to take from it, otherwise we would die. When agriculture is at its best, the people performing the necessary extraction double as conservationists as a matter of course. It's like the bison: by nature they harvested the grasslands in a way that ensured the plants would come back equally strong the following year. But the system we have built is not agriculture at its best, it is agriculture at its most productive. As has become increasingly evident in recent years, that system comes at a significant price: the health of the land.

The American environmental movement was born out of responding to exactly that problem, beginning with Rachel Carson's indictment of DDT used on fruit trees in her book *Silent Spring*. In the nearly forty years since its publication our solution as a nation has been to ask agriculture to continue producing food in a cheap and dirty way, then to have the environmental movement follow close behind to sweep up the mess. There is a growing effort to make agriculture an integral part of the green movement, but so far its reach has been selective. Smaller-scale growers and those within range of major cities have been embraced, even decorated, but the vast majority of farmers and ranchers remain on the outside. It's hard to see how they would ever fit in.

Virgil contends that we need an altogether new approach. After telling me the story of his heated exchange with the environmentalists, he did a quick calculation of all the money paid to executives of the Sierra Club, all the money spent on lawyers and lobbyists to fight people like him. "Can you imagine if that money was instead put where the problems are? What we have to do is invest in the people on the land, expose them to alternatives, new management ideas—give them tools." His voice was rising. "The people on the land, *they're* the ones who are gonna turn it around. We're not gonna turn it around by walking away from them."

Virgil does not mean plunging more money into the subsidies that prop up the current system. Nor does he mean giving a pass to the bad practices the system encourages. Rather, his vision is to trust in the experience of people who have lived on and worked with the land for their whole lives, and invest in the creativity that can come from their knowledge. Our society has a surfeit of people who know how agriculture *should* be, but a dearth of people who know how agriculture actually is—who have lived it in years of drought as well as in years when it seemed to rain more often than not; who have seen debt and worse, yet still come back the next year. That experience could translate into superior leadership, but for a long time now it has been overshadowed by the constant need to produce more, faster, just to stay in business. If the people on the land could lead again, Virgil says, just imagine what could happen.

8

THREE DAYS AFTER the calf sales and cattle processing at Ghost Ranch, I'm riding a toolbox between the two seats of Virgil's white flatbed truck. We're going to the mountains to round up his cattle from their summer grazing, a journey that begins with a bumpy drive through the outskirts of Abiquiu and then gradually turns into wild country. Virgil tells me over his shoulder we are on either the worst or second worst road in the state. I can feel it.

In the passenger seat is Leonard, a man about thirty years old who strikes me as a young Virgil. He's shorter but with the same goatee, same white hat, same working body and mind. For fifteen years he was employed at Ghost Ranch. These days he's a free agent doing jobs here and there. Virgil hires him when he needs extra help with his cattle, but I sense there's a deeper exchange, an unspoken apprenticeship. When Virgil is talking, Leonard is listening.

We leave the last houses and pass into the communal lands of El Merced del Pueblo Abiquiu, the *ejido*. Virgil points out the window to a fortress of rocks stacked into neat walls, with two wooden crosses standing inside. He tells me (Leonard already knows this) that it's a *descanso*, a shrine marking a place where long ago people from Abiquiu were ambushed by nomadic Indians.

From the *descanso*, the road climbs up through the *ejido*. It then runs through various sections of the Santa Fe National Forest, including what used to be the *ejido* of the land grant his father's family lost in the 1930s. The demarcations between owners are subtle: a wire fence and a cattle guard, a brown post with the letters USFS, a green sign that reads ABIQUIU LAND GRANT, PLEASE STAY ON THE ROAD. I'm unaware as we switch from one place to another. To me it is just one big stretch of hills under a very blue sky.

We are seven thousand, five hundred feet above sea level, but that isn't apparent in the way you'd think. There are no snow-capped peaks, no great valleys spreading out below. The land is simply a series of rises and dips, yellow ground here and soft blue ridges in the distance. The earth is covered with dry, white Western grasses, chewed to the ground and dusty green at the core. Trees cover the surrounding hills, but here there are few. Mostly just dark green juniper bushes, red rocks with mint-colored lichens on their shady sides. One dirt road leads in and out.

When the road splits in two, we head left. Before long we reach a corral, a no-frills affair with pens made from metal-pipe fencing and a perimeter reinforced with the corrugated steel used in high-way guardrails. The ground inside is dirt and dried manure, soft-ened by countless hooves. Waiting for us are two men, and before we turn off the engine one is at Virgil's window, talking.

"This is Pepo," Virgil says in the last second. On the way up here he had given a vague caveat about this guy. Virgil owns the rights to graze on this section of the forest, but during the drought he too sold off dozens of cattle and hasn't yet replenished his herd, so he lets Pepo fill out the allotment with his animals. They make an odd couple, to say the least. Pepo is a friendly barrel of a man with red-brown skin, gray hair, and a black hat. His jowls are fleshy, and he has shaved his gray moustache to run straight down in an unusually long line, past his mouth, past his jawline, into scruffy ends below his chin. He describes himself as a cowboy who likes to raise hell. Deep laugh lines extend out from his eyes, and in the quiet mountain air his huge HA! laugh is like a bullhorn.

For now his companion is hanging around the edges of the scene, keeping to himself. His name is Humphrey and I think he's Anglo but it's hard to tell. His face is red with sun and beer, leathery from years of the combination. He has a longish white beard and a thin gray ponytail held together with a blue rubber band like you'd find on a head of lettuce. He wears a brown knit cap, a plaid shirt, jeans, and spurs so worn they are dull.

Pepo has hired Humphrey to help him, but really they're old friends—Pepo says he's known him longer than his wife and his ex-wife put together. The third member of their team is a petite, white, mud-crusted dog who is bionic, jumping from the ground and onto the back of Pepo's horse in one shot. Her name is Jingles. The three have been up here since Saturday, slowly rounding up cattle from the far corners of this Forest Service section. They've been sleeping in an old trailer on the hill behind us.

"It was so cold the first night, everything froze," Pepo says. "Everything except the whiskey, that is. HA! And that's only because it was already in my stomach!" He doubles over in laughter.

"Hey, Lisa!" he says, walking across the yard and toward an empty pen in the corral. "We heard you was comin so we got you this. HA!" I follow him over and he points through the fence to a little plywood box with a wooden top cut in the shape of a toilet seat. He is heaving with laughter, and nearby Leonard and Humphrey chuckle. Virgil has his back turned. He is loading his horse. "Oh, please don't be offended," Pepo says to me. "I just like to raise hell. Ha ha ha!" He explains that they think a hunter left it here, and (this last part Pepo acts out) when they arrived on Saturday a calf had stuck its head in there and couldn't get it out, was just walking around with the box over its head.

"HA! Okay then, who wants a beer? Virgil?" Virgil shakes his head. Pepo repeats the offer to everyone and then to Virgil again. Never losing his patience, Virgil says, "*Estoy bien*," and keeps working.

Leonard stays behind as Virgil, Pepo, Humphrey, and I set off on horseback to round up the last clutch of cattle and look for strays that might need to be rejoined with the herd. (Pepo and Humphrey have already gathered some, who are now in the corral.) It's better to do this job early or late, when the cattle come out from under the trees to graze in the cool air. Right now they would be hidden in the shade, but it will have to do—this is one of few precious days that Virgil gets off from Ghost Ranch to do this work, and we're off to a late start.

With Jingles running alongside, we ride through a series of dry, wide meadows with grass the color of beach sand and flowers in matching, muted tones of yellow and white. Nearby, a nuthatch examines the trunk of a lone tree. In the distance a coyote runs from one shady cover to another. A hawk circles above. This place is not majestic the way the Piedra Lumbre is, but it feels more divine. Ghost Ranch feels like being inside a bowl, the shining cliffs your spectacular walls. Up here, the bowl has been turned upside down and we are on top of it, on top of the world. Down there traffic is constantly running through on the highway, but up here we are the only people for miles.

After a while I hang back to photograph and I think of my mother, who heard about this trip and joked about what would be my *City Slickers* moment. I'm embarrassed that I'm feeling it like Mitch Robbins did, flush with my own moment of making believe this is my life. The sense of freedom is intoxicating.

Pepo's teenage son Juanito has ridden ahead on a four-wheeler, and he calls in on the walkie-talkie to say he has found the remaining herd. Pepo and Humphrey split off to join him and collect the cattle. Virgil veers onto a hill to look for strays, and he kindly instructs me to follow him. The slope is thick with boulders and trees, and as he cuts a jagged path in and out of sight I keep as close as my rusty horse-riding skills allow. When I fall out of sight, he stops to wait. I am all but deadweight, but it doesn't seem to matter to Virgil.

"If I had my way, I would be up here every day," he says dreamily. "It's all I would do."

"What would that take?"

"A lot more cattle."

I ask how many and he tells me two hundred and fifty total, maybe more. Since the drought he has dropped to just eighty, though his permit up here would allow one hundred and forty. But he has a plan. Unlike the guys who sold their calves at the scales on Saturday, Virgil will keep back his calves this year, at least the females. That would get his herd up to about 125, and in a year those heifers will be having calves of their own. It's a risk, one he had to clear with his banker, since it means he won't get the paycheck those other guys did. But if it works and he can do it again next year, he'll have his herd back up to fill the Forest Service permit. Of course that would be only one hundred and forty, not close to a full-time living, but at least closer.

Not finding any strays, we head down the backside of the hill and into another wide meadow. Coming down a hill on the other end are Pepo, Humphrey, Juanito, and a swarm of twenty-odd cattle, plus their calves, plus Jingles. We join them and start driving the herd home.

The pace is fast at first, to make it clear to the cows that we're going, not staying. For animals that have lolled up here for six months, the sudden urgency creates a sort of frenzy. They are a moving mosh pit, one great shifting mass of fur and legs and swinging tails, and dust. Two of the cows are in heat and as they walk they're humped by anyone who can get near them—bull calves just coming into testosterone, but also full-grown mothers caught up in the chaos, their udders swinging as they mount.

Our work is to keep the group moving forward, work that is mostly a suggestion: the riders position themselves two in the back and one on each flank, a loose half-circle whose open end is whatever direction they want the cattle to go. As I ride flank, Virgil pulls me back and tells me to think of the herd as a single body; never get in front of its shoulder, for it is the pressure from the backside that makes them go. The riders in the rear cut back and forth to re-inforce the momentum and make it clear to possible defectors that there is no back door. With those two things in place the drive stays a remarkably calm affair, one big group of cows and riders moving forward down a rutted dirt path that most have traveled before. Pepo calls to Humphrey to throw him a beer.

Pepo's horse is burgundy-brown, brushed with white. Between sips he tells me that six months ago he castrated the horse himself, and while it is gradually learning to accept its position, it still has the heart of a stud. Pepo rides him easily, beer in one hand and in the other the simple blue ropes that act as his reins. When a cow breaks out of line in his section, he calls Jingles in one sharp syllable and a second later she is on the cow's heels, running at top speed, nipping and barking. The cow jumps back into line. "What a nice job you did," Pepo will coo to her, as if to a daughter. "That's great, Jingles."

Humphrey is working the hardest, in part because he's the only one being paid but I guess also because he seems to live for this part of the job. If there's a stray cow, chances are Humphrey is on it. He likes to spring into a gallop and make the catch on a renegade, even better if it's a whole group breaking away. He rides mostly in the back position, I think so he can stay moving at all times, cutting back and forth. There's a coil of rope on his saddle but no lasso, just a frayed end that he waves and slaps at the cattle's rumps as he clucks at them, "Git! Git!"

After one dash for a mother and calf he ends up next to me and laughs. "Yeah, let the old man get it. That's what they say, *Let the old man get it.* Ha! Would you believe I'm sixty-six?"

"Really?" I say. He does look ancient, but then again how could such an old body manage that? "How long have you been doing this?"

"Since I was thirteen years old."

"That's a long time."

"Oh yeah, I know this country," he says. "I know it backwards and forward. Take me anywhere, any time of night, blindfold me, gimme half an hour and I'll tell you exactly where we are." He's not joking.

Still, no one looks more of this place than Virgil, riding the muscular, black-and-white horse that he bought for his son. Her name is Estrella, Spanish for star. A few minutes ago Pepo spotted something a ways off the trail that was attracting vultures, and Virgil rode over to see if it was a dead calf. As he rides back toward us I see him alone for the first time, framed against this flat, open plain of grass. He looks majestic. He's not doing anything special, and in fact, aside from trading his denim shirt for one of crisp canvas, he is dressed no differently from on the days that I've seen him working at Ghost Ranch. But this place completes him; it makes him make sense. The slouch that I've seen behind the wheel of the Frankenstein truck or walking a tape measure from here to there, it's the slouch of being in the saddle, the loose hips that make a long ride possible. All his words about the land find their melody here. Riding back toward us in this wild country, he is the cowboy from the painting on his office wall, the lone rider on his dress shirt. No, better. He is real.

———◆———

Earlier today, as we were driving to the corral, Virgil, Leonard, and I detoured off the road and onto a faint track headed west. After some twists and turns the land opened up into a wide, flat space. At the far edge of it, where the land started to slope up, there was a little settlement, unexpected in this wild place. As we drove near, three spotted cattle dogs came bombing toward us, barking like mad.

I didn't know where we were going. The only building was a dusty travel trailer with brown and orange stripes, which someone must have hitched onto the back of a truck and pulled up here decades ago. Back across the open field was a grid of old barbed wire fences, their posts made of long, rough branches. Dozens more posts from other fences since removed were leaning against an open shed with a tin roof. Otherwise, the land was empty, open.

As we walked from the truck to the door of the trailer, Virgil stopped. He pointed to one of the barbed wire enclosures, within which there were two sets of old posts still standing in the ground. To the side of one post, a cook stove sat rusting. "This is where my dad was born," he said.

We walked in, ducking to pass through the doorway into the trailer's tiny interior. At the far end was a small sleeping area with a mattress, and beside it two ancient cots folded up against the wall. Next to the small stove and sink were stacked cases of Dr. Pepper and somebody's favorite sports drink. Empty cans of chicken noodle soup hung in a plastic grocery bag tied to the stove. The clear centerpiece of the room was a once-white Formica table with rounded edges and a few brownish stains. It was up against the wall, in front of the window that looked onto the barbed wire enclosures and the field beyond. Around it three chairs whose up-holstery was peeling off. Virgil seemed a little sheepish to show me this place, perhaps not sure how an outsider would receive it. "It's not much," he said, "but it's functional—for an escape, at least." I told him I thought the whole place was beautiful, meaning the land more than the trailer. He knew what I meant. "I like to say it's a little piece of Heaven."

Sitting at the table in the bright morning light, looking out the window, was an older man with a cup of coffee. Floyd Trujillo, Virgil's father. He had wavy, gray-and-black hair and a weathered face, with eyes intensely blue. His belt had a big, rough buckle made of carved white bone. As he blew his nose into a paper towel, I saw that the tip of his index finger was missing. Virgil introduced me then left with Leonard, and as I stood there I didn't know quite what to say.

His voice was soft and kind. He asked me to sit down, and as he talked we looked out the window. I said that Virgil told me he was born here. "Yup, right there," he said, pointing to the posts within the enclosure, all that remained of his family's house. There had been a community here since at least 1807, and his family lived here until he was six years old. After that they lived the school year in Abiquiu, but each spring they would come up here to plant the year's crop of wheat and vegetables, then live here through the summer. When he was twelve or so, in the mid-1940s, the family left for good. "Too many droughts," he told me. "There just wasn't enough water to survive up here."

Floyd lives in town with Virgil's mother but comes here as of-ten as he can and stays as long as possible. "My father gave me this place because he knew I loved the land," Floyd said. "He knew I would plant a garden." And until two years ago he did, in the long, narrow enclosure that runs between the trailer and the old home site. For years he came up in spring and planted corn, broad beans, and Mexican squash. But the recent drought finally got to be too much; the last year he planted a garden he had to haul barrels of water up from town in order to keep the plants alive. What would it take for him to plant it again? "Just water," he told me. "It's not worth it if you have to watch your plants wither away, but if there's water I'll do it for as long as I'm able."

Floyd will likely pass this land on to Virgil, so evident it is that his son loves it as deeply as he does. He recalled to me how young Virgil would join him here on weekends and help with his cattle, the way Chavela likes to come up now. "Finally he got some cattle of his own, then he got his own permit to graze them, then another and another. I guess he figured it takes time, but it takes about as much time to raise twenty as it does to raise a hundred, so he kept getting more and more."

I asked Floyd if he once had this many cattle and he shook his head no. He did it just as a sideline. Virgil, making a business of it, has gone far beyond the herd he ever had. As he told me this, the late-morning sun hit the table and reflected up on his face. His eyes were bright and proud.

———•———

The herd is now about thirty cows plus their calves, which includes some strays picked up along the way. We keep driving them down that rutted dirt road, Pepo on the west flank, Humphrey and Virgil in back, me trying to stay behind the shoulder on the east. The dust is so thick and the sun so bright that at times I can't see to the other side of the herd, and even near me their bodies turn into dark figures that fade in and out of the shifting, murky, moving cloud. There's dust in my nose and in my eyes, on my lips. I can feel the sun searing my cheeks. Virgil's uniform—shield sunglasses, broad hat, full-coverage clothing—I get it now.

As we turn west off the mesa and into the trees, the trail turns into a black diamond. "This is a pretty rough trail," Virgil says with the coolness he always uses to keep a situation calm. No doubt. It would be treacherous even without the trees, the ground covered with small, shifty rocks and big, chunky boulders. What's more, at this elevation the trees stay fairly short, their limbs beginning at the height of a horse's head. Just a moment ago the world was as open as could be, but here it is a multi-tiered maze of branches, boulders, and the odd spaces between them. A clear spot on the ground might have low-hanging branches above, and a blessed opening in the airspace above might have an impassable rock underneath. After ten minutes the whole space narrows to about twenty-five feet wide, with a barbed wire fence on the left and on the right a short but that-would-be-the-end-of-your-life kind of cliff made of blocky granite. It starts to slope downhill, steeper by the minute.

"The cows don't want to go, but they always make it down," Virgil says. "We just have to keep moving them." Pepo and Humphrey are out of sight, in the rear. Virgil and I are with the front of the group, making sure the train keeps chugging. The cattle abandon the herd formation, instead going forward any way they can. There are only suggestions of paths, patches of bare dirt that must be pieced together like connecting the dots. Quickly they plug up the space, one reluctant cow causing a bottleneck of ten bodies. The whole operation stops. Calves start to nurse. Forward movement seems impossible.

I'm useless, at this point no more than a very tall member of the herd. My horse is leading me, choosing openings mostly for her feet even though they don't always match with what's best for my head or torso. In the worst moment she moves under a tree especially thick with branches and I get truly stuck. With cows at our sides and rocks at our back, I give up trying to steer out and instead break every branch I can and emerge from the spot in a rain of detritus. There is lichen in my hair, a long branch stuck in the saddle. Later, at a hotel in Albuquerque, I will find twigs in my pockets and feel the humiliation of the moment. Right now, all I care about is getting out in one piece.

Together Virgil and Estrella make one massive body, but they move nimbly through the spaces. Virgil holds his lasso yet never uses it, just waves it gently at the animals when necessary. The only noise he makes is an occasional whistle, and in extreme cases, a high, sharp *Hey!* When a cow wanders toward the cliff and then starts a precarious walk along the edge, he spins Estrella around and steps her deftly in a zigzag path toward the cow, choosing the right spots as if they were lighted up before him. He comes up behind the cow and she moves straight back up to the rest. In that moment a group of three cows takes Virgil's absence as an opportunity to retreat to the top of the slope, along the barbed wire fence, and stop. Virgil spins Estrella again and makes a beeline for them, surging up a sixty-degree slope of shifting rocks. He does it without a blink, merely waves his lasso, gets them walking, and moves on to the next charge. Never once do I see Virgil crack—not when Pepo is drinking beer after beer, not when there's a dead something that could be one of his calves, not at any of the numerous times when it's evident that I am not qualified to be riding his horse or driving his cattle. His composure and focus are tremendous, but it is the easiness of them that is truly striking.

At the bottom of the hill the land opens up, the trees thin out, and one by one each rider and cow passes back into open air. Leonard and Floyd are waiting at the bottom of the hill. They have been riding elsewhere, looking for strays but finding none. Leonard seems anxious to get in on the action, and he rides up into the trees to help with the last of the herd. Floyd's three cattle dogs follow suit, running through cow legs and barking. Floyd sits and watches.

The corral is straight ahead, just on the other side of an irrigation ditch the width of a small river, and the cows already in their pens are mooing, calling us in. Outside of me every person here has done this ride numerous times. Still, there is a sense of homecoming, a slight sense of triumph, as the cattle plunge into the ditch and splash across, and then we lumber through, water touching our boot heels. Floyd avoids the ditch and instead rides around the long way, slipping through a gate and emerging at the front of the corral. He sits on his horse there, looking back over the cattle, smiling and quiet.

Once the cattle are in, everyone leads his horse away and gets on foot. Everyone but Virgil. He must separate his cattle from Pepo's, business he can conduct better from aloft. Leonard is on foot in the corral wielding an old broom, taking Virgil's directions to shoo certain cows through a gate to the left, others to the right. Dust kicks up and the sun goes down behind the blue hills. It's getting cold. Finally, once the cattle are in their proper pens, the party begins.

"Who wants a beer?" Pepo has both hands in Humphrey's saddlebag, pulling out warm cans of Milwaukee's Best and handing them all around. Leonard takes one and leans against Juanito's four-wheeler; Floyd, still on his horse, tips one back. Virgil declines, but pulls out a pack of Swisher Sweets cigars and passes them around.

While Floyd's cattle dogs take turns humping Jingles, Pepo holds court beside his emasculated horse. He is telling an animated story about an annual parade in Española that he used to love, but had to stop attending because every time he did he ended up in jail.

"What did you do?" I ask.

"Oh, I was just raising hell, drinking beer, being a cowboy."

As the story goes, in the final year, he rode his horse in the parade with his rifle packed into the saddle, just like it is now. A cop stopped him and asked if it was loaded, to which he replied no. What ensued was something about charges of a concealed weapon, charges that Pepo denied by spurring his horse in the side and taking off down the street. He might have gotten away, but there was a roadblock for the parade, and before he knew it he was surrounded by officers with guns pointed at him. "They said, *Unload your weapon!* And I said, *You come unload it!* Imagine that asshole's face when he looked inside and saw that it was really empty. HA! Anyway, they threw me in jail for resisting arrest or some shit." He takes a puff on his cigar.

Virgil listens to the beginning of the story then takes the last cigar from the box and walks a ways down the corral to smoke it. He has a black jacket on now and his sunglasses off, and as he leans his forearms against the rail I can see he's studying the cattle. Leonard drifts over and they stand side by side, eyes on the corral, talking quietly to each other.

I want to go hear what they're saying, but Pepo is not done yet. He has decided that he should write an autobiography, to tell all the crazy shit he's seen in his life. He even has a title: *Poacher's Dream.* Now it occurs to him that I should write his book for him, that I must cancel my flight home and come back to the mountains in the morning. "Tomorrow we start branding," he says. "You want to have some fun? That's the day. It's great, you get kicked in the face, shit sprayed on you. We'll even make you some Rocky Mountain oysters."

Above us a few streaks of clouds are turning soft pink. A set of contrails follows a plane straight down in the sky. The dust has settled around us, and now the air is cold and clean. Pepo turns to philosophizing. "A lot of people think money is it, that's the goal. But no," he says. "No, no, no! That's not what matters. As long as you can get out here and ride and drink beer and yell and scream and get the cows in the corral, then life is good. You've got to just enjoy every day, 'cause you never know, it might be your last."

Virgil silently approaches and catches my eye. "We ought to get going," he says. "I have to pick Chavela up from her basketball game."

Pepo and Humphrey will stay up here tonight but the rest of us are heading out. They load the four-wheeler onto the truck along with the saddles and various tools. Floyd slips off his horse to put on a pair of green coveralls for warmth, then gets back on and quietly says goodbye as he rides back down the road toward his trailer. Two of his dogs follow, but the third is romantically attached to Jingles, their rear ends stuck and both of them looking up at us for some way out of the situation. Nobody helps them.

Instead we load into the truck and Pepo steps up to Virgil's open window. "Hey, tomorrow morning, no?" He takes a sip of his beer. "If I end up branding your calves, too bad! You got here too damn late! HA!"

Virgil replies in a tired voice. "*Bueno, hermano.*" He rolls up the window.

The sun has long since set and the mountain has turned from blue to black. Virgil worries out loud about his father riding at this time of night, nervous that it's too cold, or that somehow the old man won't make it back to town. But he knows there's nothing he can do, and besides, he's already late to pick up Chavela. As we drive off, the headlights shine forward and down, giving an unusual attention to the first six feet of dirt before us and making the rest of the world disappear by contrast.

LaMoure, North Dakota

Our farmers rush themselves to raise more wheat to buy more land to raise more wheat. This is keeping them so busy that they and their families haven't had time to live. It is no home if with a fertile soil, the yard is barren and wind swept with no windbreak to give protection, no trees to shade the yard and porch, no wealth of shrubbery and flowers to furnish a succession of blooms, and no garden or orchard for the nourishment of its occupants.

—Ernest Hilborn,
speaking to the Minnesota State Horticultural Society, 1913

1

For most drivers on the interstate, the prairie is no more than a giant ellipsis in the middle of North America. When I first drove across the country, all I could see in Kansas was that it was corn, then wheat. When I drove back, this time across North Dakota, same thing: crops, as far as my eyes could see. It seemed to be a place characterized by being unremarkable.

But over time my eyes and mind learned to penetrate this land-scape. My first lesson came in the form of a snowstorm in south-east North Dakota on the second day of April. A week before it had been seventy degrees, and even just earlier that afternoon the land had been soggy and turning green in places. Driving west on Highway 13, I could see the white tundra swans against the black ground from a half-mile away. But as I entered LaMoure County a gray curtain pulled down from the sky, announcing what seemed to be an executive decision that winter was not over just yet. Over the next twelve hours three inches of snow fell. The swans vanished and the world became overrun with pheasants, their dark bodies naked against the backdrop of white.

The snow itself wasn't shocking—a person doesn't have to know North Dakota intimately to know the winters here are brutal and long. What struck me instead was what the snow did after it had fallen. Over the days that followed it drifted without rest, a tireless white migration from north to south. It flowed over the east–west roads like a sideways waterfall, low and steady, stopping only to pile up at the rare tree or stand of withered cattails. As I watched it I realized that what I was seeing was really wind, wind given body by the snow. And when I realized that, I began to comprehend this land for the first time. In my mind I saw this same wind coming off the Canadian Rockies, blowing across the plains of Alberta, past here and all the way down to the prairie of Oklahoma. Hundreds of miles of rich farmland connected by one long cord of air. The vast flatness became vivid.

When I returned in summer, I found that there are in fact ups and downs within the flatness, slight as their rhythm may be. Walking, a person might not even feel the land's rise and fall, but I could see it in the corn: in the undulating line where the stalks meet the earth, where the tassels meet the sky. The plants are so uniform—their rows so disciplined, their bodies so identical—that altogether they record each vague motion like a heart monitor, like a picket fence.

This uniformity was my second lesson in comprehending the modern prairie landscape. By uniformity I don't mean the big blah you see through the window on the interstate, a single stretch of corn blurring between distant exits. I mean this corn as seen at fifteen miles an hour down a dusty road, not as one endless mass but as billions of homogenous individuals, perfectly aligned by a

GPS-guided planter. I mean a whole landscape sectioned into countless individual blocks but painted with a palette of only three colors: the gray-brown of corn tassels, the sandy tan of dry wheat, and golf-course-green, the color of soybeans. It's not that every view here is the same; there is an endless recombination of the three crops. It's that the pieces comprising the view are indistinguishable from one another. The same act has been done over and over, the same decision made so many times it has almost ceased to be a choice.

This led to my third lesson about this place: the fewer choices there are to make, the fewer farmers there are needed to make them. The very nature of these commodity crops is to eliminate people from the rural landscape. It works this way: In order to survive, the farms that grow the crops are forced to expand. Because there is only so much arable land, that expansion requires a certain cannibalism within the community; either you buy out your neighbor's farm or he buys out yours. Here in LaMoure County, that has played out with eerie exactness: since 1950, farms have doubled in size and the number of farmers has been cut in half.

As the people have gone, their place in the landscape has been filled by crops. Once I started to notice it, I saw it everywhere. In Valley City, the worn entrance sign for Marty's Sky-Vu II Drive-In now leads to a field of corn, with twelve hulking grain bins where lovers used to park. At an old homestead near Litchville, a two-story house now floats in a sea of soybeans, the green plants flooded over its driveway, its lawn, its front walk; driving by, I could picture the planter scraping against the wooden shingles. The road map still calls out towns like Marion and Dickey, but they are no longer discernible to anyone but the few who live there. In front of a house in one such lost place, I saw a handmade sign by the road: SLOW DOWN! it said. WE'RE STILL HERE!

One town that has not disappeared is LaMoure, the county seat. While the county has lost about a thousand people each decade since 1930, putting it at just over four thousand people in 2007, the town itself has stayed between eight hundred and eleven hundred people since before the Depression. Today it has eight hundred and sixty residents and many signs of a healthy small town: three banks, a newspaper, a drug store, a movie theater, and several restaurants, none of them chains. At the west end of town is a thriving farm implement dealership, its yard parked with combines and sprayers and planters, all in John Deere green. Lined up together the machines look like a battalion of giant insects, standing sentry at the gates to the city. The east end of town is guarded by an International dealership, a mirror image but with all the machines in red.

The grandest building in town is the county courthouse, a beaux-arts design from 1910 complete with an octagonal dome roof whose windows face in eight directions. What commands the skyline here, though—what *is* the skyline—are the two grain elevators standing by the railroad tracks. They are, by design, places of perfect geometry, all right angles and circles of exacting roundness. The elevator on the John Deere side of town is old, not so different from those still standing in otherwise empty towns around the county. The main building is the size of a living room but three stories tall, fashioned of square sheets of steel that are riveted along the seams and now rusting. Clustered around it are four skinny cylinders with pointed roofs; at the top of each, a circle opening into

which grain was once poured. The complex is abandoned, lonely—
the kind of place where teenagers would sneak between the buildings to smoke cigarettes.

A few blocks down the railroad tracks is the newer elevator, the
real one. Its towers tower, four stories tall with steel sides gleaming in the sun. The bins in which they store grain are huge, close
to one hundred feet high and nearly as wide—and those will soon
seem small by comparison. In the spring of 2007, American farmers
planted more acres of corn than ever since World War II, and the
owners here are expanding in anticipation. All summer the elevator's dirt yard has been full of dust kicked up by cement trucks and
construction equipment brought here to build bins that are eleven
stories high, 105 feet in diameter, and hold 682,789 bushels of grain
apiece. Before each one was begun they dug out the ground where it
would stand and poured a concrete pad twelve feet deep to support
the weight of all that grain. Looking back across the railroad tracks
at the old, abandoned elevator, it is amazing to think that the four
skinny cylinders there were once sufficient.

Alongside the new bins, the owners are building an even taller
new grain dryer. Using propane-powered heat, it will dry out harvested grains until they have lost enough moisture to be stored without spoiling. On paper it seems like a boon for the community—
more grain dried is more grain ready to sell. But fast-forward four
months from now, when the dryer goes into use at harvest time.
Because of a malfunction, it sends a daily shower of dust and chaff
over the houses in town. The air is full of beeswings—skins shed by
corn kernels that float down from the heavens. Citizens complain
of respiratory problems and the state health department confirms

their grievances. They raise their concerns at a city council meeting, but in the end the episode doesn't go far. It can't. In a letter to the editor of the *LaMoure Chronicle,* one man calls for an end to the complaining as a matter of sheer survival.

"I am concerned about the message we might be sending to the Agribusiness and their farm customers," he writes. "Our community is 100 percent dependent on the agriculture industry and we should do everything we can to make sure it keeps going and growing." His letter acknowledges the inconvenience of industry, but it then weighs that against the greater damage of scaring industry away. Losing agribusiness would have a domino effect on the town, whereby schools, churches, and jobs would all fall. Between the lines of his letter lies an image of the rest of the county, the landscape from which people have effectively vanished. If we want our town to stay alive, his words imply, then we had better just shut up.

———•———

There's no sign on the road for the Podoll family's farm, just a mailbox bearing a metal sign that says EAT MORE TURKEY. Above the words is a little figure now almost lost to rust, but if you look closely you can see it was once a tom turkey with his tail feathers fanned out in full courtship display. The sign is from the first years after William Podoll bought the farm in 1953. He had decided he wasn't going to farm crops like the neighbors did but instead would raise breeder turkeys, the ones that lay the eggs that are then hatched into the birds raised for meat. He set up flocks of a size that were unprecedented in these parts, up to five thousand at a time.

People thought he was crazy; some locals had a pool going on how fast he would go broke. But six years later he had paid off the whole farm, especially remarkable considering that the place had had four previous owners over the forty years prior, and not one of them had paid off the bank. His son David tells the story of a time when you could pay a bill in town with a chicken. Well, this farm was paid for with turkeys.

Including David, the Podolls had five children. Once the eldest few of them were old enough to drive tractors and such, the family started growing crops in addition to raising turkeys, eventually expanding the farm to four hundred and eighty acres. After high school David joined his father in the business, and in time he took the reins completely. To this day he lives in the family house, the only one where he has ever lived in his fifty-four years. Sometimes when he goes to his basement, he remembers when the whole family hid there, while outside a tornado ripped the roof off the turkey barn and sent five thousand birds flying into the air.

The baby of the family, Dan, born after the tornado, joined David back on the farm after finishing college at North Dakota State University. With him came his wife, Theresa, who grew up on a potato farm in the rich Red River Valley, near the Minnesota border. They had met in college, where Dan was (as he puts it) a little wild, that is until Theresa (as she puts it) straightened him out. They bought the place next door to the farm, and over the past twenty-odd years have raised a son and a daughter there, and now another, younger son, Neil, who currently plays basketball for the LaMoure Loboes junior high team. More recently, older brother David married Ginger, who was raised on a farm in eastern Montana and now teaches school in LaMoure. With David and Dan's father deceased, and their mother moved to town, today these four adults and Neil are the family farm.

Passing by the turkey-festooned mailbox, off the road and onto their dirt driveway, you enter a place unseen by the outside world. Thick evergreen trees are planted along the drive and around the house and the farm's work buildings, with openings only where tractors would need to go out to the fields or trucks would need to come in from the road. While the trees were planted to shelter this place from the prairie wind, perhaps equally precious is the privacy they grant. Not that the Podolls have anything to hide, but in this wide-open land it can be hard to find room to do things differently. The scrutiny of neighbors here registers deviation like the corn plants mark the slightest hill.

Within the fence of trees is the house where David and Ginger live, and in front of it a thick elm tree, which throws a cool shadow all summer long. The farmyard is remarkably neat and junk-free but otherwise average-seeming. While they haven't raised turkeys commercially for a decade, the long, red barn where they used to house them still stands to the right. There are two lines of grain storage bins and a long metal-roofed Quonset hut where the guys keep tools and work on machinery. In the center of it all are two giant vegetable gardens, their tall fences covered by bushy grapevines and climbing beans.

When Theresa and I arrive here after dinner on the last evening in July, Dan and David are standing at the edge of the yard, facing the driveway, waiting and starting to worry. Dan had come home for dinner but he grabbed only an ear of corn—no plate—and sat halfway off the chair, his eyes toward the door. He didn't want to lose his focus. A truck was coming to pick up some grain they had sold, and he had to be there to help load it. He slipped out before Theresa and I were half-finished eating.

As we get out of the car, David and Dan are going over the possible reasons why, with the sun going down, the truck still has not arrived.

"Maybe it took that one corner too fast and got stuck in a ditch?"

"It was supposed to be here twenty minutes ago yet."

"Theresa, did you see it stuck in a ditch up the road?"

The brothers stand there, arms crossed in front of their chests, leaning back on their heels. They are both looking in the direction of the road even though there's no view from deep inside the trees. Theresa joins them, looking at Dan, looking toward the road. Behind the turkey barn the sun is quickly falling, hot pink behind a haze of heat and wet air. The color of the light is brilliant, rich like sherbet, and I ask to take a photograph of them in these last few moments of sun.

Dan looks down at his work clothes, shrugs his shoulders, and says, "Sure. Why not?" Theresa gives a little laugh and lines up next to her husband.

David is acting shy. "Can we hide behind something? Is that okay?" He takes his place in the photograph, on Theresa's other side.

Click. All the whites in the frame are golden.

"Theresa, you have to have a blade of grass," David says. "You wouldn't be a farmer without a blade of grass."

Theresa and Dan keep smiling at the camera, but David breaks the line and steps out of the frame, hunting for a suitable piece of grass. He plucks the biggest one in sight, maybe sixteen inches long with a fluffy seed head, and sticks it in the side of his mouth. As he gets back in the frame, he starts to chew on it and crosses his arms in front of his chest.

Click. The light is receding by the second.

"'The New American Gothic,' that's what you should call it," David wisecracks. "I should have a pitchfork."

Click.

That last frame was the one. In it Theresa is the picture of a farmwife: strong body, strong hands—Dorothy from Kansas in real life. She wears a sleeveless, red-checked shirt and jean shorts, her straight brown hair tied back in a ponytail. For the photo she has taken no pose, instead stands as plainly as she would on a doctor's scale, arms hanging straight down at her sides. She is flanked by two tall, slim brothers, both in jeans and white shirts with smudges from the day's work, both in boots and white caps over short brown hair. Each has a simple wedding ring on his left hand and skin toned by the sun. If you knew them only from this photo, you'd have to go to the details to tell them apart: Dan has a moustache, not a full beard like his older brother; David is the one wearing a watch. Together the three appear to be a portrait of the Heartland straight out of *Farm & Ranch Living* magazine.

Pan out, though, and there are clues that this place is different. For one, there's no big American pickup truck in sight. David drives what farmers around here would call a rice burner— a small, gray-blue Mazda with a measly four cylinders and a cap on the back. The only four-wheel drive on the farm is Dan's red Nissan, maybe fifteen years old with rust creeping up from the wheel wells. It's useful for some things, but Dan tells me he'd like to get an electric golf cart to drive between his place and the farm, to save on gas. He talks wistfully about a sports car he had years ago, a Mazda Z240. "Forty miles a gallon in 1980, can you believe that? That was before they gave up on fuel efficiency standards." So beloved was that car that after it ceased to be road worthy he ripped out the passenger seat and used it on the farm to transport loads of pumpkins; when it finally stopped running, chickens moved in and lived in the back seat until it decayed into scrap metal.

Also beyond the frame of this photo is the old-fashioned granary where they've stored the load that the truck will pick up tonight. They also have a dozen of the modern plastic and steel grain bins seen all over this countryside, but I'd guess the Podolls are one of a few families who haven't ripped down the clapboard buildings where their fathers and grandfathers stored their harvests. The modern bins are an obvious upgrade in terms of labor, since they work with simple gravity: pour the grain in the top of the cylindrical bin and unload it through a hole in the bottom. The granary building instead requires two arms and a shovel, work that the trucker who comes for this load will watch in wonderment. During the forty-five minutes it takes the brothers to shovel, scrape, and sweep it out completely, the trucker will casually say that his clients with the newest equipment can fill his truck in three minutes; once he timed a guy at one minute and thirty-six seconds. The brothers won't say much back.

But that's not yet. For this moment, David, Dan, and Theresa are standing still in front of their garden, the grain bins far in the distance. They are presenting themselves to the camera: David with his arms tight across his chest and a piece of grass sardonically gripped in his teeth; Dan with his thumbs hooked into his jeans and a loose smile on his face; Theresa out in front, body straight up and down, facing the world. Click. And then the rumble of a truck—in this stillness, you can hear it even before it turns up the driveway. The moment disappears like swans into snow. Everyone goes back on the clock.

2

OVER THE WINTER of 1974, David set out to prove organic agriculture wrong. He had been hearing about it in the media and what he heard disturbed him, because it ran counter to everything his high school teachers and his community had told him about how agriculture should be. David has a penchant for thoroughness that borders on obsessiveness, so when he says he spent the snowy months reading anything and everything he could find on the topic, I imagine the towers of books, magazines, and newspaper clippings that must have passed through his hands. Instead of finding holes, though, he inadvertently proved organics right in his own mind. As soon as he took over the farm from his father, he converted the entire operation.

Before I met David, someone told me: "I hear he's kind of intense." While that proved to be true, he is not unpleasant, just raw. Pleasantries and trivia don't make it onto his radar; when he's done with a sit-down conversation he will often stand up and leave without a word. His mind seems to be constantly focused on the Big Picture, at times tortured by it. His deep, almost Biblical sense of morality exempts nothing, least of all himself and the farm. "I've always had to feel some sort of moral and ethical purpose in what I do," he once told me. "I couldn't just do something to make money. There had to be some higher value."

When he converted to organic farming he didn't know what he was doing, nor was there anyone around to help him—he didn't know another person in North Dakota doing it. But the greatest obstacle wasn't learning how to rotate crops or build the soil. It was the psychological barrier. "Every time you listened to the farm news on the TV or radio, or looked at the paper, there was some assault on organic farming, just sheer ridicule," he said. "I mean, imagine, a person has farmed the same way all of his career, then someone comes in and shows him a different way, one that might confront or invalidate what he's done? That's a powerful psychological confrontation. So there was a backlash against us—it was like the early Christians being fed to the lions. When us organic farmers finally found each other, we'd sit around the table and tell our stories like we were at AA."

Things have changed since those early days. Organic food has become mainstream and organic farming methods have been proven in many people's eyes. American agribusiness has replaced its bullying with a strategy of disdain and dismissal rooted in the certainty that organic farming cannot feed the world the way it does. In 2007, the Chairman of the House Agriculture Committee, Collin Peterson, reflected the new attitude: "For whatever reason, people are willing to pay two or three times as much for something that says 'organic' or 'local,'" he told the *Financial Times*. "Far be it from me to understand what that's about, but that's reality. And if people are dumb enough to pay that much then hallelujah."

As the rest of the world has changed its relationships to organic farming, so has David changed his relationship to the world. He no longer cares what people say. Nothing could sway his conviction that the concepts behind organic farming are right. Instead now what he deals with is the tradeoff for having enlightened himself. Every day he is acutely aware of how tragically shortsighted the conventional system is.

"Sure, if you take it from the standpoint of human labor efficiency, there is nothing more efficient than American agriculture," David once explained, his voice rising as he spoke. "Just imagine driving one of these massive combines! There's how many bushel-a-minute of corn coming into the hopper? It's like gold coming out of the tube. You can combine a hundred and fifty thousand dollars worth of corn in a day—one person can! Holy smokes! It is a marvel, an absolute marvel of science that this can be done. When it comes to human labor, it is *the most* efficient agriculture the world has ever seen, by far. But from the standpoint of energy, there is nothing more *in*efficient. It is completely and absolutely, *irrevocably* unsustainable. It cannot endure past the oil age."

When David describes the agricultural system he is working to create as an alternative, he doesn't use the word *organic*. Nor does he use its sequel *sustainable*, a word he thinks is both overused and misapplied. The word he prefers is *enduring*. He would like to build a kind of farming that will last beyond the next season, beyond the next House Ag Committee appointments—beyond his own lifetime.

—◆—

Midsummer morning, blue skies above. As the sun climbs higher it brings on the heat, but nobody complains. Sun means dry, and dry means the brothers can get the grain out of the field and into the bin. A few days ago they cut down the crop on the north side of the farm and laid it on the field in swathes to dry out, and ever since then they have been watching the weather radar and praying it doesn't show rain on the way.

From the air this crop could be taken for wheat, but from the road, it's clearly something different. As pickup trucks pass by, the drivers will often slow down to see, something that seems to happen with every field on this farm. In the midst of this landscape sung in the three flat notes of corn, soy, and wheat, here there will be a field of minty green buckwheat or an expanse of proso millet the color of celery. In the dark afternoons of last fall, when the black soil everywhere held nothing but ragged brown corn stalks, this field on the north side shone like a green lightbulb, lush with slender blades of triticale.

A cross between durum wheat and rye, triticale is actually a not-so-distant cousin of the wheat that grows all over this area. In the field, though, the two plants have entirely different habits. While the triticale is seven, even eight feet tall in places, the wheats grown around here are mostly semi-dwarf varieties that stand less than three feet. Being compact, dwarf wheat spends a lesser percentage of its energy making leaves and stalks and roots—plant material that you can't sell—and thus more energy making the part that you can. Smaller plants also mean a combine can harvest the crop in one fell swoop, no need to cut the crop down into swaths and wait for it to dry while watching for rain clouds.

If being tall and bushy makes triticale a nuisance to harvest and a problem if it rains, in David's eyes the inconvenience is worth it. He focuses not on the crop, but the whole farm system. The more abundant a plant's foliage is, the better it can shade out weeds that compete for nutrition and water. This triticale crushed the opposition, good not just for the crop itself, but for reducing the weed population on the farm as a whole. Big plants like this also grow commensurately big root systems, which means that during a drought they might find water while the neighbor's dwarf wheats and their small root systems dried up and died. Finally, all that plant matter above and below is crucial to building the soil. After harvest, it's disked back into the earth, where it feeds microorganisms and helps the soil retain water.

None of this matters much to the guys growing dwarf wheat. They don't need the plant to shade out weeds because they have herbicides. They don't need biomass for the soil because they have fertilizers. In fact, the dwarf varieties are desirable specifically *because* they can take up vast quantities of fertilizer, which increases yields; given the same fertilizers, the triticale would grow unmanageably tall and fall over. David once called their farm an oasis in the "biological desert" of conventional farmland; judging from the two different crops, it's as if they are actually a parallel universe.

This morning David is harvesting the swaths of triticale in concentric circles, from the field's outside border in. From far away he appears like any other farmer who is driving a slightly older, smaller combine, but as he gets closer to where I'm standing it's clear something is different. He looks like a minister behind the wheel, his thin torso stiff and straight, his brow hardened with thought.

Closer, and I can see that his eyes are fixed straight ahead—on the crop before him, on the machine lifting and rolling it, but seemingly also on an additional dimension in which meaning and consequence are visible, like all the roots of the earth exposed aboveground.

In the middle of the field is a truck, which will transport the grain from field to bin. David pauses the combine beside it, moves some levers, and the grain in the hopper comes streaming out the top spout and into the back of the truck. As the grain downloads, I climb up the ladder on the side of the cab, open the door, and seat myself as well as I can on the metal ridge next to the driver's seat. David says nothing, keeps his eyes fixed on the stream of brown kernels. When the hopper is empty, he shifts the gears and starts moving again, eyes forward. In time, he begins to talk. Or rather, because the combine is loud and he is wearing earplugs, David shouts.

Listening to him is like looking through someone else's eyeglasses and finding the lenses turn the world to fractals. Any familiar topic regarding the environmental impact of modern agriculture unleashes from his brain a flood of facts and figures that fill the cab like a swarm of bees. I already know that modern agricultural machinery compacts the soil; he cites engineering studies from the University of Indiana, talking out mathematic equations of gross vehicle weight and the pounds of pressure per inch applied to the soil's surface, explaining how the earth feels this heavy footprint four feet down. He shouts about how he read that some Japanese farmers wear moccasins in their rice paddies, even go barefoot. He motions to his brown boots and says, "It's because they figure shit-kickers like these will damage the land! My God! Here we are driving eighty-thousand-pound machines all over the ground, and the Japanese farmers are worried about clod-hopper shoes?" Any other farmer I have met who drives a combine would dismiss the comparison as irrelevant; the American economy simply does not allow for that scale of production. David is anguished by the idea.

Of course, while few farmers think about these issues as constantly as David does, on some level everyone involved in agriculture is aware of the harm. It's well-known that the natural world that agriculture relies on is exhaustible, especially when not cared for, but there is simply no place for that concern within the economic equation. Conventional agriculture works like any other capitalist system: it succeeds only if it grows. As such, it depends on what Wendell Berry has called "the doctrine of limitlessness," the delusion that the resources necessary for that growth are infinite.

"Every person, I believe, possesses in their soul an inherent moral code." They are delicate words, but because David must shout them over the engine they turn heavy and blunt like rocks. As his voice strains, the message pares down to elemental truth. "We know deep down what's right and what's wrong, but to judge between the two we have to stop and think about it. Instead, most people just accept things. Well, I don't just accept things. I've *got* to stop and think about them. And when I do, I realize how much in our society is just based entirely on a money economy, with no thought for a moral or ethical response to what we're doing."

As we chug slowly around the field, scooping up grain, David tells me a story. It's from an era that predates his organic awakening. During these years he was in high school ag class happily being trained for his future role as a conventional commodity farmer.

Even then he sensed that something was going wrong. Up to that point, people had been content with what they had. "They didn't want more land, they didn't need more land," he says. "Then all of a sudden, they *had* to have more land—it was like a fever."

Throughout the country, agriculture was rapidly consolidating into fewer and larger farms. As David saw it, his neighbors were embracing a sort of personal Manifest Destiny, whereby their need to grow trumped preexisting values like community and cooperation. The only way to get more land was to take it from someone. Covetousness, once a sin, became a survival skill.

David was in the high school's Future Farmers of America club at the time. When they held a speech contest he took it as a chance to speak his mind about the shift. "I gave what I thought was a pretty damn good presentation slamming the greed that I saw growing in the community. It was difficult for me to understand the feeling of greed, and that's the way I described it—I didn't mince words." The contest's judge was the school's English teacher, a woman married to one of the farmers who was leading the charge to get big—a man who "expressed his greed very overtly," David says.

"So here I was saying all this, and I can imagine her thinking, *This kid is describing my husband, and I don't like what I hear.*" David gives one of the first laughs I've ever heard from him, a high, loud *ha ha ha!* As would be expected, he didn't even place in the contest. But that didn't faze him. The following year, as salutatorian of his senior class, he gave nearly the same speech at graduation.

The swaths of triticale before us now are thick, which forces David to pause so the combine can process the clump. Silently we watch the teeth spin stalks and leaves and grain, drawing the mass into the machine's inner chambers where it is digested—the grains stored in the hopper above, and the rest spit out the back. A rabbit springs forth and dashes off through the swaths.

David refers to the farming that the money economy requires as "brute-force agriculture." It is in direct contrast to the artfulness he values, instead a sort of farming-by-numbers by which a person plants, sprays, and harvests according to a predetermined schedule.

"It's telling that farmers have grown rather girthy," he shouts over the noise of the engine. "Farmers today with the big machinery go from one half-section to another without ever getting out of the cab, without ever smelling or feeling the soil, or even getting it on their boots. They sit in their tractor cabs, they have their little refrigerators—they don't even have to steer because they have global positioning. Just have to put in the coordinates and off they go."

Given that we're riding in a combine that is gradually approaching its own maximum gross vehicle weight of thirty thousand pounds, I must ask: "Is what you're doing brute-force agriculture?"

"To some extent, yeah. I try not to be very brutish, or as little as possible, but it's unavoidable when you're out here with big machinery." He says it easily, willing to convict himself. "You're not touching the soil, you're not connected to it. If we'd had a lot of rain and this low spot here was wet, and I knew I wasn't gonna get stuck, of course I'd roll right through it, knowing full well that in doing so I'd compact the soil. I mean, you have to do it for convenience sake, because of the economic pressures of the age. You just have to make those decisions . . ."

Until a few years ago David had been driving the same combine since 1969, a red Versatil machine with an open cab, no windshield, nothing to protect a person from the sun and the cold, the chaff and the dust. As he put it, "You just hoped the wind was blowing in your favor." It was miserable at times, but David was deeply reluctant to put any more separation between himself and the land.

In 2003, he upgraded to the current machine, which has a fully enclosed cab and offers the relative silence that allows the person driving to listen to the radio on headphones. This new combine is smaller and lighter than anything in the county—most people around here are working thirty-foot headers, double the size of this one. Even so, the switch seems to have come with a certain resignation. I ask why he upgraded and he shrugs his shoulders. "I guess you just get to be so old and you can't help it."

David tells another story. This one is from the Bible, but David tells it almost like he's recounting something that happened to a guy he knew. The city of Nineveh is going to hell because its residents are so bad and immoral. God tells Jonah to warn the people to change their ways, but Jonah resists and instead gets on ship, is thrown overboard, eaten by a whale, rescued by some miracle of God, etc. Then, even after all that, he's still not sure he wants to be a prophet of God. He does go back to Nineveh, reluctantly, but he tells himself, and he tells God, *It's not going to work. The people are beyond help. And besides, they're not going to listen to me— who the hell am I?* But he goes ahead and preaches, walks from one end of the city to the other preaching—and this is the largest city in the ancient world, so it takes him days. When he's done with his mission, he sits down outside the city under a shady tree and says, *Aw, these people are going to hell anyway, the city's going to be destroyed, just like God said.* And then lo and behold, the people take his message. They reform their ways, and God does not visit fire upon the city.

At this point David starts to chuckle—he had introduced this to me as a funny story. When Jonah sees that Nineveh is spared he's pissed off. He was just waiting for God to destroy the city, he wanted to see it happen—he wanted to prove God wrong. But then when it didn't happen he was pissed. "PISSED OFF!" David says, laughing. "*God, you were supposed to destroy Nineveh!* Aw, that's some pretty hilarious stuff."

Neither of us has to acknowledge the metaphor, Nineveh so close to home, the doctrine of limitlessness about to expire. Within moments the weight of the world returns to the combine's cab. David's face clouds over. "We made a bad turn in our culture when we took food production away from women and gave it to the men," he says, "when we went from the hoe to the diesel engine. Ever since then we've been on a power trip, and I think it's been really bad for the land—it's been bad for a lot of things." His voice softens. "Honestly, I guess I'd rather just be a gardener."

3

WHILE DAVID DRIVES the combine, Dan's job is to drive the harvested grain from the field to the farmyard and unload it into a storage bin, a job that takes a fraction of the time the combining does. Sometimes he does other tasks while David is harvesting; often he just sits in the truck in the middle of the field, waiting. It works this way for several reasons, not least of which is that even in his forties, Dan remains the younger brother. To this day, David calls him "Danny."

If the farm has a single person in charge it is older brother David. That said, Dan has carved out a role for himself. He is the numbers guy, the one who does equations in his head and works out the engineering details of their on-farm experiments. He is also the "guy" guy of the farm. He likes cars. He likes sports. When Dan found out that I grew up in Boston, he dug up a videotape about the history of baseball, stuck it in the VCR and fast-forwarded to a piece on the 1986 World Series. It is the bottom of the tenth inning of the game that should have won the Red Sox the World Series for the first time since 1918, and they're ahead five to three. With one out to go, first baseman Bill Buckner lets an easy groundball bounce through his legs. The Mets score, then win the game, then win the Series. It is perhaps the most humiliating error in baseball history, a wrenching memory for any Boston fan. Watching it I groaned out loud. Dan was tickled.

This afternoon in the triticale field, I am waiting with him in the truck. It's a hefty '59 Ford with a cab the color of the sky and a worn bumper sticker that reads, in barely legible letters:

EAT TURKEY

HIGH IN PROTEIN, LOW IN FAT!

Originally a gas truck, at some point it was put to work on the farm and the extra-long flatbed was fitted with a tall wooden bin for carrying grain. Every forty-five minutes David stops the combine and unloads through the spout into the back of the truck. He could go longer and fit more in the combine's hopper, but forty-five minutes' worth is the truck's maximum capacity.

After David fills the truck and returns to combining, I ask Dan if there's time for me to photograph the grain in the back. He says sure, gets out of the driver's seat, walks around the front of the truck, and opens my door, an act I realize later is not so much chivalry as necessity—the truck's door is prone to sticking. He suggests I climb onto the roof to get a bird's eye view of the grain, so I hoist myself up and stand on top of the cab. It's quite something to behold, like an aboveground swimming pool filled with more than a hundred million tiny kernels, all golden and shining. For me it's a wonderful moment, to witness that field of plants become this deep box of food, or at least what will become food.

"This part must be exciting for you," I say, "to have the harvest in and see it all before you in one place."

"Sure," he says. He takes a couple grains and pops them in his mouth, crunching the hard kernels.

Dan drives us off the field and parks the truck in a grassy lane between two rows of grain bins. They're the kind you see all over farm country: cylinders with pointed tops and bottoms, an opening in the top and a ladder running up the side. These ones are sixteen feet tall, but they can get to more than twice that. On the ground in front of the bins is a wide bucket. Running between the bucket and the top of one white grain bin is an augur, a forty-foot metal tube housing a metal spiral that's like a giant drill bit. The spiral is flush with the inside of the tube, so as it spins whatever grain is taken in at the bottom moves up the augur and out the angled top, into the grain bin. As it starts up I can hear the metal grinding inside.

Dan backs up the truck so the rear end hangs over the bucket on the ground. Next he powers the hydraulic pump that lifts the front end of the truck's grain box, which slides the triticale toward the rear. In the back of the truck is a door the size of a folded newspaper. He lifts it a crack and grain gushes into the bucket and is immediately sucked up by the augur. The grinding noise is drowned out by the sound of all those millions of kernels pouring out of the box, the sound of hard rain.

As we watch, I try my question again. "I'm not sure if I said it quite right before. Isn't this time of year exciting? You know, sixty acres of triticale harvested? After all that work and time you put in, now to have the payoff in the back of the truck?"

"Yeah," he says in the same shoulder-shrugging tone. "I guess it's exciting."

After the box empties out, Dan cranks it back flat and looks at his watch. "I think David's got another half round to go in the field. Come on," he says. Suddenly his voice is excited. "Do you like raspberries?"

We drive past the bin and away from the field, to the garden. Dan parks alongside a patch of raspberries that runs almost the length of the fence, a good thirty yards. He starts picking, handing me berries and motioning for me to do the same. It's a sort of fantasy treat for me. I love raspberries but live in a place where they are precious—available at the farmers market for about a month each year, and four dollars for a half pint. Having been here for twenty years, the patch is thick and the dark canes are loaded with so many berries that some are starting to turn bad and fall off. They're as delicious as any raspberry I've ever had: sweet, fragrant, soft, warm from the sun. Unaccustomed to the abundance, I'm shy, picking carefully and curbing my greedy impulse to make a pouch in my T-shirt and load it with berries. Dan tells me not to worry—there are plenty. So we pick and eat and talk and pick. In time he feels the pull back to the field, knowing the combine has probably finished its rounds and might even be waiting for us.

"We should go," he says, heading back to the truck. "Here, put your hands together."

He tips his big palm over, carefully transferring every last berry into the bowl of my hands. We drive back to the field and park in the middle. As David comes around the last bend, we sit in the truck and eat. Our hands are stained pink. Dan can't help but smile.

For the Podolls, the farm's first priority is to feed the five people living on it. In this corner of North Dakota, that is radical.

"The idea is simple," David told me. "We live on a farm, so why not grow our own food? It seems so illogical to grow a bulk commodity, send it out, then go to the grocery store and buy everything we need to eat."

This is a primary reason why their farm plan runs perfectly counter to those of their neighbors. Rather than continually grow, they have designed the business so that the farm can stay small. If it got too big, they wouldn't have time for the garden. They've seen it happen to more or less every farm around: The husband focuses only on cash crops and the garden is left to the wife. In time the wife is needed elsewhere, whether hauling grain, going to town for parts, or taking a job to help pay the bills. Inevitably, the garden is abandoned and the job of feeding the family is outsourced to the people at Super-Valu Grocery in LaMoure.

Here, though, the garden is the root of the farm. With a laugh, Theresa says that when it comes to the garden she is actually an interloper; tending it is David and Dan's work. I asked them what they grow, and Dan chuckled—turns out it's a big answer. Tomatoes, sweet corn, cucumbers. Muskmelon, watermelon, summer squash, winter squash, pumpkins, parsley, peas, and celery. Dry beans, pole beans, carrots, onions, beets, and potatoes—that's off the top of Dan's head. They store long-lasting foods like potatoes and carrots in the basement, and freeze and can as much as possible. They also grow strawberries, raspberries, and grapes, which they turn into jam and jelly. Apples from the orchard become apple juice and applesauce. Theresa has four goats and at the farm there are scores of chickens for eggs and meat. Some years they have a flock of turkeys in the old turkey barn, some years Dan raises hogs or beef cattle. The only thing missing is a milk cow, and they're working on that.

It's not as if they are affecting some nineteenth-century pioneer fantasy. They have DSL and television, they have cars and a grocery store less than twenty minutes away. And they do buy food: oil, butter, nutmeg, ice cream—that sort of thing. It's just that, given the choice, they would always rather produce it themselves. Likewise, they would rather cook food themselves than eat out. Everyone in the family participates. David and Ginger cook nightly at their house, the rule being that whoever comes home first makes supper. The brothers annually make a batch of sauerkraut and grind flour on a hand mill. Theresa prepares three meals a day for their side of the family, often with Dan's help.

In the kitchen, Theresa is natural and unpretentious. She makes bread without measurements or timers, instead judging the dough with her eyes and her fingers. There are no cookbooks on her shelves, and I suspect the food she makes is strikingly similar to what her mother made, and what her grandmother made before that. Perhaps she gets elaborate on holidays, but for everyday meals there are few sauces and nearly everything is served as a single ingredient. Most things end up only one step away from how they were harvested: corn is boiled, beans are steamed, turkey is roasted. The food is so flavorful it doesn't need much help.

Meals are composed of whatever looks good in the garden that day, plus whatever is left over from previous meals. Corn on the cob, sliced tomatoes, turkey refried with onions and garlic, and bread and butter—always bread and butter. Whole, steamed beets, raw cabbage with a simple dressing, Dutch meatballs, mashed potatoes, beet greens in a bowl. Winter squash, spinach, chicken, salsa, sliced tomatoes, chopped cilantro. Cornbread made from sweet corn that was left to mature in the field, then ground into meal and mixed with eggs, butter, milk, and honey. For dessert there are raspberries or winter squash mixed with milk and sugar. Over and over I was amazed to look at their dinner table and think that nearly everything aside from the salt and pepper came from this farm. I think back to California, where some people I know started the "locavore" challenge, aka the hundred-mile diet: for a whole month, eat only food grown within one hundred miles of your home. With some exceptions, Theresa and Dan have been on a one-mile diet since they were married. Neil has been on it since he was born.

Three meals a day, Theresa and Dan sit down to eat together. Neil is there, too, whenever he is not at school or a friend's house. For every mealtime when I was at their farm, the family simply assumed I would join them too. At times when I resisted out of modesty, they insisted—to them it seemed absurd that I would leave and eat somewhere else.

Grace is said before meals, but after that there is no more formality. The meal has no courses, neither entrees nor side dishes, just the moment's array of different foods in bowls and on plates and in pots and jars. You eat what you want, you don't eat what you don't want. At the end of each meal, every plate is clean.

It's especially striking to see eleven-year-old Neil at this table. Theresa does not tell him that he must eat something because it's good for him, and rarely must she nag him to finish something on his plate. He likes ice cream as much as any kid, but at dinner he'll help himself to green beans and eat them with his fingers. What he does not like is the food at school. Once the subject of Theresa's grape jelly came up, and he told us that the grape jelly at school tastes . . . funny.

"Is it the kind that comes in those little plastic rectangles?" I asked.

He wrinkled his nose and nodded.

"Funny? What does it taste like?" Theresa asked him.

"I don't know, it's just *gross*. Some kids will slurp it right out of the dish, though." He wrinkled his nose again and smiled, the very thought so totally disgusting it made him giggle.

This reminded Theresa of how when their oldest son, Nic, left the farm to go to college, the dining hall burned down days after he arrived. For his whole freshman year he ate food cooked in a trailer and served in a makeshift mess hall.

Dan confirmed, shaking his head, "On plastic plates, with plastic forks."

"It was awful," Theresa said. "I mean, it's one thing to go from eating bad food to eating good food, but from good food to bad? The poor kid. Was he ever glad when he came home for Christmas break."

———•———

I was first introduced to the Podolls' garden on a snowy winter day, while eating lunch at Dan and Theresa's house. David was there

244

and our meal lasted for hours, the three telling me how the garden is the hub of their farm and about all the things that radiate out from it. As they spoke of the garden I was struck by the tenderness in their voices and the words they chose. When Theresa referred to a time the grapes had been infested with flea beetles, it sounded as if she were recalling a time one of their kids was ill. The love was especially apparent in David. The world weighs on his mind like lead, but as he talks about the garden his spirit is untied and left to rise in the wind. Hope returns to his face. "The world's salvation is in the garden," he said over lunch that day. "All the world's good is there."

At some point in the conversation I admitted that my gut response to their emphasis on gardening was the same as, I guessed, many Americans' would be: that gardening is nice, but it feels dramatically less important than farming—less legitimate. David looked at me solemnly in response. "Gardening," he said, "has taught me how to farm."

The garden allows for intimacy, he explained. It is food production brought back to a human scale. "In there you're close-up." His voice was warm, almost giddy with the topic. "You crawl around on your hands and knees, picking weeds, and you see things, little things, and you smell things. All your senses are used. Being a careful observer like that gives you a better sense of where to plant what, how to rotate things. With that level of awareness you have an infinite ability to finesse the production of your food."

The garden is the gold standard against which everything on the farm is measured. For instance soil. In the garden it is light, rich, and moist, and never feels weight greater than what's borne by a pair of boot heels. When David rides some big piece of equipment into the fields, scrutinizing as he goes, he compares that ground to the garden. "Because of the garden I know what the best soil looks like, feels like, smells like. As long as I'm sitting on a tractor it will never meet that standard, but the standard is always present in my mind. It's something I'll always strive for, even agonize over."

The experience of the work is different, too, because it's done together in the dirt, not solo under the roar of an engine. In the garden, David and Dan spend hours weeding and talking about "religion and the world and things of meaning." They have accepted the reality that they must create surplus values in the crop fields, laboring in order to pay for phone bills and doctor's visits. As much as they try to make their work there thoughtful and careful, they recognize the need for compromises and flexibility— thirty-thousand-pound combines and the like. But the garden gate is a boundary between worlds. Inside is a place where a sort of moral economy presides.

"Both Danny and I are not businessmen," David said. "We are running the farm as a business, but we don't like to sell stuff—we think money perverts everything. So we decided that the garden is a sacred place, and we would not let the money economy intrude upon that space."

They do not calculate the hours spent in the garden versus the pounds of food produced there. They choose the vegetables they plant by what tastes best, not by what will have the highest yields. If there is excess beyond what they can eat and store themselves, they give it away. In the garden they make all their decisions and apply their work according to an equation of values—generosity, fulfillment, health, ecology, diversity—rather than numbers. As much as any technique of land management, this is what was learned when David says that the garden taught him how to farm.

That afternoon at the dining table he recalled an epiphany that came to him after he had been growing his own food for some time. By nature he made the food in his garden as good as possible, believing that by giving it the utmost care it would be healthy for the land and nutritious for his own body. How could he then turn around and apply a lesser standard when growing food for other people? To him that would be more than a contradiction. It would be morally indefensible.

4

THE DOWNSIDE TO the garden philosophy is that it has created a bit of a paradox for the Podolls. One of the core values they aim to foster is community, and yet in the community of LaMoure County their belief in a farm system based in moral currency has often isolated them. Theresa says that when she brings up alternative ideas she can watch as a veil comes over the face of the person she's talking to. David senses that many neighbors don't even consider him a real farmer.

I once asked him if he ever thought to leave and go to a place where these ideas would be received better. He shook his head no, definitely no, as if the thought had never crossed his mind. "We've lived here for fifty-four years," he said. "This is our home."

And so they do their best to live like fish out of water. Over the years they have earned the respect of some neighbors, have even been told privately that what they are doing is the right thing. Others remain suspicious, even derisive. The brothers respond by not mixing much, staying on the farm most days and finding their companions in the community of organic farmers spread across the state.

Theresa takes a different tack. On a Tuesday morning in the end of July, I am following her through the roasting streets of town as she posts yellow signs announcing the LaMoure Farmers Market's second season, which begins tomorrow. She buys tape at the drugstore and then uses it to post a sign on the counter. She hits the hardware store, the post office, the soft-serve ice cream shop, the tearoom, even Nogo's Tapper, a dark bar with a deep stench of stale beer and unemptied ashtrays. As she pins a sheet next to the pool table, she laughs and says, "Yeah, I'm not sure this is quite perfect. But who knows? Maybe they'll talk about it after they leave here and someone will overhear them. We might get a customer or two."

Theresa posts the last sign at the first gas station in town, then realizes she wants to put one at the other gas station. So we return to the bar and reclaim the sign there, agreeing that it will be more effective elsewhere. As we go Theresa chides herself for not having made more signs, for not having made a list of where she wanted to post them, for not having put them up sooner. It's the way she is: always thorough, but always wanting to do better.

Before the bar we went to Wanda's, a diner where a few older farmers were drinking coffee and talking about engines they'd had in their time. Theresa wound around the counter to the bulletin board in back, which was crowded with signs announcing auctions and puppies for sale.

"Keepin' out of the heat?" one of the men at the counter asked her. In this town, everybody knows everybody.

"Actually, I've been in Minneapolis," she said back in a small-talky way, looking for available tacks on the board.

"Ohh"—he tipped back in his chair—"the big city." I could have sworn there was a trace of scorn in his voice.

"Oh yeah," she said flatly. If that was bait, Theresa wasn't biting. "At least it didn't get as hot down there."

Theresa is known in town as being something other than a farm wife. She travels often, certainly more than anyone else on the farm and probably more than most people in LaMoure. As a director and then board member of various farmers' nonprofit groups, she has spoken at meetings in England and California and has briefed the press backstage at Farm Aid in New York City. She and Dan joke that her frequent travel stems from her being almost completely stationary while growing up. Her Dutch-immigrant father was so driven as a farmer that during her whole childhood the family took only two trips: to Bismarck, the third biggest city in North Dakota, and to see an uncle in Manitoba, two hours away.

On her family's seed potato farm near the Minnesota border, she grew up with pesticides as a way of life. She was warned to not breathe the white dust they used at planting time and had strict orders not to go into the poison shed. (This rule, of course, was broken. She and her siblings would sneak in there, take out the old herbicide barrels, and build forts out of them.) Theresa says she always knew something was wrong with the way they were farming, but it was not until college that she learned there were alternatives. During a lecture in ecology class her professor talked about organic farming, and she was so excited that after the bell rang she ran to find her boyfriend, Dan Podoll, and tell him about it. When he responded quietly that his family farmed organically, Theresa's mouth dropped open—she couldn't believe he hadn't ever told her.

Looking back, though, she gets it. In the early '80s, you didn't talk about it, you just did it.

When she and Dan were first married Theresa played a more traditional role of wife and mom, taking care of their two babies and making crafts at home for extra money. In those years her support for an alternative agriculture was more passive. She volunteered for nonprofits, helped with the farm, worked in the garden when she could. Years later, when she was pregnant with Neil, she took the job of director of the Northern Plains Sustainable Agriculture Society, a nonprofit representing and organizing farmers in Minnesota and the Dakotas. It was then that she found her voice and became an outspoken critic of conventional agriculture and the stranglehold it puts on farmers, families, and land in the Northern Plains. She still looks like a grown-up Dorothy from Kansas, but in casual conversation she will reference pointed facts and statistics and studies as easily as if she were speaking before a Congressional committee.

Since leaving the nonprofit in 2005, Theresa has been staying closer to home, in part to work on a master's degree in community development at Iowa State University. Two years ago, she started the farmers market in LaMoure. Though it has become her project, it wasn't her idea initially—an older woman in town with health issues wanted local produce and she knew Theresa could be convinced to fill the need. "I'm never someone to back down when a person asks, *Do you think we can do this?*" Theresa said. "I mean, when I hear someone say something can't be done, it's like waving a red flag in front of a bull."

Now that the market is up and running Theresa would like to pass it off to someone else, but so far no one has stepped up. In the meantime, she looks on the bright side. She says it's fun, and that it's exciting for her to have conversations about food in a place where the subject doesn't come up very often. As she sells at the market, people ask her about the garden and respond with their own stories. When she tells them that the bread she's selling was made with grains that she and her family grew and milled themselves, people are stunned. She says that last year the little old ladies would show up before the market opened and wait in line while she set up her stand, just to make sure they could get a loaf before she sold out.

The irony, of course, is that there's wheat growing within a mile of any point in town. Most of these customers were probably raised on farms that grew it or at least next to those that did. But then, most of them, at least the elderly, also used to have a garden. Indeed, that's why they come to the farmers market: they know from experience the difference between the food at the Super-Valu Grocery and the food sold here.

———•———

The market takes place on a stretch of grass right on Highway 13, the two-lane road that leads in and out of town. Selling goes from four o'clock in the afternoon until six, but on opening day Theresa arrives just after three o'clock so she can clean the area and still have plenty of time to set up. It's a humid ninety-two outside and the prairie wind is blowing hard, restlessly, more nuisance than relief. She sets up her card table in the shade of a tree, beneath the tossing branches. On the highway a Buick Skylark slows down to a roll. Inside is an elderly couple, and the woman calls out the window to ask if the market is today. "Four o'clock!" Theresa calls back, smiling.

Before long a big black Ram 2500 turns in and backs up under the tree, next to Theresa's table. The truck bed is packed with boxes of tomatoes, laundry baskets filled with cabbages, also peppers in three colors, dill, and some onions in a Tupperware bin. The driver is Denise, a redhead wearing a ball cap and a sleeveless shirt made of fabric decorated with horses, wind blowing through their manes. She and her husband raise horses on his family's farm, and this year she's supplementing the business by expanding her garden and selling at three farmers markets. Theresa is delighted to have her, since her own offering is modest: beets and beet greens in a bucket, green beans in a small cooler, twelve loaves of bread baked the night before. The only other grower, Angela, is a thin, pretty woman with wavy, gray-brown hair. She has a nice, also small selection: green beans, Nanking cherries, collard greens in Ziploc bags, and low-sugar apricot jam made from North Dakota fruit—"Not from California or Washington," she will tell each customer. "They're from here. They're ours."

Ten minutes before four o'clock, Theresa is helping Angela arrange her jams and Denise is moving the boxes of peppers and dill to a card table, deciding whether to move the cabbages and tomatoes to the grass or leave them on the truck's tailgate. Theresa realizes she is the only one to have brought a scale, so she moves her table closer to Denise's truck in order to share. This puts her beets in the sun, and immediately the tops begin to wilt, but there's no time to solve that. As she's moving, the Buick couple returns and parks. The husband is slow to get out of the car, but the wife makes the speediest beeline her old bones will allow. It is no deterrent that the market is only half set up. She goes directly behind Denise and starts picking through the tomatoes in the truck.

Within moments four cars arrive, then two more, all of them carrying elderly women with glasses and hearing aids and curlers in their hair, all of whom follow the first woman's lead. There is a swarm around the back of the truck, and women are reaching over each other to get tomatoes, sticking cabbages under their arms, barely talking except to ask where the bags are so they can fill them up. They hand their loot to Denise, to Theresa, to anyone who doesn't appear to be shopping, while others still at the boxes call into the air, *How much are the tomatoes? Is there any corn?* A man in a meaty pick-up slows down and yells out the window to ask if they have watermelon. The question passes person to person down the line to Theresa, who answers *No, they're not ripe yet* without looking up. The tomatoes are causing a frenzy and in the rush Theresa weighs produce for Denise, who is busy trying to keep track of all the people trying to pay her. Her cash box is still somewhere in the truck, so as people hand Denise bills she holds up her pocketbook and makes change out of her wallet and coin purse.

Forty pounds of tomatoes and thirty minutes later, the lawn is empty. Theresa looks at her watch: 4:20. "Okay," she says, "that was a rush!" For the next hour and a half people trickle through, mostly one at a time. They buy jam or beets, always tomatoes. By 5:10 Theresa sells out of bread. More people ask for corn and watermelon and are told it's too early in the season. One woman asks for peas, and it is all Theresa can do to mask her amazement. A springtime crop, peas have been done for six weeks now; in this heat, they would be as limp as wet newspaper. "Well, no. No peas," Theresa answers her, and the woman leaves. The wind continues to blow.

Some customers stop to talk. One woman tells how her husband was diagnosed as diabetic and has taken up a new diet: veggie burgers instead of hamburgers, plus lots of vegetables. She beams as she talks about how much weight he has lost, how much healthier he seems. A teller from the credit union shows up before 5:00 and is delighted to see that Theresa still has bread for sale. As she puts two loaves in a bag, Denise jokes how her husband refuses to eat wholegrain bread because he's convinced it's made from "screens," the weed seeds and other trash screened out of wheat after it's harvested. This leads to a conversation about white bread—"air bread"—and how you can't find it without high-fructose corn syrup these days; how you can't find anything without high-fructose corn syrup these days. Angela mentions a woman she knows who serves her kids soda at dinner because it's cheaper than milk. The rest of the women look aghast.

"Instead of milk?"

"What ever happened to just drinking water?"

As the clock nears six o'clock, Theresa, Denise, and Angela agree that it's okay to pack up a little early. It has been slow for a spell now, and the wind and the heat have sapped what energy they had to spare. They trade some of their remaining vegetables and pack up their tables, and at a few minutes past the hour each woman is in her car, leaving.

As we drive back to the farm Theresa assesses the market, saying it was a good turnout for the first day of the season. She saw a lot of devoted customers from last year as well as some new faces. Plus, she believes the crowds will only grow as word travels—and as sweet corn comes into season. She's candid that for her, the market is more an act of community service than a moneymaking opportunity. In fact, between gas and little expenses like bread bags, it actually ends up costing her money to participate. Last year she found herself up before sunrise just to fit the work into her already busy schedule, digging carrots in the mud and groaning to herself, *Why am I doing this?* But she is convinced that the community needs it, and that all the talk in the world is useless unless people like her actually do something about the things that need to change.

———

By the next day at lunch, the farmers market sign at Wanda's restaurant has been covered up by flyers for the Ladies' Country Club Card Marathon and a demolition derby. To be fair, this is the busiest bulletin board in town. The only posting whose space seems to be sacred is a Farmers Cooperative Creamery Association calendar from 1972, whose theme is "dessert-a-month." It's permanently opened to June, month of the Lime Loaf, a white frosted cake with blue-green crème between the layers.

Wanda's used to be part of the local creamery, first the co-op's egg storage room and then a café called the Dairy Bar. When the creamery closed in 1974, the café stayed on under a series of new owners. Last year it changed hands again, but it remains a classic small-town luncheonette. The décor is country kitchen, with green-and-white Formica counters, matching green stools, and ruffled curtains the color of cooked spinach. The menu is familiar: hamburgers and cheeseburgers, corn dogs served on a plate. Egg salad and potato salad, both the bright yellow of a legal pad, are available by the pint. For dessert waitresses scoop ice cream hidden in a silver freezer. At any given time you can find at least one group of men assembled around the U-shaped counter or in one of the booths, drinking coffee from bottomless mugs and talking about the weather, maybe playing cards. By the door is a hat rack (where they do in fact hang their caps), and next to it is a framed poster of a cow printed with the motto: COWS MAY COME AND COWS MAY GO, BUT THE BULL IN THIS PLACE GOES ON FOREVER.

There is a Wanda's in every small town from here to Ohio that's big enough to have a restaurant. Or rather, there's a place *like* Wanda's in all those towns; that's the draw: it's not a chain. For locals it feels like a private social club, but even for outsiders the place feels personal, intimate in a way that McDonald's inherently is not. I seek them out any time I'm on the road, and I'm not alone—there are legions of travelers throughout the country who scour the blue highways for diners and cafés and trade their tips with other devotees. The food is important, especially pie, but what matters most is the experience. People are hungry for authenticity.

It was strange, then, to have the Podolls point out to me that in all those diners, all that food—the hamburgers, grilled cheese, ice cream, corn dogs—is exactly the same. A cook might bring individual talent to the Sunday special, but the ingredients were all hauled in by a truck from U.S. Foodservice, which stops at every other joint along the way to deliver the same array of foodstuffs in card-board boxes. In the walk-in at Wanda's you'd find a case of half & half from Glenview Farms, on its carton a woodcut image of a barn and silo. Under the counter would be a box of Hilltop Hearth Saltines, its logo a shock of wheat. Both are brands owned by U.S. Foodservice. Both trace back to Columbia, Maryland—before that, who knows?

It is possible that corn from LaMoure ended up being fed to the milk cows that produced the half & half, or that it was processed into the high-fructose corn syrup used in the crackers. But even if so, it would be nearly impossible to know. Just as these foodstuffs arrived in cardboard boxes from a distant place down the highway, so did last year's harvest disappear into anonymity the moment each farmer emptied his semi at the grain elevator. At this point nobody even questions it. Ever since the gardens disappeared from the farmstead, farmers have not concerned themselves with food in the small sense of feeding themselves. They are too busy feeding the world.

5

THE LAST WEEK in July the roads leading out of LaMoure feel narrow, hemmed in by dense stands of corn. From the flat road they are green walls, eight feet tall, and they give this open land an unusual sense of privacy, even suspense. Then comes one of those fractional inclines, hardly noticeable when the ground is bare. As your line of sight rises the landscape shifts open and becomes a plain of brown made entirely of corn tassels. This week, all of the corn in LaMoure County—indeed, all of the corn in southeast North Dakota—is in bloom.

Almost all of it. Drive past the Podolls' and you'll see a whole different approach to the crop. The plants are not in bloom just yet; they were seeded later intentionally so that they wouldn't cross-pollinate with the neighbors' corn, most of which is genetically engineered. The tall green stalks here are healthy-looking but not remarkably uniform—the same only enough to prove that each planting is a single type of corn. And while the rest of the fields around here are planted with rows so tight a person could hardly breathe between them, the rows at the Podolls' are spaced with dark alleys wider than a big man's shoulders.

Today, in those alleys is a path of footsteps looping up between two rows and then down between the next, the pattern of a heating coil. At the far end of one long alley is the tiny figure of Theresa, in shorts, a sleeveless pink T-shirt, and tennis shoes. At the end of the next alley is Dan, same as ever, with white T-shirt, white ball cap, jeans, boots. Their shoulders are tilted down and their heads face earthward, but neither bends. Instead they deftly use the whole range of the hoes in their hands, wielding them lightly to sever the stem of any weed found between the corn plants. They walk silently, alone, sometimes crossing paths and moving together for a moment before drifting apart again, eyes always on the ground beneath them.

Every so often one will stop to address some purslane, a recalcitrant weed that has evolved an ability to search out water and suck it up like mad. Left alone, these little succulents would take over this field. At times Dan has torn them up and watched them lie in the sun against the hot, black earth for a week, then, with a light rain, reroot themselves and start growing again. For this plant, hoeing is not enough; it must be diligently hacked to bits. (I once went to a posh, Alice Waters–style restaurant in Manhattan with Theresa. When the waitress announced that the chef was featuring a salad of purslane, Theresa almost spat out her drink. She ordered it just so she could tell Dan she had.)

Alongside the corn are winter squash, watermelon, and tomatoes, plantings that altogether total three acres. This is the farm's latest venture, growing seeds for gardeners. On their small acreage, grain farming alone can't support two families; they need a high-value crop. For years David and Dan followed in their father's footsteps and raised turkeys. While Mr. Podoll had made a profit by raising birds by the thousands, after David took over, flocks that size had become standard for the industry. Rather than grow even larger, the brothers made turkey farming profitable again by raising the birds organically and selling them to distant health food store chains. Business boomed until 1995, when they were hit by a double whammy of consolidation: Both of their buyers were bought by Whole Foods, which at that point was not buying organic poultry and so ended their contracts. At the same time, the local slaughterhouse went out of business, leaving them nowhere to have the birds processed. After four decades, the turkey barns went empty.

The following year, the Podolls began growing vegetable seeds for a company in Montana. In the years since then they've developed relationships with several other companies, the sort whose racks you see in garden stores. The work was a natural fit for the Podolls. They have always gardened, and this was more or less an extension of that. "We didn't fit the mold for traditional agriculture anyway, so it wasn't like it involved any kind of mind shift," Theresa explained. "It was probably more traumatic for the neighbors, because they had to figure out what the heck was going on. When they'd drive by they'd slow down and be just, *What are they doing now?* You'd notice pickups taking the long way around, just to get a good look."

Odd as it may appear to the neighbors, the business perfectly matches the Podolls' vision for their farm. It allows them to keep things small, as the revenue from three acres of seeds roughly equals that from the farm's three hundred acres in grains. And while the grain business requires ever-bigger equipment on ever-larger acreage, growing seeds instead demands attention to detail, their greatest strength. Today Dan and Theresa are swamped with things to do, getting ready to leave for three days, but weeding the seed plots was at the top of the list. Even in that quick absence, Dan wants to be sure the weeds don't get ahead of them—normally he walks the plots with his hoe three times a week. As he weeds he studies the plants: how rain is impacting the germination of the squash seeds, whether the corn shows signs of rust or other disease. I bet the seed plot will cross his mind more than once during their vacation.

They began growing seeds long before it became their business—it's part of the whole garden system. As much as possible, the vegetables they grow are planted from seeds saved from last year's harvest. When Theresa and Dan cook they keep a bowl to the side into which they scoop out the seed cavity of a squash or the jelly innards of a tomato. If the squash or tomato or whatever they're eating that day tastes particularly delicious, they save the seeds and sow them the following year. It is plant breeding at its most basic: a person finds a plant with desirable traits, saves its seeds and grows them, repeating annually to steer the plant toward what he or she wants it to be. Called "selection," it is how agriculture began. Corn, rice, wheat—all were just wild plants to begin with, selected by humans over millennia to become what they are today.

David has been doing it in the field for thirty years. He and Dan make selections based on a plant's fortitude against disease and other pests. Sometimes they are looking to improve a variety of plant that already exists, aiming to make their version of it ideally suited to the particular conditions of their four hundred and eighty acres. Other times they make selections to create an entirely new variety. Back in the 1970s, David grew a small, early-maturing variety of watermelon next to a large, sweet, southern variety. When they cross-pollinated he kept the seeds from the progeny and planted them the following season. The next year he selected the best watermelons and planted their seeds the following season. He repeated this for years, until finally what grew was a unique variety perfect for their garden: a medium-sized watermelon that does well in a short, cool season yet still produces sweet, bright-red flesh that's juicy enough to dribble down a person's chin. They named it Dakota Rose, and today you can buy seeds for it at garden stores.

Over the years they have come up with numerous other unique varieties, most of them identifiable by the signature "Dakota" name—Dakota Tears onions, Dakota Black popcorn, Uncle David's Dakota Dessert squash. If it sounds unusual for them to be saving seeds and creating new varieties of plants, it is; the vast majority of American farmers and gardeners buy their seeds from a catalog each year and leave breeding to the professionals. But David insists that it's only our modern context that makes what they do extraordinary.

"The whole of agriculture has evolved from just gardeners selecting seed that they liked," he says. "It's only within the last hundred years that farmers have been left out. Every farmer or gardener previous to this time did so just as a matter of survival—they needed to do it to eat. And it's not long before we're going to return to doing things that way." He says it matter-of-factly.

David's reasoning follows the same logic as modeling the family's farm after their garden. In his view, modern breeding is mostly crude and myopic; genetic engineering, which many consider to be the most advanced form, he calls "brute-force breeding." He values instead plants guided by the intimate observation that happens every day on the farm or in the garden. It's a matter of morality—artfulness and care rather than forceful imposition of will—but it's also a matter of pure physical logic. He believes that this approach to breeding is the basis of an agriculture that will endure past the oil age. This, in fact, is what will feed the world.

———•———

The shift away from farmers breeding officially began in 1900, when scientists rediscovered the work of the nineteenth-century botanist Gregor Mendel. He had been the first person to recognize that specific traits could be tied to individual genes, most famously peas having purple flowers instead of white. It's a lesson familiar to many from high school biology—the Punnett square showing how two parents' genes combine to determine the genes of their offspring. But as basic as the idea might seem in the twenty-first century, for plant breeders at the turn of the twentieth century it was a revelation. Until then, plants had been treated not as individuals, but as populations. Their characteristics were thought of not in terms of yes-or-no—purple flowers or white—but rather as degrees on a scale that went from most to least. Breeding was done by the technique called mass selection, in which a person selected the plants whose desirable characteristics were strongest and replanted them, steering the population toward more of what was desirable.

The heart of the process was observation: understanding a place's particular growing conditions, recognizing what characteristics were beneficial, selecting desirable plants, noticing how the plants and the growing conditions changed over time, and how that shifted the whole equation. It followed that the people doing this work were the same people who were growing food—as David explains, the acts were intertwined. Beginning with the earliest British colonies and onward through the American frontier, farmers and gardeners were the ones who adapted food crops to the new lands of North America, work that settled the wild country acre by acre.

Critical to the settlers' work was genetic variation within the seed supply. Some people refer to this variation as "genetic breadth." David thinks of it as memory. He believes that in the genes of each seed lies a record of everything its forebears endured—extreme temperatures, diseases, drought and flood. To face the challenges brought by each new microclimate's growing conditions, these early American farmers' plants drew on all the different memories within their population. The more memories they had, the more adaptable they were.

But the rediscovery of Mendel's laws changed everything. Now that it was possible to attribute a trait to an individual gene, plant breeding became a matter of singling out desirable genes and cementing them in place. Once a specimen had the desired genetic composition, it could be replicated indefinitely. Increasingly over the course of the twentieth century, the new standard was purebred varieties whose plants were identical.

This new approach went hand in hand with the overall industrialization of agriculture. The more plants acted the same, the more the process of growing them could be automated and conducted on a larger scale. In a paper written in 1968, two USDA researchers put it well: "Machines were not made to harvest crops; in reality, crops must be designed to be harvested by machine." What mattered was that all the corn plants mature at the same time and that the wheat plants be the same height. Not only did the genetic variation that earlier farmers had depended on now cease to be valuable, it became a liability.

It followed that farmers' skills as plant breeders also ceased to be valuable. What they brought to the process was the power of intimate observation, which allowed them to produce plants highly adapted to a particular place. But industrial agriculture had chemicals and fertilizers to mitigate climatic variations; what it needed was seed that would act predictably in a whole range of situations and locations. The traditional technique of observation over the course of many seasons was increasingly replaced by methods that allowed a person to skip ahead and instead know in advance what the plant would do. Breeding passed into the hands of professionals who had the tools and training to seize on technological advances in plant science—advances that farmers couldn't have employed in their breeding without quitting farming and becoming professional breeders themselves.

Fast forward to the twenty-first century. Genetic uniformity is now such an integral part of conventional agriculture that it has become the standard of beauty among farmers. A good-looking crop field is one where all the plants are the same height and color;

individuals that stick out are an embarrassment. A breeder I know came up with a wheat variety whose genetics were intentionally diverse, and while its yields were strong the test plot it produced was visually erratic. He showed it to a local farmer, who was not impressed. "If my fields looked like this," he said, "my neighbors would think I was having marital problems."

The reason for this preference is simple: uniformity means greater efficiency and predictability, and in turn higher yields. A farmer can plant a thousand acres of a single variety and know that each plant will behave more or less exactly the same. When breeders create a single plant that is immune to a disease, every acre that's planted with its purebred offspring will be safe. However, the flip side is dangerous. Because nature is not static, this insurance of uniform immunity is temporary. When a host plant stops a disease at the door, the pathogen does not just die for lack of a place to grow. Instead, it evolves to overcome the plant's immunity. When this happens, suddenly all those thousand acres of a single variety are struck by a new version of the disease—one to which they are not immune. They all act the same, but this time they will suffer, even die.

It has happened before, most famously in the Irish potato famine. In 1845, the majority of Ireland's potato crop was planted with a single variety, the lumper. When the fungus *Phytophthora infestans* ("plant killer") arrived from North America, the lumper proved to have no immunity; every potato succumbed and famine ensued. Never one to soften the edges, David does not rule out the chance that we may face just that sort of scenario—and not in the distant future.

"Modern plant breeders have been able to succeed in what they've done only because the ten thousand years before them they had gardeners selecting seed through pure observation," he says. "The modern breeder has taken that material and narrowed the genetics down to the highest yielding strains. Sure, it's produced a lot of food, but it has also backed us into a corner. Because of this narrow genetic composition, our food supply is *very* vulnerable to collapse. If we don't change something soon, we're going to be caught with our pants down."

———•———

As both a plant breeder and a farmer, David values beauty—it's a top criterion in his selection process. But probably it is no surprise that he doesn't define beauty the way conventional farmers do. In fact, he doesn't define it all. When I once asked him to, he recoiled. "It's NON-QUANTIFIABLE," he said, "and this is VERY IMPORTANT in this age when we want to quantify everything to the nth degree. I mean, everyone knows what beauty is, you just can't define it. You shouldn't have to."

And that's just the point. Beauty is unquantifiable in part because each person has a different sense of what is beautiful. I remember an autumn afternoon when David, Theresa, and I stood around the hundred or so pumpkins they had chosen to save seed from. It was another Podoll original in the works, though to my eyes they looked like just a group of plain, orange pumpkins. Then David pointed out his ideal individual. Theresa wrinkled her nose and said she didn't like the color.

"What do you mean?" he said. "It's the perfect punkin orange!"

"I think it's puky." She pointed to another as the perfect shade.

"But that's the same color!" David said.

"No," Theresa replied. "It's less brown, more orange."

My favorite was a tall one with smooth sides and full shoulders. Theresa picked one that was fat and round, with deeply grooved "Cinderella ribs." David stood by, hands on his hips, pleased by the impromptu experiment. It demonstrated perfectly the role beauty plays in plant breeding, which is to maintain variety within the gene pool.

"If you have all these gardeners saving all these different seeds, you have this whole range of beauty," he explains. "Doesn't this just add to the earth's life force, and grandness, and greatness? Creation is a wonderful thing, but what are we doing to it? We need to allow it to flourish and express itself in a lot of different ways. Instead we're inhibiting it."

There is a sort of parable about the reductive nature of modern plant breeding. It is the story of the Crimson Sprinter, a tomato that the Podolls have been growing in their garden since the 1970s. David got the seed through Seed Savers Exchange, an informal, nationwide fraternity of people who save seeds. Each year they publish a catalog of who has what, which members use as a guide for trading seeds by mail. Thirty years ago, whoever had the Crimson Sprinter didn't want to grow it anymore, so David adopted it. The tomato's seed was stored in university and government seed banks in the United States and Canada, but as far as David could tell he was the only person actually growing the plant.

Created in the 1960s by plant breeder Thomas O. Graham, the Crimson Sprinter was released to the public in 1969. Graham did his research at the University of Guelph, in Ontario, the region that produced the lion's share of Canada's tomatoes. His work was to breed varieties that would perform well in Ontario's short growing season, which went from cool, sometimes frost-bitten springs, to sweltering summers, to early falls. Because Ontario's growers were still picking tomatoes by hand, he also sought to make varieties that would enable mechanical harvest: plants that were low and compact, and matured all at once.

Graham was known as a tireless worker who spent his nights in the office and his days doing manual labor in the test plots. His specialty was creating purebred tomato varieties, then crossing them with themselves and others repeatedly to reduce the genes down to exactly what was desirable. The tangle of inbreeding that produced Crimson Sprinter involved varieties such as Pink Tanggula, Campbell #128, Guelph #81, Early Bird, and Earliest of All, many of which came from the same stock of genes. If you likened the map of them to a human's family tree, the incest would be arresting— great-grandparents mated with children, then two generations later the progeny crossed back to a parent.

One lineage in particular kept returning, in varieties including the child High Crimson, the grandparent Kannatto, and the great-grandparent Philippine #2. These all descended from the Narcarlang, a tomato that was sent to Ontario in 1948 from Bangued, in the far northern Philippines. It wasn't a lab-bred variety, but rather a wild tomato from the jungle whose habit was described as an "ungainly" sprawl. Narcarlang's fruits, which were small, rough, purplish, and "muddy"-colored, had no commercial value in North America. It was the plant's vigor that was desirable. Graham wrote that Narcarlang plants had been witnessed to survive and bear fruit in areas with one-hundred-inch rainfall, remarkable to anyone who has tried to grow tomatoes during a rainy summer. The plants were sent to North America in hopes that through breeding, some of the plant's finer genetics could be extracted and placed into tomatoes with more marketable fruits.

Initially the idea had been to breed Narcarlang with North American varieties to produce a canning tomato that would withstand the Philippines' extreme humidity. If the work was successful, this variety would then be returned to the Philippines in order to enable a canning tomato industry there. But Graham and others found that Narcarlang had things to offer them as well. The plant could handle both drought and dampness. It was tolerant of phytophthera, the disease that caused the Irish potato famine and could be devastating to tomatoes. Most importantly, its ability to withstand the heat of the Philippine jungle also somehow conferred an unusual capacity to withstand low temperatures. The Narcarlang germinated even at forty-five degrees, ten degrees lower than most tomatoes, a trait that could be useful in the cold, late Ontario springs. Early on, researchers in Guelph selected out the most useful of Narcarlang's offspring, the variety that would be called Philippine #2. It became a cornerstone of Graham's breeding program.

But here was the problem: along with everything else, Philippine #2 gave its progeny "the crimson gene," which made its fruit intensely red. (Most tomatoes' color is a combination of red and yellow, but Dan tells me that tests have found Crimson Sprinter to be 100 percent red.) It makes for a beautiful tomato, but researchers soon realized that the color came at the expense of reduced beta-carotene content. Tomatoes possessing the crimson gene were denounced as having reduced nutritional value, and by and large all the varieties that had it were shelved. That included the Crimson Sprinter.

When David got his Crimson Sprinters from the Seed Savers Exchange, he knew nothing of this. All he knew was that when he grew the seeds in the garden the tomatoes they produced were delicious, and that was enough for him. He saved back seeds from the best plants and replanted them, year after year, adapting them to the farm. Today the Podolls grow a quantity of them in the plot out by the road, to supply a seed company based in New Mexico. Meanwhile, other Seed Savers have adopted the tomato. In the 2008 catalog of who-has-what, Crimson Sprinter seeds were offered by a woman in Indiana, who got hers from a fellow farmer at the Shelby County Farmers Market; by a man in eastern Georgia who claims to have grown over one thousand varieties of tomatoes and was currently offering 307; and by a woman in upstate New York, who got hers from a woman in Ontario, who had got hers from Plant Gene Resources of Canada, a government seed bank.

The ironic coda to the story is that at the same time the Seed Savers were embracing the Crimson Sprinter, the crimson gene was being resurrected by the seed industry. As it turns out, the deep red color that the gene imparted (and the consequent reduced beta carotene levels) happened because of increased levels of lycopene, a carotenoid whose best natural source is tomatoes. Breeders in the 1970s knew this, but they didn't realize that lycopene itself had any value. After researchers discovered in the 1980s that lycopene is an antioxidant with potentially miraculous anti-cancer powers, the tomato industry trumpeted the news. Suddenly ketchup makers were touting their product's health benefits—today Heinz runs a lycopene information website. The crimson gene came off the shelf and was paraded about, its promoters making it widely known that the gene increases a tomato's lycopene content by 50 percent. Today, the gene is found in production varieties for Heinz and Campbell's Soup and has been bred into commercial varieties grown by all the major vegetable seed companies.

The lesson of this parable is, of course, be careful what you throw away—you never know what you might be losing. Indeed, the Crimson Sprinters in the Podolls' garden may be proving to have another valuable characteristic: resistance to the fungal disease septoria. Also known as leaf spot, the disease thrives in damp conditions and attacks tomato plant foliage. In advanced cases, it causes leaves to fall off, allowing the fruit beneath to be scorched by the sun and fail to mature.

Professional plant breeders have not come up with a tomato that resists septoria; then again, they haven't paid much attention to looking for one. More serious threats are diseases like phytophthera, and spraying fungicides for them will take care of any septoria spores. Plus, for professional breeders the money is in producing varieties for commercial production, and septoria doesn't impact those as much as it does heirlooms and other "garden" varieties. But suppose you wanted to grow old-fashioned tomatoes in a damp place and not spray them with fungicides. What variety could you grow? That's what David and Dan are working on.

Their technique is old-fashioned observation and their laboratory is, predictably, the garden. In mid-summer you cannot see the ground in places, it is so thick with plants. Tomatoes, potatoes, sweet corn here, flint corn there. Feathery carrot tops, young leeks, bushy asparagus. Vines of purple-flowered shelling beans and skinny green beans cover the high fence surrounding this place, weaving themselves through the wire mesh. Stalks from last year's corn stick up through the mulch. A frog sits in the shade of tomato leaves.

The brothers' growing medium is rich black soil covered in last year's leaves and stems. David calls it a "stew of disease" they have created intentionally by mulching with last year's plants (including those that had septoria) and by cloistering this humid garden within walls thick with beans. Every other vegetable in the garden rotates through the rows each year so it won't be directly exposed to pests from the previous season. But for the purpose of breeding better tomatoes, the brothers replant them in the same place every year. They even place a sprinkler in the row to set the right conditions for septoria. The brothers figure that if they smother the place with disease, the tomatoes will be forced to draw on their genetic memory of how to resist it.

When Dan toured me through the tomatoes, he began by handing me a ripe one to eat. He then brought me to a patch of tomatoes that had succumbed completely to septoria, a variety called Silvery Fir Tree. In the mess of dead leaves, a volunteer plant had pushed its way through, looking perfectly healthy. It was a Crimson Sprinter. Dan grinned.

Next was a whole patch of Crimson Sprinters, the best-looking tomatoes in the garden. He told me they were planted from seeds taken off last year's sickest plants. Kneeling beside them, he snapped off a leaf and brought it two inches from his nose. He tipped his head down and inspected the specimen, looking through the slit between the top of his glasses and the brim of his cap, as if there were an invisible microscope there. He showed me that around each septoria spore the plant had decommissioned a ring of cells, like a moat. Sequestered like that, the disease could live but not reproduce. Its damage was controlled.

The brothers may never know why or how these things happen, and that's okay. They aren't concerned with isolating the single gene that confers resistance to septoria and breeding it into a line of plants with commercial qualities. Their objective is simply to create a stronger population of tomato plants, one that can survive septoria as well as all the other stresses of life in the garden.

Down the row is another patch of plants, these ones packed together tightly, all tall and leggy as they compete for sun. It's an experiment aimed at encouraging the plants to turn on mysterious internal coping mechanisms such as transposons and epigenetics. More commonly known under the broad term "mutation," this sort of transformation comes in response to extreme environmental stress, such as the severe disease pressure they've created in the garden. To survive, a plant can reshuffle its DNA or express it in a different way; it's how an individual plant that is genetically isolated is able to evolve. The professional plant breeding community is divided over whether this is possible, but the brothers feel sure. Their Crimson Sprinters have already produced one unique new plant, what's known as a "sport," and this experimental plot reflects the hope that they might produce another that is immune to septoria. It's a rare occurrence, nothing a person can induce, but the brothers figure the more times they try the more likely it will be. So in spring, when they transplanted the young Crimson Sprinters that they had started in the greenhouse, they sowed this patch directly with seeds—three thousand of them at once. Now they just have to wait and see.

———•———

The Podolls are not, as they say, rocket scientists. All their breeding work could be replicated by anyone with enough interest, patience, and space in the garden. Their process is informed by modern science, but at the core it is the same as what farmers and gardeners have done for millennia. There is one hitch, though. In order for the process to work, a person has to stick with the plants year after year, shepherding the slow change. But the vast majority of people who grow plants don't do that anymore. Most rely on professional breeders to make the changes for them, and instead buy their seed new each year. A century ago that would have seemed odd to a farmer, even silly; buying seed would have been like buying bottles of water when you could get it free from the well. But over time, breeders have learned how to design varieties with benefits so substantial that they make the expense of buying seed worthwhile.

The first example of this—the thing that laid the foundation for the modern seed industry—was hybrid corn. In the early twentieth century, after years of trial and error, researchers showed that hybrid corn varieties reliably yielded more than any corn the world had seen before. The only problem was that if you save seeds from a hybrid and plant them the following year, the offspring won't necessarily be the same as the parents; in order to get the same, high-yielding plants, farmers would have to buy the seed every year. Initially farmers were reluctant, but because their yields increased so substantially the trade-off was soon seen as worth it. The first commercial hybrid corn was introduced in 1923 and became widely available in the 1930s. As even just a few farmers bought the new seed, their yields increased enough to raise the bar for everyone. It took only a decade for adoption to spread across the Corn Belt, and by 1965, 95 percent of United States corn acreage was planted with hybrids—adoption of the new varieties had become necessary simply to stay in the business. Today, you'd be hard-pressed to find a conventional American corn farmer who doesn't buy seed every year.

A similar compromise has taken place more recently with genetically modified, or GMO, plants. These plants are engineered to have traits they couldn't possess naturally, for instance, to be resistant to herbicide. Normally a farmer would control weeds by running a mechanical weeder through a crop multiple times each season. With the GMO version, the farmer can simply spray the field with herbicide, which kills everything except the crop. The greatest benefit is time saved, which allows the farmer to farm more acres and thus, the logic goes, have a better chance at staying in business.

Again, there is a catch: GMOs work the way they do because they are given certain genes, which are patented by the corporations that breed them. Because those companies' profit comes from selling farmers seed and herbicide every year, to ensure this annual sale they have farmers sign a contract stating they will not save seed. To monitor and enforce this prohibition, the contract grants the corporation access to the farmer's fields and accounting records—even if the farmer stops buying their seed. Farmers agree to use only that company's herbicides and other chemicals on the plants. They also waive their protections under the Federal Privacy Act. The contracts are non-negotiable and farmers must agree to them before making their purchases. In case they don't, there's a safety clause: opening the bag of GMO seed constitutes signing on the dotted line. Between 1997 and 2007, the world's largest seed company, the Monsanto Corporation, brought 112 cases against a total of 372 farmers for violation of its patents. At last count, the company had been awarded more than twenty-one million dollars in damages.

Monsanto's contract is called a "Technology/Stewardship Agreement," an ironic choice if you believe, as David does, that the patenting of plants is in fact a direct assault on the very concept of stewardship. When farmers lose the right to save seed, they can no longer care for plant populations from year to year and adapt them to their land. The plants cannot evolve. Equally important, the farmers cease to be stewards of those plants. Instead they become like contractors, hired to do the piecework of growing out someone else's seeds each year. "The very essence of agriculture is this act of participating intimately in the ongoing evolutionary process of these plants," David says. "I mean, that's the way it all started! With patents and ownership, you lose the essence of farming culture at its core."

And yet the numbers speak for themselves. The adoption of GMOs has increased steadily since they were introduced in the

1990s, and in 2008, 92 percent of all soybean acres in the United States were planted with genetically engineered varieties, along with 86 percent of cotton and 80 percent of corn. In North Dakota the numbers were even higher: 89 percent of corn and 94 percent of soybeans.

The decision to sign the necessary contract is individual to each farmer. Plenty do so without a moment's thought, even with great conviction in the value of biotechnology; others struggle with the sacrifice they feel in forfeiting their right to save seed. In the end, though, all those papers for all those acres are ultimately signed. Taken as a whole, they are stunning evidence of the change that has taken place over the past hundred years. Whereas farmers began the twentieth century as essential stewards of the seed they planted, they enter the twenty-first century almost entirely dependent on the seed industry for this critical resource. Today, the vast majority of farmers wouldn't believe that it is within their power to do the work of breeding plants themselves. Indeed, most have forgotten they ever did.

6

Before July 15, 2007, nobody had seen anything like it, at least not anyone around this part of North Dakota. A hailstorm fifty-four miles long and at times fifteen miles wide, five separate tornadoes within its sweep. Hail the size of golf balls whipped around in eighty mile-an-hour winds. It took vinyl siding off of buildings and bark off of trees.

The majority of the land in the seventy mile-long strip that the storm hit was cropland, and for most of that, the "white combine" brought the end of the season early. Corn stalks as tall as grown men were reduced to six-inch skeletons. Fields of spring wheat not long from being harvested looked like they had been plowed under. The storm knocked out two hundred and fifty thousand acres in Cass County alone, one of four counties where the governor declared a disaster and called in FEMA. According to extension agent John Kringler, the losses later proved to be a "double whammy" for the farmers: when commodity prices skyrocketed during the following winter and growers around the country were cashing in like never before, these guys had nothing to sell.

Dan told me the storm passed just north of their farm but brought them only rain. He is a devoted home-meteorologist, a guy who can tick off a half hour looking at online radar maps to see what high-pressure system is moving where or how dew points are pooling. For him, the storm was a fascinating anomaly. Watching his eyes, wide-open as he recounted the storm's details, I guessed there was a sliver of him that wished he had witnessed it himself. But in another way it was not surprising at all, rather a predictable link in a larger chain of events. For the Podolls, the hailstorm was just one more piece of evidence that in LaMoure County, North Dakota, climate change had begun.

That was not the prevailing opinion. Locals agreed that it was a "severe summer storm" and an "unusually large system," but in these parts, climate change is still largely considered a theory. A 2008 editorial about global warming in the *LaMoure Chronicle* ended with, "This could go on and on but the main thing is that people are jumping to wild eyed fear mongering conclusions on something that will probably never happen." In an earlier Associated Press article with the headline "Talk of global warming gets chilly reception in N.D.," a LaMoure farmer told the reporter, "I don't know where this global warming comes from . . . We've had hot summers, we've had cool summers . . . I think it's just somebody trying to start something."

David was quoted in the AP article, too, as an "organic farmer and gardener . . . who does believe global warming has arrived on the Great Plains." What the article didn't mention is that he had been recording the farm's meteorological details every day since 1973. He was meticulous about it; if he went out of town, someone had to cover for him. Over time, he saw clear shifts in the farm's climate. So clear, in fact, that he stopped keeping the records. "We know what happened," Dan explained. "At a certain point there was no need to track climate change anymore, because it was here."

Spinning off of the hailstorm story, Dan gave me evidence of climate change that to him is staggering. "For starters, pooling dew points are higher every year," he said. "Just last week, there was a dew point of eighty-three in Saskatoon." When I told him that was not something that registered with me as shocking—that in fact, it didn't register at all—he nodded. "Well, yeah. Weather is something you experience every day, but you don't notice it unless you mean to. That's true even for farmers."

What has happened in their area is not the simplistic, literal translation of global warming that makes for a nudge and a wink every time it snows in April ("Doesn't feel like global warming to me!"). What they're experiencing is more accurately called a climate change, in that the climate that southeastern North Dakota has had for as long as anyone can remember is changing. It is, in a word, wetter. As Dan explains it, higher temperatures across the West and a heating of the upper atmosphere are making it so moisture that would normally stop at the Rockies is sailing over and landing in North Dakota. On the radar, he can see the huge vapor trail streaming over from the Pacific. Likewise, moisture from the Southern Plains is heading north into the Dakotas and Manitoba. Since 1992, rainfall on the Podolls' farm has been 150 percent of normal.

You can feel the increased moisture in the air—dew points, just like Dan said. You can also see the rain in the landscape. This area is called the "prairie pothole" region for the land's many small natural depressions filled with water and cattails. The potholes are shallow, and as the rains have increased they have spilled over in every direction. Now each year entire sections of cropland are abandoned to standing water, left as flat mirrors to reflect the blue sky all summer long. Here and there among them are big trees rotted, dead, their long limbs stretched out in what seem like illogical positions now that they are bare of leaves. Along the side of the road sit bales of hay just sagging, folding in on themselves.

One reason the Podolls recognize climate change more than their neighbors is because of the way that they're farming. Nearly everyone around here deals with weeds by spraying herbicide. It knocks down everything except their crops, which are genetically engineered to withstand it. The Podolls rely instead on cultural practices such as crop rotation, which manages weeds by alternating crops to suppress them. For instance, the first year of a rotation they'll plant a crop that's sowed early in the season. Its weeds, such as mustard, will also be early, and they'll go to seed along with the crop. The next year when those mustard seeds come up early in the season, the Podolls will till them in and then plant a different crop, one that's planted later. Along with that late crop will grow a late weed such as pigweed, which will also go to seed. The next year they'll switch back to the early crop, so that by the time the pigweed germinates the crop will be tall enough to crowd it out. Every year, bit by bit, the weed seed bank is diminished.

Or at least that's the way it's supposed to work. With the wide temperature swings they're having because of climate change, they see pigweed germinating two months early because April is so warm, and then mustard seeds coming up in July when the temperature is at fifty—thirty degrees below normal. And it's not just the weeds. Torrential spring rains have kept their vegetable seeds from germinating in the seed plot. Summer humidity and low temperatures are what brought on septoria in their tomatoes.

The biggest loss has been wheat. Beginning in the 1990s they had to plant the crop later each year because of the increasing springtime moisture. By the time the plants started forming the heads that produce grain, the temperatures were reaching the eighties—too hot for grain to form well. Planted late the crop was also more susceptible to disease, a threat doubled by the rising humidity. For years they planted a variety that could fend off the pathogens, but eventually its resistance broke down. The neighbors who kept growing wheat sprayed fungicides to fight disease, but the Podolls ran out of options. In 2005, after growing wheat for more than fifty years, they had to give it up.

———

Less than a year after the hailstorm hit southeastern North Dakota, the world began to panic about food. Hungry people rioted in Mexico and India, Haiti and Yemen. Before the end of March, more than one newspaper had declared 2008 "The Year of the Global Food Crisis." The dire circumstances reverberated in newspaper headlines across the world:

"High Food, Fuel Prices Drive up the Number of Hungry People"

"Hoarding Countries Drive Food Costs even Higher"

"Food Aid to Poorest Countries Slashed as Price of Grain Soars"

"Hungry Hordes Storm Border"

"Is the World Food System Fixable?"

"Will the Food Run Out?"

Of particular concern was wheat. In April, U.S. Secretary of Agriculture Ed Schaefer told the International Food Aid Conference that the world had "never been less secure about the near-term future of wheat." Global stocks had hit their lowest point in thirty years, and U.S. wheat stocks were at sixty-year lows. In Pakistan, paramilitary troops had been assigned to protect trucks transporting wheat and flour.

There was a tangle of reasons why the world's wheat supply was in trouble. Over the long term, industrialization had changed global diets and increased demand for wheat. In the short term, high prices for corn and the demand for ethanol in the United States had switched acreage out of wheat production. As supplies dwindled, players in the commodity market drove prices higher with speculation. A rapacious disease called African stem rust was making its way across the Middle East and into India, laying waste to all the wheat it touched. Perhaps most importantly, there had been a series of crop failures in major wheat producing areas. A too-dry fall and too-wet spring had ruined the American winter crop harvested in 2007. In Australia a seven-year drought left colossal grain silos empty. Britain's Special Representative on Climate Change told Reuters that the drought was "almost certainly, or at least very probably" the result of climate change.

Agriculture Secretary Schaefer responded to the crisis with a three-point plan, which he presented in June 2008 at a meeting of the United Nations' Food and Agriculture Organization. He called for improved plant breeds that would boost yields, specifically hybrids and new genetically engineered varieties of major food crops. The seed industry followed suit. The day after Schaefer's speech, Monsanto released its own three-point plan, also focused on creating crop varieties with increased yields. "In short, the world needs to produce more while conserving more," Monsanto's CEO, Hugh Grant, said. "As an agricultural company focused on increasing crop yields, we will do our part." It was the traditional fight song of agribusiness: *More*, Schaefer and Grant said, nearly in unison. *We must simply figure out how to make more.*

With regard to wheat, the statements were particularly provocative. Currently there is very little hybrid wheat and no commercially grown GMO wheat. That is to say, wheat remains one of the few crops with which farmers still save back their seed each year. They generally aren't involved with breeding or "evolving" the wheat they keep—they buy new seed every few years to take advantage of new, improved varieties—but they also aren't tied to the cycle of buying new seed every single year. Indeed, this is central to why wheat is also one of the few commodity crops that is not yet grown as a GMO: farmers have not wanted to give up that right to save seed.

There have been attempts to introduce genetically engineered wheat, but it has never gotten off the ground. This is in large part because it came on the scene later than the GMO versions of other major crops—which is to say, after wheat farmers had already watched consumer rejection of GMOs cripple exports of those other major food crops. When Monsanto's herbicide resistant wheat was nearing commercial release, farmers resisted it. In North Dakota, the significant organic grain-growing community was particularly vocal in the opposition. (Theresa, of course, was on the front lines.) After months of argument, Monsanto shelved the product because of what it called "a lack of widespread wheat industry alignment."

With climate change, genetically engineered wheat may have another chance. Researchers are trumpeting a new solution for the challenges of growing food on a warming planet, in the form of a new generation of GMO crops that are "climate ready." Hundreds of patents have been filed around the world for the use of genes that might help food plants withstand the extreme conditions that climate change will bring. For wheat that means varieties that are drought-resistant, designed either to withstand drier conditions or to produce consistent yields despite fluctuating amounts of moisture. To a farmer who has watched his crops wither and die while waiting for rain, such a promise is tantalizing. In Australia, where the multi-year drought has left massive grain silos empty, field trials have already begun.

———

Meanwhile, in North Dakota, David and seven other organic farmers have been devising a solution of their own. Working with two researchers from North Dakota State University, the farmers formed a group called the Farm Breeder Club. They, too, intended to breed a wheat for the future, but using a totally different set of priorities. As they saw it the current food crisis was linked to a much bigger issue. Over the past century the industrialized world built an agricultural system using a scaffold of external supports: cheap fuel to run machinery; fertilizer manufactured from natural gas; imported water for irrigation; pesticides to eliminate insects, weeds, and diseases. With these inputs, fantastic yields were achieved, the likes of which the world had never seen. When turned into vast quantities of inexpensive food, those yields allowed the world population to grow exponentially. That, in turn, created greater demand for more food. The problem was that the scaffold became inseparable from the system itself. Agriculture could not function—the world could not eat—without those external supports, yet suddenly they were running out. Oil and gas reserves were dwindling, aquifers were being drained. And, in spite of the skeptics in LaMoure County, climate change had already begun to amplify the challenges.

According to David and his comrades, more of the same scaffold-supported, yield-fixated production was not the solution; to feed the world now and in the future, agriculture would have to learn to stand on its own two feet. Likewise plant breeding: for decades, the focus has been on creating high-yielding crops designed for the conventional system. Called "prima donnas" by detractors, these breeds thrive only in a narrow environment supported by chemical fertilizers, pesticides, and often irrigation. But the Farm Breeder Club wanted to create just the opposite: workhorse varieties that would thrive without the scaffold and be resilient enough to withstand whatever curveballs climate change threw them.

The Podolls were already growing a plant that could serve as a model—one that was, to use David's words, truly enduring. It was a proso millet called Crown, which the family had grown and saved back every year since they bought the farm in 1953. On most modern varieties the head of the plant is tightly closed, but this one's is a loose, open spray of stems, which allows it to shade out weeds below. It also makes for a beautiful plant, whose thick, grassy understory of green is topped with a dapple the color of lemons. The slightest breeze turns a field of this millet into a rippling yellow ocean.

More importantly, this millet has muscle. Its seeds are smaller than the head of a dressmaker's pin and yet they can emerge from four inches down in bone-dry soil. Once grown, it can kill off Canada thistle plants that dare to emerge in its midst. And because it has adapted itself so perfectly to the farm, in fifty-five years this millet has never failed the Podolls. In years when it has not rained a drop, this millet still produced a crop of excellent quality. In 1982, when it was hailed down to the ground in mid-July, the stalks grew back and made a crop that was harvested in September. As David and Dan watched their wheat crops succumb to disease, they couldn't help but think about the millet and wonder, *What if we had a wheat like this?*

The natural place to go with such a concern would be North Dakota State University (NDSU), the state's land grant college. But for years their public breeding efforts have been geared toward serving the conventional wheat industry. Aside from a few rogue researchers, the university has shown little interest in breeding for organic farming systems. So David and the others have instead done what farmers do when they need something accomplished: they figured out how to do it themselves. First they conducted scientific comparisons of dozens of wheat varieties, modern releases from NDSU as well as heirloom varieties, some of which were more than a century old. Guided by two NDSU researchers, Steve Zwinger and Pat Carr, the farmers replicated the sorts of tests done in university research fields, right down to the tedious data collection. The difference was that they executed the tests on their own farms, without chemicals, and judged according to their own criteria—bushels per acre, yes, but also things like how quickly the plant emerged and how well it shaded out weeds. They were looking for varieties that might work on their farms without the scaffold, as well as for those that they might crossbreed to create new kinds of wheat.

Before they ever reached that point, luck brought a new variety to them. It came in the hands of a professor emeritus at Oregon State University named Mat Kolding, a white-haired plant breeder who is long since retired but still goes to the test plots every day of the growing season. He was born on a farm in Shawnee, North Dakota, a few hours north of the Podolls, and before his university career he, too, was a wheat farmer. Perhaps that's part of the reason why as a plant breeder he still values the old-fashioned methods of observation. For him, being out in the field just looking at what happens naturally is an essential part of the work. "If you listen to the plants," he says, "they'll tell you a lot."

The town where he grew up no longer exists aside from a sign on the railroad tracks, but the farm is still intact and until recently his mother lived there. In 1993, while Mat was visiting, he took a walk through the forty-acre field next to the house. It was rented to a local farmer and, like every other field in North Dakota that year, was infested with a disease called head scab. Mat says when you walk through a crop you can tell how good the yield will be by the feel of the plants. As he walked through this field, it felt like nothing more than a bunch of grass, his pantslegs barely registering the scrawny leaves and stems.

"And then, aha!" He loves to tell the story. "There was a plant shouting, *Here I am! Take me!*" Estimating one hundred and twenty thousand plants to an acre, Mat guesses there were close to five million wheat plants in that field, and in the middle of them all was a single one untouched by the disease. Mat pulled it out, brought it home to Oregon, and seeded it in his garden in the spring. For ten years he selected out the best offspring and planted back their seed the following year. In time he came up with a strong variety, which he gave the unceremonious name KW960175.

When Mat heard about the Farm Breeder Club in 2004, he sent them some seed. There were no strings attached, he just hoped the farmers would be able to make something of it. "Everything we do is built on something somebody else did in the past," he explains. "Borrowing material, building on others' work—that's the only way you can start making progress. After all I had learned from farming in North Dakota over the years, I figured it would be good to give something back."

After a few seasons of making selections on KW960175, the Farm Breeder Club came up with its own variety. It was high-yielding and resistant to diseases including stem rust and fusarium head blight. When they tested it for industrial milling and baking qualities it came up somewhat short, but when they tested it with artisan bakers it got high marks for flavor and quality. Most of all, it grew well without chemical fertilizers and herbicides. It wasn't the perfect wheat; to begin with, because it came from a single parent it lacked genetic variation. Still, it was a good starting place.

In 2006, three farmers in North Dakota grew it on 68.1 acres. The next year their harvest was sold as seed under the name FBC-Dylan—"FBC" the acronym for the Club and "Dylan" for researcher Steve Zwinger's son. In 2007, FBC-Dylan was planted on close to four hundred acres by fifteen farmers: eleven in North Dakota, one in South Dakota, and three in faraway Maine. In 2008, twenty-five farmers in six states (now including Vermont, New York, and Minnesota) planted it across two thousand, four hundred acres.

The Podolls themselves cannot share in the accomplishment directly. Most growers in the Farm Breeder Club are west of LaMoure, where it's drier. Even FBC-Dylan isn't disease resistant enough for the Podolls to plant it on a commercial scale in their wet climate, at least not yet. Still, David has a patch of it planted near the garden, alongside several other varieties of wheat. He will select seed from the best plants and hope for a gradual improvement, however slowly it comes. He will also make sure to walk among the plants as they grow, just in case there's a plant looking different, looking better, trying to get his attention.

Really, though, David measures the value of FBC-Dylan in terms much bigger than the success or failure of his own crop. For him it is significant as a first step toward restoring the vital partnership between farmers and the plants they grow. Consider again the scaffold of dependency built around modern agriculture. As artificial inputs and external supports have become integral parts of our food production, they have eliminated the farmer—the steward. Of course farmers are still called upon to perform the perfunctory acts of buying seeds and applying fertilizer and driving machinery, but no longer are they asked to think or care or protect. When

David agonizes over how farmers drive their combines from one field to another without ever touching the soil, this is the loss he is mourning.

While the Farm Breeder Club aim is to create food plants that can stand on their own two feet, without the scaffold, it is equally about restoring this essential human role of stewardship. That's because when the scaffold is taken away, what replaces it is the farmer. The real value of the Farm Breeder Club's wheat is that it is designed to begin that restoration. To make FBC-Dylan an enduring variety will require the humans who grow it to steward it from year to year, watching its habits and changes and helping it to become something better. To use David's words, the farmers will need to reestablish their intimate participation in the evolutionary process.

What makes that possible is a single, small but salient point: FBC-Dylan belongs to no one. Instead of a corporate contract, each shipment of seed comes with a letter from the Farm Breeder Club. In it the Club encourages recipients to save organic seed and to promote it with their neighbors. They also ask that if the recipients sell some of the harvest as seed, that they collect a 10 percent development fee and return that to the Club to support its future work. The whole thing is done on the honor system. At the bottom of the letter, instead of a dotted line to sign, there is just a quote: "Seeds are our past, present, and future. May we always posses the wisdom and knowledge to use them appropriately."

7

OCTOBER. LOW SKIES and drizzling rain. It's ten o'clock in the morning but it could be mid-afternoon or first thing in the morning—one of those days when only the dimming of dusk reminds you that the sun did in fact rise. As I drive in to the Podolls', the farm appears to be deserted. I park and get out, not sure where to go until I hear a thumping noise coming from the old red turkey barn. The whole building stretches about eighty yards and is composed of two separate areas that each once housed about one thousand birds. Connecting them is a much smaller room, where last year the Podolls raised a small flock for themselves. As I walk up to the outside of the barn, the thumping is joined by a whirring mechanical sound. I slide open the doors.

The room is the size of a three-car garage, with walls of plywood and high ceilings supported by rafters. Someone has pulled in a halogen shop light on a ten-foot stand to cut the darkness, and its blaring light makes this room look like a Hollywood set. In its spotlight are Theresa and Dan. He is a cold-weather version of himself: safety-orange sweatshirt over various layers of T-shirts and sweatshirts, white baseball cap as always. She is determined not to be cold: jeans tucked into rubber boots; a thick, long denim jacket whose metal buttons say SEARS; a gray fleece tube that rises from inside her top, around her neck and over her head, the drawstring cinched tight around her face. Both are wearing blue plastic gloves. Both have a round stain of mud and grit caked onto their outerwear, right on their bellies. Behind them is the red Toyota pickup, its bed filled with dark green winter squashes the size of volleyballs.

Today is one of several days to harvest and clean the squash seed they will sell to two seed companies this year. They have done watermelon and pumpkins for years, but this is the first time they've grown and processed winter squash. This particular variety began forty years ago, when David started selecting from some buttercup squashes in the garden. Since then the family has tasted every squash they ever saved seed from, and the result is a rich, orange squash with a creamy feel. They selected it away from the buttercup's round shape and toward having square shoulders, which store more flesh and make for a higher yield of edible parts. They also selected for diversity, each year dividing the crop into groups from most desirable to least and keeping seed from across the board. Last year they named the finished product Uncle David's Dakota Dessert; last spring they planted a crop out by the road, and now, in late October, it's ready to harvest and sell.

The next challenge, the one they face today, is how to turn twelve thousand pounds of dirt-clod-covered squash into a package of tidy white seeds that the seed company will buy. They know some parts of the process just from having done it for their own

consumption over the years. When the squash ripened earlier this
month, they kicked the fruits off the vine and left them in the field
for a few weeks, during which time each one's juices redistributed,
making the skin thicker, the flesh sweeter, and the seeds firm and
plump. But now that the crop has been "cured," the question marks
begin. Big growers harvest the seeds with what is essentially a giant nut grinder, into which they feed the squash whole. While the
machine's crushing ruins many of the seeds, for that scale of production it's an acceptable loss. Dan figures they could do the same
if they bought a small mechanical separator, which might make
sense if they could also use it for watermelon and pumpkins. Then
again, they would lose maybe half their seeds to crushing, meaning
they would have to grow twice as many of all three crops, and that
doesn't make sense to them. As Dan explains, the goal here is to get
the maximum from the minimum.

If it were sunny today they would drive into the field and do
the work there. Instead, on this drizzly day, they are collecting the
squash truckful by truckful and bringing it into the barn. Next to
the truck, they've constructed a makeshift workstation consisting of
one steel barrel as a base, and on top of that a wide, shallow steel
bin. Dan tells me the bin used to be part of a turkey water can, then
was cut down to this size to serve some function with the truck.
Today it's a basin containing two wooden stumps and a mound of
squash.

The process they've devised is straightforward, with one person
opening the squash and the other person scooping out the middle.
They started off using a sledgehammer for the first step, as they do
with pumpkins and watermelon, but quickly found that it blew the

little squashes into unpredictable chunks, whose inconsistent size and shape slowed down their mini-assembly line. Now Theresa uses a small axe to break the squash into quarters, whacking it gingerly, like she is splitting kindling. Next they go to Dan. His tool is a vacuum hose, the black nib on its end cut into a scoop, which he runs along the walls of the squash's cavity. Everything inside—stringy pulp, bits of hard flesh, seeds plump and skinny—is sucked into the thick hose, then up through a white extension hose suspended from the ceiling by a loop of twine, then back down through a Shop-Vac top that's fitted onto a rusty barrel. The rest of the squash is tossed in a garbage can.

After I arrived I picked up an axe and we all worked together, talking as we split and scooped. Now we've drifted back into quiet, the only noise the thump-and-roll rhythm of axes, the whirring hum of the vacuum. The door slides open and in walks David in beige coveralls and a sweatshirt with the hood pulled over his head. While Theresa vacuums and Dan splits, David reports on a phone conversation he just had with one of their seed buyers. Among other things, they talked about poppy flowers, and specifically how the buyer will pay three hundred dollars an ounce for the seed. Dan starts working out the numbers of what kind of money that could mean and the room perks up for a second. I can't help but think of the curious neighbors—imagine the traffic jam a field of red opium poppies would cause.

The room goes quiet again. Together they complete the splitting, then the scooping, and finally only scraps remain in the bin. Dan runs his vacuum through, hitting spots of pulp until the bin is clean. David drags a garbage can full of squash hulls outside and a draft of cold, wet air slides in. As Theresa waits for them she goes through the seeds that have fallen outside the bin, bending down to pick some off the ground. She spreads them out on her hand and sorts out a few that seem flat and immature. The ones that are plump and white, about a dozen total, she carries across the room. She slides them off her palm and into the barrel with the rest. The group breaks for lunch.

———•———

The corn harvest in LaMoure County is on hold today because of rain, but yesterday it was happening in earnest. Combines were outfitted with pointed attachments like bird beaks, designed to nose their way through rows of corn, and all day long they went up and down field after field, sucking up the grain. Every so often each combine would stop to pour its grain into the tractor-trailer truck parked beside the field, and at the end of the afternoon all those trucks drove into town to unload at the grain elevator. By the time I arrived trucks were jammed up at the entrance, their cabs turned in toward the receiving office and their trailers stuck out at all angles across the street, like a jumble of pickup sticks dropped on the ground. As they sat there waiting their turns I watched the gray-blue sky of evening grow darker, bringing out red taillights, orange streetlights, and finally rain turned pink against the dusk. One by one the trucks drove in and parked in front of the office. Under the yellow floodlight, a cloud of steam rose as each new one opened the vent in its bottom and unloaded one thousand bushels of grain into the pit below.

In the yard beyond the office, things were noisy and alive. Trucks *beep beep beeping* in reverse and grain dryers moaning *wanh wanh wanh* like a band of lazy washing machines. Motors grinding to spin drive shafts that spun augurs that sucked grain from one place and shot it to another. The grating of metal against metal. The giant new storage bins had been completed on schedule and it looked like both would soon be filled to 682,789-bushel capacity. Above the yard hung an American flag, and another for North Dakota. On the ground below, splashes of corn like yellow paint.

Down the street, the lights were on at Wanda's. The café in the front had closed by then, but happy hour had begun in the back room, called Wanda's Bar and Supper Club. When I arrived two women had just sat down at the dinner tables with their husbands, but otherwise it was all men at the bar, alone and talking casually to their neighbors, never taking their eyes off the television above the shelves of liquor. I sat down next to an older man in a flannel shirt, jeans, and cowboy boots, who was drinking Coors Light and smoking long white cigarettes. While fumbling with the remote control in search of Monday Night Football, he told me about his day spent hunting pheasant. He wasn't a farmer, but rather the owner of the restaurant.

"So that would make you Mr. Wanda," I said. He didn't laugh.

In walked a tall, hefty man in a black jacket and black cap. He greeted Mr. Wanda, signaled the waitress, and in a moment drinks appeared before all three of us without a word.

"For me?" I asked.

"I don't like to drink alone," the new man said. He pushed the straw in his cocktail to the side and took a long draw from the glass.

He said he was from South Dakota, ran a custom combining business and was hired to come up for the corn harvest. Farms around here are so big a grower can't possibly harvest all of his own grain by himself, so every fall there's a migration of men and machines for these few weeks of work. Normally he'd stay close to Aberdeen for harvest—there's usually plenty of work right there at home—but last year was so dry they didn't even have a crop down there and he had to come up here for work. This year there was corn at home, but he came back out of loyalty. Said he'd rather be out pheasant hunting, but it's good work just the same. He hired his crew locally, mostly young South African men. They work on farms back at home, but come here from April to November to learn the ways of bigger acreage. This year there were thirty in LaMoure alone, and as far as Mr. Wanda was concerned they were all welcome—there simply aren't enough people here anymore.

The combiner left and in his place a younger guy in an army jacket and a camo hat sat down. He had glasses perched on his round nose and his long hair was in a ponytail. He ordered an Old Milwaukee and Mr. Wanda introduced him to me: Chad, a farmer who has lived here his entire life. He works six hundred and fifty acres and except for this time of year, when he hires someone to help him combine, he does all the work himself. Since March he had not had a day off, but the day before he had finished his harvest. That night he was there to celebrate having the time for a schedule that was more than just work, sleep, repeat. He drained his beer quickly and ordered another.

After a while I left the bar and walked down the railroad tracks to the old grain elevator. In the quiet night, the only evidence of recent human activity was a mountain of corn covering the grass. This often happens in fall. There isn't enough room to store all the grain properly so it's dumped on the ground until a better place opens up. Newspapers love to run photographs of these grain piles to illustrate the enormousness of a recent crop, but until you stand next to one it's hard to appreciate the true volume. This pile was twelve feet high, pyramidal in cross-section and sprawling the length of three train cars. A sand dune made of billions of kernels of corn. Parked alongside it were several tractors and an augur in position: one end down low to receive more grain from the bottom of another truck, the other end high above the mound, ready to pour it out.

As I stood there I thought back to the first time I saw this landscape from the interstate, how the endless string of crop fields blurred into one nameless green horizon. By slowing down and looking closely I had learned to see those fields as groups of individual plants, billions of them. Now I saw this grain pile as one of perhaps thousands throughout the middle of the country, all in towns like LaMoure. I had learned to see the forgettable flatness of the prairie as a vast and amazing expanse of land. Now I imagined the countless farmers spread across that land, who give their lives to growing corn that ends up in a pile on the ground in the middle of a deserted railroad yard.

I thought about Chad, who was happy to finally have time to drink beer and watch Monday Night Football. I wondered to myself if he wanted more than just that. I should have asked him, but then it's not exactly barstool talk for strangers. Instead I asked him about his crop. He predicted this year's harvest would be below average, thanks to a hot, rainless spell during summer. He knew incentives for ethanol production would bump corn prices higher than they'd been in a long time and that that would help, but he didn't think it was going to be the bonanza everyone had predicted. His face said *whatever*. Harvest was harvest, and in a month he'd be escaping the North Dakota winter in Arizona. He nursed his second beer and stared into space.

———•———

After lunch at the Podolls, the real challenge begins. Now that the squashes' insides have been scooped out, the seeds must be extracted from the pulp and then cleaned. It's wet work, too wet to do inside, so even though it's still raining the threesome puts on extra clothes and switches to an outdoor workstation. In front of the barn, they've set up an old laundry sink with a custom-made screen on top of the basins. This is where they do a final rinse on the seeds, a process that Dan has mastered. He uses a hose to perform a sort of winnowing, tilting the screen so that as the water sprays, the seeds go down and the remaining gunk goes up. When the seeds have been separated out and rinsed to lily white, he slides them off the screen and into a white bucket.

But before the seeds reach the final rinse, these three must figure out how the hell to clean off all the pulp. Picture the second stage of pumpkin carving, when you dip your hands into the bowl of pumpkin innards and squeeze the seeds off with your fingers. This is just like that, except it's not a bowl of seeds in a cozy living room but rather several garbage cans full in the rain. What's more, the innards of this squash are not mushy like a pumpkin's, they are dense

and cling to the seeds with force. The most effective way to separate them is the familiar one of putting the end of the seed between
thumb and forefinger and squeezing to sever the bond, but if the
Podolls did it that way they would be here until Thanksgiving.

That is not to say they haven't tried that approach. All three
have sat with hands in blue gloves and arms in buckets, squishing
the pulp with their fingers. But the work is tedious and inefficient,
not to mention cold and wet. They tried soaking the seeds for a few
days to loosen the gunk, hoping that then they would clean with less
effort, but it didn't work, as they are now finding out. Dan dumps
a bucket of soaked and hand-squished innards over the screen and
sprays the mass with the hose. Theresa and David look on as the
disappointing results are revealed. Water splashes out the bottom of
the sink and onto their feet. A collective head-scratching begins.

They retreat to the barn and run the seeds and pulp through
the vacuum a second time. No improvement. They try it again, this
time adding water to the squash mixture, which produces a goopy
orange soup—also no improvement. Dan has a vision involving a
customized wire basket and a pressure washer, the only problem
is that they don't actually own a pressure washer. They reconvene
outside by the sink, figuring they might as well work the seeds by
hand while they come up with another idea. At three o'clock the
five-gallon bucket at the base of the sink is about one-eighth full of
shiny white seeds, which by all accounts is not very much. A barn
cat sits on the hood of the truck parked next to the sink, keeping
warm and watching.

"Could we ferment it?" David says. "Pour a bunch of sugar
and yeast in there?"

When Dan and Theresa don't respond, he continues talking to himself. "I guess the problem would be is you'd get into staining." He keeps working the bucket before him, staring off toward the barn. Rain is dripping off the sloped roof and onto garbage cans full of seeds. Inside the cans is orange stew, but where the drips hit there is a line of white—clean seeds.

"Hey! How about that?" David says. "What if we put the screens under the eaves? We could build a twenty-nine-foot screen and the rain would do the work for us."

"But you'd have to have rain," Dan says. "Today, sure, but by the time we built the screen it might be sunny again." He thinks for a second. "How about washing them with a hose? We could use a front-loader to get the seeds onto the roof and with the pressure they'd just slide down off."

"That could be great!" David says, his eyes bright. But as he's working out the details aloud, his voice fades off.

"How about that fermenting?" Theresa says. "Could that work?"

David mentions that he's heard about people running pumpkins through a combine, but that doesn't go far either. Before long the solutions turn from how to do this more efficiently to how to do it the same way but just not be so cold. An on-demand hot water source? Warming gloves underneath the blue plastic ones? Water is creeping up David's pantslegs. Theresa's denim jacket is heavy with wet pulp. Dan is just plain soaked. And yet no one complains. "Y'know, on a sunny day this wouldn't be bad work," David says optimistically. No one replies.

As dusk closes in the whole scene turns almost to black-and-white, the only colors the bright blue gloves and the orange pulp.

Nobody is talking now, they're just plowing through the seeds so they can finish and get dry. I step back to take a photograph and David looks up. "You can entitle that one 'Slave Labor.'" He looks back down and keeps working the bucket.

And then it's over. Or at least what must be done today is finished. I follow David as he takes the last bucket of cleaned seeds to the far end of the barn and opens the sliding doors. The room is huge and dark, more or less empty aside from the old 1969 combine parked at the other end. Here by the door, though, there are a dozen long screens propped up on bricks. On the screens lie almost all the year's harvest: black, tear-shaped seeds from the Dakota Rose watermelon, ears of sweet corn in white, yellow, and purple, ears of flint corn in red and blue, ears of black popcorn. And now there is a growing pile of white squash seeds, wet but slowly drying under the soft breeze of an electric fan. In the near darkness they are gleaming.

David closes the door and we head back to the group, ready for dinner of beef, fried potatoes, salsa, bread, and, of course, squash. As we walk I ask him if they have achieved everything they want with this latest creation, if Uncle David's Dakota Dessert is "done"?

"It might just be perfect!" he says, half seriously but also with a cutting sort of humor, as if to ridicule the act of wanting such a thing in the first place.

I reconsider my question. "I guess if you reached perfection, well then, what would you do with yourself?"

"We'd sit on our laurels, I suppose. That would be nirvana, right?" He laughs. But as we keep walking, his brow hardens and his face becomes dark. He seems worried that he has made light of the situation and wants to be sure that I understand the true gravity. "No," he says, shaking his head. "We'll never just sit on our laurels—we can't. There's far too much to be done."

ACKNOWLEDGMENTS

THIS BOOK WOULD not exist without the courage and vision of the families it depicts. My deepest gratitude goes to Harry, Billye & Wynton Lewis; Virgil, Isabel & Chavela Trujillo; David & Ginger Podoll; and Dan, Theresa & Neil Podoll. Not only have you been generous with your time, you have opened your lives to me and trusted that I would tell your stories with the respect they deserve. This book is as much yours as it is mine.

In many ways this book is also a reflection of all the farmers and ranchers who have shared their time with me over the years. Thanks to each of you, in particular Roger & Holly Harjes, Loretta & Martin Jaus, Tony Malmberg, David Evans, and David & Jan Lawrence.

My thanks also to the following people: The Marin Arts Council and Cynthia & Jim Meketa lent critical financial support. Nancy Schaub offered the perfectly quiet place I needed to finish and revise the manuscript. Holly Blake and the Headlands Center for the Arts provided a creative environment and a warm community. Steve Jones, Bill Tracy, and especially John Navazio gave valuable expertise and insight, which helped me navigate the complicated terrain of plant science and genetics. Bob Scowcroft and Fred Kirschenmann shed light on various other topics with their own great wisdom. Kathy Wilhelm and the Mill Valley Public Library graciously filled my countless requests for obscure books and articles. Writers Sam Fromartz, Deirdre Dolan, Claire Cummings, Melissa Nelson, and Chera van Burg all entertained my many questions, answering each one with solid advice and words of encouragement. My agent, David McCormick, was essential in finding the right home for this book and counseling me throughout the publishing process. My excellent editor, Roxy Aliaga, was exceedingly perceptive, perspicacious, and patient. And Jack Shoemaker always had time to talk, listen, and offer support, even on his busiest days.

Special thanks to my dear friends William Brangham, Holly Link, Valerie Hamilton, and Julene Bair, whose intelligence and honesty helped me to improve the manuscript tremendously. Also to my mother, whose enthusiasm and encouragement are boundless. And most of all to my husband, Tucker Nichols, who offered me strength and comfort, wisdom and clarity, trust and love. Without you, impossible.

RESOURCES

In the words of Mat Kolding, "Everything we do is built on something somebody else did in the past. . . . Building on others' work—that's the only way you can start making progress." The following books served as fundamental resources for this one, and for that I thank their authors.

Gilbert C. Fite, *American Farmers: The New Minority*

Bobby MacDonald, *Plowin' Deep*

Thad Sitton and James H. Conrad, *Freedom Colonies: Independent Black Texans in the Time of Jim Crow*

Ken Meter, *Green Isle: Feeding the World, Farming for the Banker*

Lesley Poling-Kempes, *Valley of Shining Stone: The Story of Abiquiu*

Paul Kutsche and John R. Van Ness, *Cañones: Values, Crisis, and Survival in a Northern New Mexico Village*

Raoul Robinson, *Return to Resistance: Breeding Crops to Reduce Pesticide Dependence*

Jack Ralph Kloppenburg Jr., *First the Seed: The Political Economy of Plant Biotechnology*